THE
ELEMENTS
OF LIFE

A CONTEMPORARY GUIDE TO
THAI RECIPES AND TRADITIONS
FOR HEALTHIER LIVING

SU-MEI YU

PHOTOGRAPHY BY ALEXANDRA GRABLEWSKI

WILEY

JOHN WILEY & SONS, INC.

Photography copyright © 2009 by Alexandra Grablewski

Published by John Wiley & Sons, Inc., Hoboken, New Jersey

Published simultaneously in Canada

For general information on our other products and services or for technical support, please contact our Customer Care Department within the United States at (800) 762-2974, outside the United States at (317) 572-3993 or fax (317) 572-4002.

Wiley also publishes its books in a variety of electronic formats. Some content that appears in print may not be available in electronic books. For more information about Wiley products, visit our web site at www.wiley.com.

Design by Vertigo Design NYC

LIBRARY OF CONGRESS CATALOGING-IN-PUBLICATION DATA

Yu, Su-mei.
  The elements of life : a contemporary guide to Thai recipes and traditions for healthier living / Su-Mei Yu ; photography by Alexandra Grablewski.
     p. cm.
  Includes index.
  ISBN 978-0-471-75707-8 (cloth)
  1. Cookery, Thai. 2. Medicine, Thai. I. Title.
  TX724.5.T5Y872 2009
  641.5593--dc22
                                    2008033331

PRINTED IN CHINA

10 9 8 7 6 5 4 3 2 1

To my husband, Dr. Robert Nichols

and my mentor, Dr. Pennapa Subcharoen

CONTENTS

ACKNOWLEDGMENTS

This book is based on the teaching of Dr. Pennapa Subcharoen, the director of the National Institute of Thai Traditional Medicine, to whom I owe immeasurable gratitude for her wisdom and friendship. She was supportive of my endeavor until the final days of her life. Dr. Pennapa died of carcinoma of the gall bladder on April 2, 2008.

In addition, the writing of this book would not have been possible if it were not for the support and dedication of my Thai and American family members and friends.

I am especially grateful to M.L. Sirin Rongthong and her daughter, Paramapon Chotibut, for introducing me to Dr. Pennapa and for making countless arrangements for me to meet other traditional Thai doctors, herbalists, historians, and cooks, including Dunphichai Gomodvanich and his wife, Yuwanucht Tinnalak of Ayutthaya, Suwanna Sangsurisai, and Jinda Jamjun of Petchburi. My research in Thailand would have not been complete without the generosity and kindness of M.L. Tri Devakul, who housed me at his beautiful Villa Royale in Phuket while giving me the liberty to work with his staff to test and experiment with healing potions for spa use. William Warren connected me with his Thai friends, including Pimpa Bencharit, Marisa Viravaidya, and Natini Sriyuksiri, who lent me their helping hands.

I am grateful to my agent, Sarah Jane Freymann, whose steadfast belief in my ability humbles me. I am equally indebted to Justin Schwartz, my editor at John Wiley & Sons, another true believer in this book. I thank Alexandra Grablewski for her ethereal and artistic photographs; Nikki Symington, my friend and editor, whose talent in bringing forth clear and precise writing is invaluable; Pam Hoenig, whose expertise in editing transformed the manuscript into a book; Lois Stanton, who turned my creative recipes into delicious dishes; and Bob Harrington at Specialty Produce for his bountiful supplies of fresh produce.

Most and foremost, I thank my husband, Dr. Robert Nichols, who lived with a preoccupied wife during our early married life as this book was being written. This book is dedicated to him for his endless hours of editing and loving devotion.

FOOD AS MEDICINE

Each morning, still lying in my warm and cozy bed, I peek through the window shades to check the weather. I listen closely for my husband, Bob, who is downstairs shuffling about, making a cup of hot tea, getting ready for his morning run; I am assured that he is feeling well. With my busy schedule ahead, my mind racing with lists of things to do, I start to think and plan what to make for dinner. A quick survey of seasonal vegetables and fruits runs through my thoughts. If the day is cold and gloomy, I think of warm, rich dishes to be made with potato and other root vegetables or winter squashes. A hot, sunny day calls for a supper with the cool and refreshing tastes of bitter greens, radishes, lettuce, and summer squashes. Bracing for what I suspect to be the end of an exhausting day, I pick dishes to be spiced with an extra measure of ginger and sesame seeds. Although Bob is always calm and serene, these added ingredients will help him sleep better.

After six decades, I have become like my mother. Migrating from northern China with my father to tropical Thailand in 1940, Mother was acutely concerned with and never truly adjusted to the country's extreme climate, which she felt could play havoc with our health. She became our house doctor. Before deciding what to cook, she too started her day by checking the weather. After surveying how we were feeling, she would step out into the street, beckoned by calls from street vendors who showed up with baskets filled with fresh vegetables and fruits for sale. If nothing pleased her, she would then instruct the servant to buy the ingredients needed for cooking lunch and dinner from the nearby market.

Food, for my mother and for generations before her, was the protector of health. Food is not only the sustenance that nurtures us; it is also a remedy, which keeps us healthy during abrupt and unexpected climatic changes. It is the medicine that heals us in time of sickness.

My mother's view on food was shared by older generations of Thai people in our neighborhood. Although there were differing opinions as to the specific medicinal properties of various vegetables and fruits, the belief in the basic principle that food is medicine was held by all. They believed that the freshest locally grown seasonal vegetables were nature's true and natural remedies to keep us in good health. They also shared the idea that sudden changes in weather called for an extra bit of protection to shield our bodies. Rainy days meant rich, warming foods to fuel the inner heat. Hot days, on the other hand, called for cooling foods to calm the inner heat.

If someone in the family developed a fever, or was out of sorts, some Thai cooks in our neighborhood would cook *yah nang* greens to cure the fever, while Mother's remedy was a rich chicken soup seasoned heavily with ginger, scallions, and sesame oil. For insomnia, elderly Thai cooks made a stew with leaves of Siamese cassia in creamy coconut milk, while Mother cooked red beans with sweet Chinese dates to calm the nerves. I was taught these various natural formulas and grew up being nurtured with foods fitted to each changing season. It was, therefore, natural for me to value and follow in their footsteps.

When I came to America at the age of 15, Western medicine seemed miraculous to me, but at the same time, its power was frightening. To make matters worse, American foods were strange and foreign, and I could not eat many of them. My mother's way was more comforting. Her wisdom about food, I have come to believe, was more than just ancient cultural tradition. I began to cook my native foods, intuitively

adopting my mother's ways. When I had a cold, I made myself some ginger-honey tea while also taking the medicine prescribed by the school nurse.

Years followed with college, marriage, and work, while my interest in food intensified. Following my mother's example, my own immediate family was fed doses of her food wisdom through my cooking. Finally, after years as a medical social worker, I decided to open a Thai restaurant. That was 24 years ago.

Being in the food business, I would go back to Thailand at least once a year in search of ancient recipes. Friends and families hooked me up with old-timers who were willing to share their cooking secrets. While we cooked together, our conversation would inevitably turn to food. They talked about this and that ingredient being in season. These were nature's medicines, they said, given to us by nature to keep us well. The healing remedies, they explained, are cleverly hidden in the tastes, flavors, and aromas of these natural ingredients. The bitter taste in bitter melon, for example, cools and lessens fever, while the sweetness in sugar palm increases the body's heat. The spicy taste of chiles enhances the appetite, while the pungent flavors in ginger and shallots reduce bloating.

Until then, Mother and I simply accepted this inherited knowledge about foods and their benefits without question. The reminiscences, however, raised a spark of curiosity in me. I wanted to know how this particular world into which I was born and raised became instrumental in shaping the Thai people's belief system about food and health. I wanted to learn how our ancestors' ideas, together with their religious beliefs, eventually created a life philosophy that guided generations of Thai peoples' views on how to live, cook, and eat.

In 2002, while on a trip to Thailand, I met Jeffrey Steingarten, the food writer for *Vogue* magazine, who was a guest of the Thai Tourist Authority. He asked me to join him at Suan Dusit College of Culinary Arts to interpret a lecture given by Acharn (Professor) Gopkeaw Naipinji. There, in the college kitchen, was an impressive spread of fresh vegetables, fruits, herbs, and spices, which Acharn Gopkeaw proudly displayed as she stated with great authority the same familiar sentiments of my mother and the older Thais I had spoken with. "Thai cooking," she said, "is based on the principle of food as medicine." She explained that a typical Thai meal, consisting of multiple dishes, is developed not only to create an enjoyable and delicious eating experience. The mixing and matching of various dishes is done deliberately. A meal is a nutritious, balanced composition consisting of natural and seasonal ingredients, each with their own unique taste, flavor, and aroma, as well as their own healthful benefit to the diner. She further explained how Thai cooks and ancient Thai doctors shared the technique of using mortar and pestle to blend numerous ingredients together. For the cooks, it was a seasoning paste, central to Thai dishes. For the doctors, it was herbal medicine.

Acharn Gobkeaw became my professional sounding board. She introduced me to several Thai traditional doctors, one of whom was Dr. Pennapa Subcharoen, the Director of the Department of Traditional Thai Medicine in Thailand's Ministry of Public Health. Trained in both Western and Thai traditional medicine, she was both my teacher and mentor. This book presents a practical approach to Dr. Pennapa's research and knowledge of the Thai natural path to health and spiritual well-being. The foundation for this belief and practice originated from the integration of three basic ideologies: the ancient principle of natural order, Brahmanism, and Buddhism.

THE FOUR ELEMENTS: EARTH, WATER, WIND, AND FIRE

Natural philosophy is based on the principle that nature consists of four elements: Earth, Water, Wind, and Fire. As a reflection of and as part of this natural order, these four elements are also present in our physical bodies. In simple terms, Earth represents the solid and tangible parts of our bodies, Water is the fluid, Wind is the breath and movement, and Fire is the energy and fuel.

When one of these four elements takes a dominant position in nature, it is believed that a change in the weather has occurred. Mirroring nature's framework, each of us is also born with a dominant or home element. It is manifested in our unique and distinct characteristics and personalities. Thai natural theory states that this dominant or home element is given to us at the time of conception. This personal identity is also our road map, directing us toward a path of good health and spiritual well-being. In other words, to achieve good health and well-being, we must reach a state in which our body's four elements (our total personhood) and our home element function in perfect harmony. At the same time, our bodies must also be in perfect synchronization with nature's dominant element (weather and time of day).

To achieve this perfect state, which rewards us with good physical, emotional, and spiritual health, we must first determine our own personal home element. Knowing our home element will lead to the process of discovering our true self. When we know ourselves, we can then learn how to care for ourselves and how to live in perfect harmony with nature.

Food is one of the keys to good physical health. Eating the "right" foods enriched with tastes, flavors, and aromas from natural, edible plants helps us meet our body's needs and requirements. This is especially vital when our bodies are made vulnerable when there is an abrupt change in the weather. However, achieving good physical health is only a part of the Thai concept of wellness. Emotional contentment and spiritual peace are also goals. When we are unhappy and depressed, we cannot eat well, and there is the potential that our health will suffer. Following the guidance of our home element, we can learn a better and more suitable way to live.

YOUR HOME ELEMENT AND THE PATH TOWARD SELF-DISCOVERY

Until recently, the only way to determine one's home element was to consult a traditional Thai doctor, who often is also a Buddhist monk. Today, thanks to the brilliant work of Dr. Pennapa, to find your home element all you need is the Wheel that she developed and which I have adapted for this book. The first chapter introduces you to the Wheel and instructs you on its use. The second chapter is Basics. Here you will find an extensive collection of foundation recipes, as well as recipes that are appropriate for all home elements or that can be easily adapted to your home element. I explain how to put together a meal

according to the influences of your own home element and nature's home elements. I also give you advice on planning a meal for people with different home elements.

The following four chapters each focus on one of the four elements: Earth, Water, Wind, and Fire. Each chapter identifies the personal characteristics related to that home element and the tastes, flavors, and aromas best suited to that element, with a chart of natural ingredients that possess those qualities. There are suggestions and recipes for breakfast, lunch, dinner, and snacks for different types of weather. Each chapter ends with recipes for natural beauty treatments, massage oils, and healing balms.

THAI NATURAL PHILOSOPHY OF HEALTH AND SPIRITUAL WELL-BEING

The teaching of Thai natural philosophy of heath and spiritual well-being has helped me understand the ways of my mother and my older friends. Their views on food as medicine, and the way they have lived their lives with great reverence for nature, are no longer simply inherited ways. They make sense. It is a good way to live.

With the help of the Wheel to find my home element, I have gained insight into myself. Having learned to trust my inner voice, I have come to rely on it for guidance. I am more in tune with my body and emotions. I now understand why certain tastes, flavors, and aromas are right for me. I avoid foods that can aggravate my body, especially when I am anxious and nervous. I know why I crave certain foods when the weather turns cold and damp and that it is important for me to cook extra-nurturing foods when there is a sudden change in the weather.

I have also come to respect and understand the individuality of each of my family members and friends. I no longer feel that we all have to like and eat the same foods. Allowing each of us to be who we are as we choose how to live or express our thoughts, while respecting and treating others with courtesy, is a good thing.

Cooking with and eating local and seasonal foods almost every day of my life has made me more appreciative of the irreplaceable partnership we humans have with nature. I am determined to do my share to care for nature, as it has unselfishly given so much to me.

I hope this very old and wise path will also open the door to a discovery of your true self, as it did for me. At first, you might find it awkward or perhaps a bit confusing and time-consuming. Be patient. After a while, you will feel as if you have found a lost friend—your home element—which you have known all your life. Trust it. Listen and follow your home element's guidance. Let it show you a path toward a healthful and contented life. In this new path, join hands with nature, and respect and care for it as you respect and care for yourself.

I usually travel to Thailand in the cooler months of December and January, but one year I was homesick for the rain. I arrived at the height of monsoon season so that I could feel the wet, heavy "elephant drops" that I fondly remember from my childhood. My friend Gobgaew Najpinij, a professor of Thai culinary arts, and I decided to attend a fair on traditional Thai medicine at the Ministry of Public Health in Bangkok. Gobgaew, a petite woman in her sixties, epitomizes the traditional Thai woman of her age, refined and genteel, always impeccably attired in ethnic Thai dresses made of iridescent silk. Short, curly black hair frames her round face and oversized glasses magnify her twinkling eyes.

On that hot, humid August day, we joined the throngs pouring through the ministry's gates and strolled past booths displaying myriad plants, herbs, and potions. Buckets and baskets were filled with shoots, bark, seeds, fresh and dried leaves, blossoms, and dried centipedes, snakes, and worms. Many vendors sold homemade remedies packaged in bottles, paper, or plastic envelopes. There were cures for just about everything, including herbs to help lose weight and tighten sagging skin.

We spotted a booth jammed with people under a large sign that read "Taht Chao Reien"—Home Element. Under the shady canopy, several elderly men and women sat behind a long wooden table, spinning a plastic wheel and consulting with passersby. Our curiosity piqued, we took a place in line and were soon ushered before a stocky gentleman who told us that he was a *moh thai,* or Thai folk doctor.

These doctors often come from generations of family healers and apprentice with Buddhist monks, who are skilled in the healing arts. In Thailand, medicine is closely related to Buddhism. Folk doctors are regarded as emotionally centered and spiritually wise. To become a healer, one must excel in both practical knowledge and religious theology.

The moh thai looked at my face and asked for the date and year of my birth. He then began to move arrows on a plastic wheel covered with numbers, turning them back and forth, moving one circular wheel, and then another, right and left. In less than a minute, he told me that my home element is Water.

"Hot weather is good for you," he said.

Gobgaew chimed in, "She lives in America."

"How is the weather there?" the moh thai asked.

"Where I live, it's good most of the time, not too cold or too hot," I replied.

EARTH WATER WIND FIRE

FINDING YOUR HOME ELEMENT

"Good, good," he said. "Your friend is lucky because cold weather is not good for her," he continued, speaking to Gobgaew. "She should be careful when it rains. Cold and rain are not good for the nasal passages, throat, and lungs of Water people. Also, your lower intestine and bladder are sensitive. You would do well to eat fruits and vegetables with sour, bland, and bitter flavors."

When it was Gobgaew's turn, she was reluctant to give the old doctor her birth date. To the Thais of her generation, one's birth date is sacred information, revealing the spirit of the person. In the wrong hands, one's spirit could be tampered with. After assuring her that he was trustworthy, she finally gave him the date.

The moh thai spun the Wheel and quickly told her that her home element was half Wind and half Water. She was vulnerable to heart problems and high blood pressure.

"You must take care of your heart now that you are older," he warned. "Meditate. Be quiet. Take care of yourself during the rain. Your body temperature goes up and down. Eat spicy foods with cool, refreshing flavors, and some bland and bitter tastes."

Gobgaew and I looked at each other, astonished, feeling as if the doctor had looked right into our souls and bodies. Gobgaew cannot eat enough bitter greens. She detests the sweet flavors that contemporary Thai cooks add to her beloved curries, ruining the rightful balance that has been so carefully crafted by previous generations. Her body temperature often fluctuates. Lately, she sometimes slips away from her busy life to meditate with her son, a Buddhist monk.

Su-Mei Yu with Dr. Pennapa Subcharoen

As for myself, since I was a child I've known to look after myself when the weather turns cold and rainy. In recent years, I have cut down on spicy and creamy dishes. Chiles irritate my system and I can no longer digest rich dishes cooked with coconut cream. I crave bitter-tasting vegetables and I have always been drawn to sour fruits such as tamarind, green mango, and tart cherries.

"It's all here on this Wheel," the moh thai told us.

I asked him who invented the Wheel, and he replied that the doctor's name was Khun Moh (doctor) Pennapa. He went on to explain how difficult it had been to determine a person's home element before the Wheel's invention. "I had to consult several books and calculate the exact astrological alignment at the patient's time of conception," he said. "Before the Wheel, I needed my books and abacus."

"How did you come to use the Wheel?" Gobgaew asked.

"Dr. Pennapa came to the town where I live. She was interested in folk doctors. She came to learn and record our practices. It was tough going for her. You know how Thai people are: We don't like to share our secrets. But we opened up to her little by little. She told us about the Wheel. At first, I didn't think something so complicated could be made so simple, but when I calculated my patients' home elements the old way and she used the Wheel, the results were the same!"

Gobgaew and I each bought a Wheel at the fair's bookstore, along with a book published by Pennapa that explained how to use it. Gobgaew told me that Pennapa was the director of the Department of Traditional Thai Medicine at Thailand's Ministry of Public Health and that a mutual friend of ours, Khun Mom (Lady) Sirin, knew her.

It would be a year, however, before I would meet Pennapa. In the interim, I started using the Wheel when cooking for friends, family, and myself. Herbs and spices that I regularly use in my cooking took on new meaning. No longer did I add them to food simply as flavorings, but also as preventive aids for my health and well-being. I soon found myself cooking like my mother and her generation of friends, and felt that I had become an alchemist as well as a cook.

When I finally met Pennapa in August of 2003, I was convinced of the Wheel's efficacy. Pennapa was in her fifties, a serious, well-educated woman. Her father was a folk doctor, and she was trained in both Western and Thai traditional medicine. She told me about her travels throughout Thailand, collecting medical texts and recording regional healing practices and herbal remedies from folk doctors.

"I've come to believe," said Pennapa, "that the path toward good health begins by knowing oneself physically, emotionally, and spiritually. It's also important to have an awareness and respect for nature. Traditional Thai medicine has a holistic approach to treating illness. It takes into account the mental and spiritual condition of the patient. In the past, Thais believed that people got sick because their body elements had fallen out of balance with their environment. They paid attention to maintaining balance in their lives. They ate food that was grown locally and seasonally. Besides planting fruit trees, they also

planted trees that have auspicious meanings around their homes. They planted aromatic herbs and flowers that are used as medicine and aromatherapy to this day."

I asked her about the Wheel. "I wanted a device that could be used by anyone to identify his or her home element," she said. "The home element is the key to understanding who we are."

Strolling through the herb garden Pennapa had cultivated at the Ministry, she said, "Your passion is food, and mine is the hidden treasures in edible plants. We make a good pair, don't you think? The Thai people owe an enormous debt to the ancient Thai cooks, whom I consider geniuses. They consciously knew what they were doing when they invented heavenly-tasting dishes by blending common, ordinary plants that have specific healing properties. A typical curry paste is a combination of several herbs and spices, and usually includes lemongrass, which is an antiseptic, and bird chiles, which curb nausea, vomiting, and diarrhea and help blood circulate."

At the end of our day together, I asked for her permission to translate one of her books about the Thai philosophy of health. She was delighted. The book would become an inspiration for me in my quest to understand the link between Thai food and folk healing practice.

Another year passed before I returned to Thailand with the partially translated manuscript. I asked Pennapa if I could use the Wheel and much of what I learned from her and her books for my own book. She graciously not only gave her permission, but also helped me revise the Wheel to make it more understandable to Westerners.

YOUR HOME ELEMENT

"The spark of life is smaller than the tiniest droplet of sesame oil on the tip of a buffalo hair." That is how a Thai saying describes the moment of conception, when our home element is assigned to each of us. Discovering your home element will allow you to use your diet to achieve harmony with nature. With the information you gain by knowing your home element, you can adjust your menus in response to the weather, the season, the time of day, or how you feel for optimum health and emotional well-being.

Your home element has a spiritual dimension as well. To discover its presence is to discover your true self. To know your home element is to know your inner voice. This light of wisdom illuminates your way as you journey through life. Its sustaining energy provides you with a sense of direction and fortifies you against life's problems. When you follow the path of your home element and listen to your inner voice, you will be rewarded with a life of well-being and a state of physical and spiritual harmony that Thais call *suk sabai:* contentment, clarity, and happiness.

HOW TO USE THE WHEEL

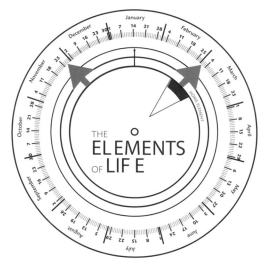

The Wheel has three overlapping disks. The large bottom disk has information on both the front and back. On the front is a calendar with the year laid out by months and days.

On the back of the large disk is a list of specific dates in months and years.

Only a small arrow is immediately visible on the front of the middle disk. When you gently lift the smallest disk up, there is an inner circle divided into red, yellow, blue, and black.

The top and smallest disk has two large arrows. The first arrow has the words "home element." Directly underneath is an inverted triangle window. The second arrow is 90 degrees to the left of the first one.

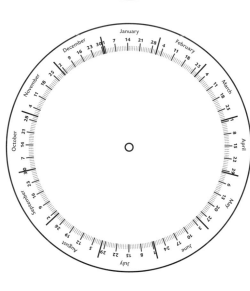

FRONT. Calendar with year laid out in months and years

BACK OF LARGER DISK. Specific dates in months and years

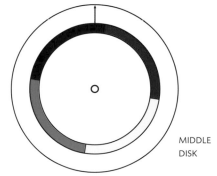

MIDDLE DISK

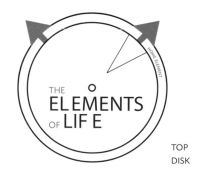

TOP DISK

TO FIND YOUR HOME ELEMENT:

1. Look on the back of the large disk and locate the year of your birth. Note the date and month next to your birth year. For example, my birthday is September 8, 1945, and the number next to it is 24 Mar. 1945.

2. Turn the Wheel over and, using the middle disk, point the small arrow to the date and month next to your birth year, as identified on the back of the large disk. I would point the small arrow on the middle disk to March 24.

3. While holding onto the middle disk, making sure it doesn't move, rotate the top of the smallest disk and point the left arrow to the actual date and month of your birth, minus one day if you were born in North America. (The Wheel was created for people born in Thailand, so for those born in North America, you need to subtract one day to make up for the time change.) I move the left arrow on the smallest disk to September 8, the day I was born. (I was born in Thailand.)

The home element arrow is now pointing to the approximate date of your conception. In my case, the home element arrow points to December 3. Dr. Pennapa says those born prematurely should add the appropriate number of days or weeks to your actual birth date before determining your date of conception. So, if you were born eight weeks premature on March 31, your birthday should be May 26, which would actually be May 25 if you were born in North America because you need to subtract one day. If you were born after your mother's estimated delivery date, subtract the number of days or weeks from your actual birthday, then subtract one more day if you were born in North America.

Underneath the right arrow of the smallest disk is an inverted triangular window. Either one or two colors will appear in this window. The colors identify your home element.

YOUR HOME ELEMENT

IF THE COLOR IS:	YOUR HOME ELEMENT IS:
Red	Fire
Yellow	Wind
Blue	Water
Black	Earth

In my case, the color is blue, which means my home element is Water. If two colors appear in the window, this means you have two home elements. For example, if yellow and red appear in the window, your home elements are Fire and Wind. If both colors appear exactly the same size in the triangle, you have two evenly weighted home elements. If more of one color appears than the other, then that home element predominates, with influence felt from the lesser home element. Having more than one home element means you should follow the guidance of both elements in proportion to their dominance in the triangle.

Knowing your home element(s) is like having a compass. It guides you toward the right path on your journey through the unpredictable terrain created by nature's changing weather and time of day. With each change, you need to adjust your direction in order to remain in balance to maintain good health. One of the ways to achieve this balance is through a diet that combines the tastes, flavors, and aromas most beneficial to your home element(s) together with those appropriate to the elements dominating the time of day and that day's weather.

A JOURNEY TO UNDERSTANDING

The bus pulled over to a clearing by the side of the road and stopped, jolting my husband, Bob, and me from our sleep. We had been on a bus since the night before, taking off from Bangkok for a small remote village in Prae, a province in the far northern corner of Thailand, with 30 other disciples of my friend and mentor, Dr. Pennapa.

Hidden in an isolated mountainous area surrounded by teak forest, the people of Chong Bhuk live untouched by most modern amenities except for electricity, mobile phones, and pickup trucks. Otherwise, their lifestyle remains basically the same as that of their ancestors. Each new generation is taught by its elders how to identify and use homegrown and foraged plants for foods and/or medicine. Chong Bhuk, according to Dr. Pennapa, would be a perfect laboratory where I could experience firsthand what I had been studying.

It was still dark when we got off the bus. The air was cold and wet, blanketing us in heavy, dense fog. Several men got out of their pickups and started to unload suitcases from our bus into the beds of their trucks. We were told to find ours and jump in. The ride in the open air over dirt roads winding through a wooded expanse, with a chilly morning wind whipping through our thin clothing, instantly banished any longing for more sleep from our weary bodies. By the time the truck came to a stop at a paved lot, we were shivering hard from the cold. Our minds had also snapped into full alertness.

Under a makeshift tent, several women wearing heavy sweaters with shawls draped over their heads and shoulders stood behind several tables. They called us to come and get our breakfast. There were steaming hot mugs of soy milk in all sizes and shapes, and enamel bowls filled with rice porridge, and cubes of taro, mushrooms, and sweet potatoes. Slivers of ginger mixed with some kind of spicy herb and chopped cilantro leaves garnished the porridge. Trays of sliced oranges were set nearby.

Warmed and nourished by breakfast and our brief welcome by the village chief, we were assigned host families with whom we would stay as guests in their homes. The early morning light had burnt off the fog, and we could see the green forest wrapping around the tiny village of Chong Bhuk. Aside from the concrete building that is the children's school, the village is laid out as a typical small Thai community. Along the single dirt road running through the middle of the village are modest wooden homes surrounded by bamboo fences covered with vines and early spring blossoms. A wide opening in the fence serves as the front gate to the homes. Across from the road is a wild wooded area with a waterfall and running stream.

After freshening up, we were divided into four groups. Each represented one of the four home elements: Earth, Water, Wind, and Fire. I was in the Wind group. Our assignment was to identify the taste, flavor, and aroma of both homegrown and foraged plants in the village and woods. We were also instructed to pick plants with the particular taste, flavor, and aroma most suitable for our assigned element. Each group was guided by a villager.

Our guide was a short, stocky, middle-aged man with an easygoing disposition. Mr. Somphun was born in Chong Bhuk, as were generations of his family before him. As a child and from the time he was able to walk, he would accompany his grandfather into the woods. He was taught how to identify and forage plants for food and medicine. As he walked with us through the village, he frequently paused, pointing at a tree, shrub, vine, or clumps of grass along the fences, in neighboring gardens, and at the edges of the woods. He would identify the plant's name, then pick a leaf, blossom, fruit, or shoot for us to taste, asking us to identify the plant's taste and aroma. Then he would ask us to name the home elements that would benefit from that particular taste, flavor, or aroma. After our answers, he would recite the plant's curative properties and how it is used either for cooking and/or as medicine. We recorded everything down in our writing pads.

At times, Mr. Somphun would use his machete to chop off or dig from the ground edible plants known to be valuable to the Wind home element and give them to one of us to carry. Several hours would pass before we came out on the other end of the wood into a vast grassy meadow.

There were four temporary lean-tos set up in four corners surrounding a central area with chairs and tables. The same women who made and served us breakfast now sat cooking and chatting merrily in each of the lean-tos. Mr. Somphun took our baskets and gave them to the women in the lean-to designated as the Wind kitchen. The air was heavily scented with spices and herbs.

When everyone had arrived, and while lunch was being cooked, Dr. Pennapa began her lecture about the interrelationship between taste, flavor, and aroma and the individual home elements, our body's elements, and nature's elements. She started by analyzing what we had for breakfast.

Although February is considered to be the beginning of hot season in Thailand, it is not so in Chong Bhuk. Located in the northern mountainous region of Thailand, the cool season lingers on a bit longer, and we had eaten our breakfast on a very cool, damp morning. The weather and time of day, stated Dr. Pennapa, are both under the dominance of one of nature's four elements. In Thailand, there are hot, rainy (monsoon), and cool seasons. The Thai cool season is generally dry and not extremely cold. Therefore, the dominant element for the Thai cool season is Water. On the other hand, in other parts of the world (including most of the United States) where winter can be very cold and damp, the dominant element for winter is Earth.

NATURE'S DOMINATING ELEMENTS

WEATHER:

Cold, damp	=	EARTH element
Cool, dry	=	WATER element
Wet	=	WIND element
Hot	=	FIRE element

HOURS:

6 A.M. to 10 A.M.	=	WATER element
10 A.M. to 2 P.M.	=	FIRE element
2 P.M. to 6 P.M.	=	WIND element
6 P.M. to 10 P.M.	=	WATER element
10 P.M. to 2 A.M.	=	FIRE element
2 A.M. to 6 A.M.	=	WIND element

On that particular morning, the climate was under the influence of nature's Water element (Thailand's cool tropical climate), Wind element (wet and damp climate), and Water element (the early morning hours between 6 A.M. and 10 A.M.). The villagers served us a well-balanced breakfast made with ingredients exuding tastes, flavors, and aromas that helped our bodies' elements maintain equilibrium with nature's varied elements, beginning with the rice in the porridge. Its bland flavor (a flavor good for Water, Wind, and Fire elements) is especially nurturing to the circulatory, digestive, and respiratory systems when there are multiple dominating forces of nature (Water and Wind, in this case). The same is true of mushrooms, another bland flavor ingredient.

Taro tastes buttery, whereas pumpkin tastes buttery and sweet (a taste and flavor for Earth element). Both fortify our bones, muscles, tendons, and skin in a cool and damp climate. Spicy and warming ginger, plai (a variety of ginger), shallot, and cilantro in rice porridge shielded us from the wet Wind element.

Orange's sour and sweet tastes (tastes for Water element) generate the body's heat. It is a protective measure for our respiratory system, especially on wet, cool mornings.

Lastly, rich and buttery soy milk (a flavor for Earth element) sweetened with sugar (another taste for Earth element) warmed all of us against the cool and damp climate.

Among those of us with Water and/or Wind as our home element, breakfast was especially restorative. This is because nature's dominant elements on that cool, wet, early morning were the same as our home elements, and these double forces called for extra fortifications. All of us, especially people with Earth as their home element, glowed from an extra protective coating for our bodies against the surprising and unfamiliar cool and wet morning. And for people with Fire as their home element, although they fare better in a cool and wet climate, their body element still needs nurturing in order to keep its balance with nature's elements.

TASTE, FLAVOR, AND AROMA AND THE HOME ELEMENTS

After centuries of observation and study, Thai traditional folk doctors have come to believe that all natural and edible ingredients contain one or more of nine essential tastes, flavors, and/or aromas.

The tastes, flavors, and aromas best suited for the individual home elements are:

- **EARTH ELEMENT:** astringent, buttery, salty, and sweet

- **WATER ELEMENT:** bitter, bland, and sour

- **WIND ELEMENT:** spicy and cool/refreshing

- **FIRE ELEMENT:** bitter, bland, and cool/refreshing

Dr. Pennapa then asked us to identify the nine natural tastes, flavors, and aromas, with their healing qualities. By then, we had learned and repeated the recitation taught to us by our guides:

- **ASTRINGENT** equalizes the elements

- **BITTER** purifies the blood

- **BLAND** aids the respiratory system

- **BUTTERY** lubricates the joints and tendons

- **SALTY** restores the skin

- **SOUR** rids the body of phlegm and cleanses the blood

- **SWEET** increases the Wind (affects breathing, emotions, and digestion)

- **SPICY** drives away the Wind (eases digestion, bloating, and flatulence)

- **COOL/REFRESHING** nurtures the heart

Dr. Pennapa went on to elaborate that some vegetables, herbs, and fruits may have multiple tastes, flavors, and aromas. For example, orange has both sour and sweet tastes, and some nuts such as almond are buttery and sweet, while other seeds like sesame are buttery and bitter. Green beans are astringent and bland, and mint is spicy and cool/refreshing. These ingredients are suitable for various home elements in which these tastes, flavors, and aromas are needed.

The distinct tastes, flavors, and aromas in edible plants, explained Dr. Pennapa, are the keys that unlock the secret passage into the depths of the healthful benefits of the plants. For example, ginger tastes spicy and warm, the flavor that regulates and drives away the Wind. This spice is known to be beneficial to the digestive, respiratory, circulatory, and nervous systems. It curbs nausea and bloated feelings and warms the chest, easing a cold. For a Wind element person with these delicate systems, ginger is a perfect spice.

Besides edible plants, traditional Thai folk doctors include traditional Thai seasonings such as salt, sugar, honey, vinegar, fish sauce, soy sauce, salty bean paste, fermented shrimp paste, and fermented fish paste in this classification of tastes, flavors, and aromas.

Several young children crept up to Dr. Pennapa and whispered that lunch was ready. Before taking us through the four lean-to kitchens, Dr. Pennapa asked us to call out together which element ruled the climate on that cool and sunny day and what tastes, flavors, and aromas were best suited for it. We all chimed together "Water," followed by calling out "bland," "bitter," and "sour." Then she asked which element dominates the lunch hours and which tastes, flavors, and aroma nurture it, to which we answered, "Fire," followed by "bitter," "bland," and "cool/refreshing."

Her lecture fresh in our minds, we followed her from one makeshift kitchen to the next.

The women in the Earth element kitchen had prepared a dipping sauce made with astringent banana blossoms, aromatic and bitter/sour kaffir lime juice, peppery green onion, buttery salted dried fish, roasted dried chiles, spicy garlic and shallot, buttery peanuts, and sweet palm sugar. An array of steamed vegetables and buttery, sweet pumpkin would be served as accompaniments.

The women in the Water element kitchen created a salad made with sour green mango and unripe star fruits, shallots, and a wild cool/refreshing herb. The dressing was made with sugar, fish sauce, garlic, chiles, aromatic herbs, and lime juice.

Cooks in the Wind element kitchen, using a variety of bitter greens, bland-flavor mushrooms, astringent/bland green beans, and cups of spicy basil, made a northern Thai–style curry called *geang khae* that is seasoned with a paste with salt and spicy chiles, garlic, shallot, lemongrass, and galangal and served with buttery grilled fish.

Cooks in the Fire element kitchen prepared several stir-fry dishes. One was made with tender and slightly astringent banana shoots, garlic, and basil, the other with a variety of bland-tasting greens seasoned with a paste made from salt, garlic, peppercorns, and coriander root. Away from the kitchens, several men were roasting large bamboo tubes over a fire. When we gathered to watch, they laid one with a charred and blackened surface on the grass and hacked it open with a machete, spilling out steaming hot newly harvested red and brown rice.

Dr. Pennapa explained that she had deliberately asked the villagers to cook dishes best suited for each of the four elements. Yet each kitchen, while using ingredients with tastes, flavors, and aromas most suitable for that particular element, all flavored their dishes with a "balancing" seasoning paste. These pastes, central to most if not all Thai recipes, represent the connection between Thai food and traditional Thai folk medical theory because they are made with herbs and spices from either opposite elements or all four elements combined, creating a balance that is necessary and suitable for all home elements and climates. For example, the curry paste for the *gaeng khae* made by the cooks of the Wind element kitchen, like most Thai curry pastes, was prepared with herbs and spices from two opposite elements, Earth and Wind, providing important nurturing and healing remedies for all. The green mango and unripe star fruit salad made by the cooks of the Water element kitchen was served with a dressing containing ingredients with tastes, flavors, and aromas from all four elements.

As we lined up to pick our selections, Dr. Pennapa reminded us that we should feel free to enjoy all the dishes from each of the home element kitchens, but she advised us to take a bit more of the dish most suitable for our particular home element. For those with Water and Fire as home elements, she reminded us of the double forces at play from nature's Water (the weather) and Fire (the time of day) elements. Because of this, Water and Fire people should eat fewer dishes from Earth and Wind elements kitchens and more from their own home element kitchens.

We partook of a typical traditional Thai meal, consisting of several dishes served together and prepared from seasonal fruits, vegetables, and herbs, a balanced and healthful meal, Dr. Pennapa concluded, suitable for all.

CREATING BALANCE IN YOUR OWN KITCHEN

No matter where you live, what climate you happen to be in, or which meal of the day you plan to cook for yourself and/or others whose home elements are known to you, your menu should include ingredients that balance tastes, flavors, and aromas based on:

1. Your or their home element(s) together with . . .
2. The element that dominates the climate together with . . .
3. The element that dominates the time of day.

Here are combinations of the different elements based on the above formula. To select the appropriate ingredients, you can refer to the chart of ingredients with their tastes, flavors, and aromas at the beginning of each element chapter.

NOTE: On a hot or cool day, if it rains, add Wind to the combination. On a rainy day, if it is hot, add Fire to the combination. If it is cold and damp, add Earth to the combination. During the winter, if it is cool (not cold) and dry, add Water.

If you plan to cook for friends whose home elements are not known to you, then your menu should include ingredients that balance the tastes, flavors, and aromas of the element that dominates the weather together with the element that dominates the time of day.

EARTH HOME ELEMENT

HOT CLIMATE (FIRE):

BREAKFAST: Earth + Fire + Water (time of day)

LUNCH: Earth + Fire + Fire (time of day)

DINNER: Earth + Fire + Water (time of day)

RAINY CLIMATE (WIND):

BREAKFAST: Earth + Wind + Water (time of day)

LUNCH: Earth + Wind + Fire (time of day)

DINNER: Earth + Wind + Water (time of day)

COLD CLIMATE (EARTH):

BREAKFAST: Earth + Earth + Water (time of day)

LUNCH: Earth + Earth + Fire (time of day)

DINNER: Earth + Earth + Water (time of day)

WATER HOME ELEMENT

HOT CLIMATE (FIRE):

BREAKFAST: Water + Fire + Water (time of day)

LUNCH: Water + Fire + Fire (time of day)

DINNER: Water + Fire + Water (time of day)

RAINY CLIMATE (WIND):

BREAKFAST: Water + Wind + Water (time of day)

LUNCH: Water + Wind + Fire (time of day)

DINNER: Water + Wind + Water (time of day)

COLD CLIMATE (EARTH):

BREAKFAST: Water + Earth + Water (time of day)

LUNCH: Water + Earth + Fire (time of day)

DINNER: Water + Earth + Water (time of day)

WIND HOME ELEMENT

HOT CLIMATE (FIRE):

BREAKFAST: Wind + Fire + Water (time of day)

LUNCH: Wind + Fire + Fire (time of day)

DINNER: Wind + Fire + Water (time of day)

RAINY CLIMATE (WIND):

BREAKFAST: Wind + Wind + Water (time of day)

LUNCH: Wind + Wind + Fire (time of day)

DINNER: Wind + Wind + Water (time of day)

COLD CLIMATE (EARTH):

BREAKFAST: Wind + Earth + Water (time of day)

LUNCH: Wind + Earth + Fire (time of day)

DINNER: Wind + Earth + Water (time of day)

FIRE HOME ELEMENT

HOT CLIMATE (FIRE):

BREAKFAST: Fire + Fire + Water (time of day)

LUNCH: Fire + Fire + Fire (time of day)

DINNER: Fire + Fire + Water (time of day)

RAINY CLIMATE (WIND):

BREAKFAST: Fire + Wind + Water (time of day)

LUNCH: Fire + Wind + Fire (time of day)

DINNER: Fire + Wind + Water (time of day)

COLD CLIMATE (EARTH):

BREAKFAST: Fire + Earth + Water (time of day)

LUNCH: Fire + Earth + Fire (time of day)

DINNER: Fire + Earth + Water (time of day)

	HOT CLIMATE	RAINY CLIMATE	COLD CLIMATE
BREAKFAST	Fire + Water	Wind + Water	Earth + Water
LUNCH	Fire + Fire	Wind + Fire	Earth + Fire
DINNER	Fire + Water	Wind + Water	Earth + Water

Once again, remember to add Wind to the combination on a hot or cool day if it rains. Add Earth to a rainy day if it is cold and Fire if it is hot. In the winter, if it is cool (not cold) and dry, add Water.

When planning your dish or dishes, begin by balancing ingredients with the tastes, flavors, and aromas from opposite elements or a combination of all four elements:

	EARTH	
FIRE		WATER
	WIND	

It can be as simple as combining salt (Earth) and pepper (Wind) or sugar (Earth) and cinnamon (Wind) or making a salad dressing of salt, oil (Earth), lemon juice (Water), mustard (Wind), garlic (Wind), and mint (Wind and Fire).

Then select seasonal ingredients to create a balance of tastes, flavors, and aromas of all elements. You can use this same guideline for putting together a single dish or for preparing a combination of dishes, as was the case with the meal served at Chong Bhuk. Here is how it works:

Let's say it is a cold winter morning and you decide to make pancakes for your family. Cold weather is under the dominance of nature's Earth element, and the morning hours between 6 A.M. and 10 A.M. are under the dominance of nature's Water element. If you happen to have two members of your family whose home elements are Earth and Water, they will be under the double influence of the Earth and Water elements.

This particular pancake recipe (Applesauce Pancakes, page 32) is made with ingredients with tastes and flavors of Earth element (buttery, sweet, and slightly salty), as well as a bit of orange juice and zest for a touch of Water element. Serving it with a sweet syrup is a good idea, as sweet is a taste best suited for Earth element. This combination makes it an especially good breakfast on a cool morning dominated by Earth element.

As a double measure of protection for the Earth element person, use buckwheat instead of oat flour and offer some buttery walnuts, almond slivers, and/or sliced sweet banana for additional toppings. To take care of a person with Water home element, sour dried cranberries, dried apricots, or slices of oranges would be a wonderful choice. For a Wind element person, shake some warm and spicy cinnamon on top of the uncooked pancakes while they are still on the griddle and offer slivers of spicy candied ginger as a topping. For a Fire element person, garnish the pancakes with shavings of bitter chocolate.

Now, let's consider what to make for lunch when the weather is still on the cool side. Look at the basic Fried Rice recipe on page 69. It contains seasonings and ingredients with the tastes, flavors, and aromas of all four elements, making it balanced not just for all home elements, but also for nature's demands. Rice is a balancer ingredient, good for all elements. Spicy garlic, ginger, and white pepper are restoratives for Wind element, cool/refreshing cilantro and cucumber for Fire element, and sour lime for Water element.

As suggested in the recipe, make one serving at a time, so that you can mix in additional cool weather ingredients to further meet specific home element needs. Remember that in the case of family members with Earth or Fire as their home element, they will need extra protection because of the double forces from their home element and nature's element (weather = Earth, time of day = Fire). You can add raisins, apple, and carrot (sweet) as well as celery (salty) for the Earth element person. For the Fire element person, add mushrooms (bland) and fennel (bland/slightly sweet). For a Water element person, add broccoli or arugula (bitter) and mushrooms (bland). For a Wind element person, add extra garlic, onion, and dried chiles (spicy).

Use the same guidelines when you plan a dinner menu with multiple dishes. A dinner on a cool evening is still under the dominance of nature's Earth element. However, the hours are under the influence of nature's Water element (6 P.M. to 10 P.M.). Consider a menu that includes ingredients with the tastes, flavors, and aromas of mostly Earth element (astringent, buttery, salty, sweet) and Water element (bitter, bland, sour), which will also take care of those with Earth or Water as their home element. Then add a couple of other dishes with tastes, flavors, and aromas suited for Wind and Fire, if you will be feeding people who have either of them as their home element.

For example, you can build a menu around hearty and warming Mussaman Curry with Chicken and Dried Apricots (page 138). It is a perfect dish for a cool, wintry night. To start, the curry paste is made with ingredients perfectly balanced and suitable for all home elements. Additional warming spices in the paste, including cardamom, cinnamon, nutmeg, and cumin, are especially nurturing to Wind element people. The curry sauce is made with rich and buttery coconut cream, a flavor that is strengthening to the muscles, joints, and tendons of all elements. The recipe includes apricots, whose sweet flavor turns fruity and sour when cooked, a taste suited for Water element people, as well as meets the need to balance the evening's dominant Water element. Sour taste is believed to warm the upper respiratory system during the cool evening hours.

Accompanying dishes might include Pear and Smoked Fish Salad (page 243), an elegant dish and excellent choice for the refined taste and desires of the Wind element person. For another dish, make Stir-Fried Chicken, Cabbage, and Bean Threads (page 297). Cabbage, with its bland, slightly sweet taste, is cooling and considered to be good for Earth, Water, and Fire element people. Finally, serve rice as a balancer for all the elements. For dessert, do as most Thais do—instead of a sweet, rich dessert, serve fresh, seasonal fruits such as sliced apple and pear. Or, for a little indulgence, make Sponge Cake with Cinnamon and Kumquats (page 180).

HARMONY

Before the morning sun rises, nature's Wind element rules, blanketing the earth with dew. While we sleep, our body's Wind element, following nature's cues, effortlessly spreads its energy through the streams of our consciousness. Some of us sleep blissfully, our bodies floating gently in the arms of a balanced Wind. Others wrestle with demons in their dreams, as the ungrounded Wind element whirls and spins off course.

When the sun rises, brightening and warming the earth, as we begin to awake, nature's Wind element lingers in our somnolent consciousness, slowly easing the way for the Water element to assume nature's watch. During this precious and transitory moment, for those of us fortunate to have enjoyed a tranquil

rest, our minds are calm and peaceful, prepared to meet the day's chores and responsibilities. For those of us who experienced a fitful or sleepless night, we wake up exhausted, with our minds and spirits battered by the stormy Wind element.

Regardless of your state of being, before getting out of bed, take a moment to close your eyes and focus your mind on the rhythm of your breath. As you draw in each breath, deep and slow, imagine streams of white light entering your body, spreading its loving kindness through you. As you slowly breathe out, focus your mind on the light leaving your body, enveloping you with its compassionate rays. In this pool of deep quiet and light, you are in the presence of your home element's guiding spirit. If your mind wanders, gently refocus on your breathing and the streams of light, guiding it back toward thoughts of loving kindness. While in this state of mindfulness, gently tap into your emotions. Make a survey of how you feel. Are you content, or are you worried, anxious, or upset? Inhale and exhale deeply, breathing away the anxiety. Recite your home element's mantra. Take in the vision of your mantra and, with your mind's eye, see yourself moving through the day ahead with grace and wisdom.

Stretch slightly and quietly, mentally checking on the condition of your body. Are you well, or are your muscles and joints achy? Are you uncomfortable from last night's dinner? Make a note of what you find. In the light of your physical, emotional, and spiritual state of being, let your guiding spirit lead your consciousness. Alert and prepared, get up and look upon the beauty of nature that surrounds you. Embrace it as your companion in the hours to come.

The early morning hours, ruled by nature's Water element, remind us that the right balance of fluid intake is like a constant and refreshing stream that keeps us well hydrated and rejuvenated. By midday, nature's dynamic Fire element heats up our world and bodies. Stimulated by the day's activities, we hunger for nourishment, a reminder to refuel our body's energy. Mid-afternoon welcomes back nature's Wind element, as our minds and emotions move into high speed. Though it may seem counterintuitive, slow down. Remember to breathe; calm your body's Wind element and keep it on course, balanced by your wise and steady home element.

By evening, nature's Water element returns. Unwind, relax, and let its pure and pristine streams cleanse away the grime and worries of the day. As you get ready for sleep, close your eyes and release your body's weighty Earth element that you have shouldered throughout the day. Get back in touch with your home element's guiding spirit and breathe evenly and deeply to slowly calm the force of the body's Fire element. Let it refuel your tired body as you drift off to sleep. Feel your guiding spirit as it wraps you in blissful sleep.

While the sun, moon, and stars revolve in their constant, quiet, and serene cyclical paths, your home element synchronizes your mind and body with the planetary cycles, illuminating its guiding light within and through you. Trust your home element to keep you on a harmonious life path, balanced within the ever-changing influences of your body's elements and nature. In this state of perfect harmony, we are truly one with nature.

CHAPTER TWO

In this chapter, you'll find the building blocks for creating balanced dishes and meals. There are the basics, ingredients you'll find across all the elements, including almond milk, soy milk, coconut milk, chicken broth, and vegetable broth, as well as stir-fry seasonings and salad dressings. Then there is a large selection of recipes for breakfast, lunch, and dinner that will work for all elements, with variations included where appropriate to tailor the recipe to a particular home element. You'll find drinks, salads, stir-fries, soups, curries, and much more.

Once you have mastered this basic repertoire of recipes, you can read on to find out how to nurture your and your family's special and unique needs in the following chapters on individual home elements.

BASICS

WATER, WATER EVERYWHERE

The quality of drinking water is different from state to state, even city to city. New York City, where my daughter, Angela, lives, has excellent-tasting tap water. In San Diego, where I live, the tap water has so much chlorine that it tastes like it came out of a swimming pool. All of our drinking water is passed through a reverse osmosis filter attached to the kitchen faucet to make it palatable. When making preparations like almond milk, use the best-quality water you can.

i first discovered almond milk as a substitute for coconut cream and milk through a Thai friend who is a physician. Trying to control her own intake of saturated fats, she had thought of almond milk as a potential substitute in Thai cooking. Since she is not a cook, she asked if I could experiment with it when making curry. I did, and today I use it not only in my own cooking, but I also offer it to customers at my restaurant, who are grateful that healthy food can also be delicious. ∼§∽ Almonds contain "good" monounsaturated fat. High in calcium, magnesium, and folic acid, they also contain resveratrol, an anti-inflammatory agent. Blue Diamond manufactures almond milk under the brand name Almond Breeze. Buy the unflavored one for cooking. Homemade almond milk, however, is richer and thicker than the store-bought variety. For an even thicker milk, reduce the final amount of water from 3 cups to 2 or even just 1 cup. Almond milk is good for all home element types.

ALMOND MILK

PUT the almonds in a large bowl, pour over the boiling water, and let sit until the water is just cool enough to touch, about 1 minute. Drain the water.

PUT the almonds in a clean dish towel, rub off the skins, and discard. Rinse the almonds and place them in a jar. Add the 3 cups water, cover tightly, and refrigerate overnight.

TRANSFER the almonds and water to a blender and process until smooth. Line a fine-mesh strainer with damp cheesecloth and place the strainer on top of a bowl. Transfer the contents of the blender to the strainer. Extract the milk by squeezing the cloth tight and hard. Store the almond milk in an airtight container in the refrigerator for up to a week. Save the leftover almond puree to use as a skin treatment (see below).

Almond Puree

Almond puree, the pulp left over from making almond milk, makes a unique base for homemade facial masks, body scrubs, and hair conditioners. Refer to your specific home element chapter and try the beauty treatment recipes using almond puree. I apply it regularly to my hands, which are often dry. After cooking or doing dishes, I take a teaspoonful from a container of it I keep in the refrigerator and give my hands, nails, and cuticles a deep-tissue massage. I do this over the sink and use the time to clear my overloaded mind by focusing on the treatment. After a minute or two, I rinse it off with warm water and dry my hands with a clean towel. My hands are softer and my thoughts are relaxed.

MAKES ABOUT 3 CUPS

1 cup raw almonds with the skins on

5 cups boiling water

3 cups water

oconut cream and coconut milk are two of the most important ingredients in Thai cooking. When water is added and then extracted from coconut pulp, the cream is the thick part that rises to the top, while the thinner, lighter liquid beneath is coconut milk. Coconut, with its buttery flavor, is good for Earth element people, while other home element types should eat it sparingly, especially during hot weather. ~~~ Canned coconut cream (this is not the same as canned cream of coconut, the sweetened product used for making desserts and mixed drinks) is thickened with flour and has a very high fat content. Frozen, pasteurized, and grated coconut and coconut milk can be used for convenience. Nothing, however, comes close to freshly made coconut cream and milk for quality and nutritional value.

COCONUT CREAM AND COCONUT MILK

PREHEAT the oven to 350°F. With a screwdriver and hammer, pierce a hole through each of the three indentations on the surface of the coconuts and drain the liquid. Discard the liquid. Place the coconuts in the oven for 15 to 20 minutes. Let them cool slightly before breaking each one open with a hammer. Drape one hand with a thick towel and hold onto a piece of shell with meat. With the other hand, use a knife to pry loose the meat. It should come off easily.

REMOVE the hard, outer peel from the pieces of coconut with a vegetable peeler and discard or dry in the sun, reserving to be used for smoking or grilling recipes. Store them in a paper or plastic bag with your other grilling equipment; they'll keep for months. Slice the white coconut meat into small pieces and put them in a blender or food processor. Add 1 cup of the boiling water and process until the liquid turns milky and the coconut is reduced to pulp. Line a fine-mesh strainer with several pieces of cheesecloth and set on top of a bowl. Transfer the contents of the blender to the strainer. Let drain until the pulp is cool enough to touch, then extract the remaining liquid by squeezing the cloth tight and hard. This is the coconut cream.

RETURN the coconut pulp to the blender and add the remaining 3 to 4 cups boiling water, depending on how thick you want your milk. Process until the water turns milky. Line the strainer with a clean piece of cheesecloth, then pour in the contents of the blender and let drain into a bowl. When the pulp is cool enough to touch, squeeze the cloth tight to extract any remaining liquid. This is the coconut milk. Reserve the coconut pulp to make Dry-Roasted Coconut Flakes (page 101) for garnish or beauty treatments (see next page).

MAKES ABOUT 1 CUP CREAM
AND 3 TO 4 CUPS MILK

4 coconuts

4 to 5 cups boiling water

WHEN a recipe calls for coconut cream and milk combined, mix equal amounts of each to combine.

COCONUT cream and coconut milk will keep in the refrigerator for a couple of days in an airtight container. They can also be frozen. Transfer the cream and/or milk to separate zip-top plastic bags, seal, set them on a baking sheet, and place in the freezer until frozen. Now you can store them stacked on one another. Make sure to date your bags; coconut cream and milk will keep in the freezer for 2 to 3 months.

Coconut Pulp

Long before beauty product companies manufactured expensive coconut-infused hair softeners and body lotions, Thai women used coconut pulp, the solid left after making coconut cream and milk, to keep their hair and their bodies smooth and soft. The application is as easy as taking a handful of coconut pulp and massaging it into the hair, scalp, and skin. For dry, unmanageable hair or rough, dry, or chapped skin, use coconut pulp at least once a week. Before showering, massage the coconut pulp over your entire body, especially around calloused and dry areas, and into your scalp and hair. Leave it on for 5 minutes or longer, then shower and shampoo.

For centuries, soy milk has been highly prized as an important and nutritious food source. It's good for all home elements. Although pasteurized and packaged soy milk is available in both American and Asian markets, there is nothing quite like hot, steamy, homemade soy milk. Dried soybeans can be found in health food stores.

SOY MILK

PLACE the soybeans in a large bowl, cover them with cold water, and let soak overnight.

DRAIN the beans, then rinse several times with cool water. Transfer them to a blender and add 3 cups of the boiling water. Cover tightly with the lid and a dish towel. Blend for 1 minute, then transfer to a large saucepan. Bring the mixture to a boil, stirring constantly to prevent it from foaming over and the bean paste from settling at the bottom. Reduce the heat to medium, stir, and cook for 10 minutes. Add another cup of the boiling water and continue to stir for another 10 minutes as it boils. Turn off the heat and add the remaining 1 cup boiling water. Stir to mix.

LINE a fine-mesh strainer with several layers of cheesecloth and place it on top of another saucepan. Stir the soybean paste and liquid well before pouring it into the lined strainer. Wait until the bean paste is cool enough to touch before squeezing the cheesecloth to extract the remaining liquid. Save the bean paste for use in other recipes.

COOK the soy milk over high heat, stirring constantly to prevent it from foaming over, for 15 minutes. Stir in the sugar, if using. You can serve the soy milk hot or cold. Let it cool to room temperature before storing in an airtight container in the refrigerator, where it will keep for 2 to 3 days.

MAKES 3 CUPS

1 cup dried soybeans

5 cups boiling water

¼ cup sugar or honey (optional)

Because of its fruity-sour taste, tamarind is a good ingredient for Water element people. For others, use it in combination with ingredients having the tastes, flavors, and aromas of your home element. Tamarind pulp, which can be purchased in Asian markets, some specialty food markets, and online, is sold in an oblong block wrapped in cellophane. Though exported by a number of Southeast Asian countries, I prefer the tamarind pulp from Thailand, as it contains no preservatives and is of a uniformly high quality. ⁓ It is also believed to ease sore throats and eliminate phlegm and relieve constipation; simply take a tablespoon of it or mix it with a cup of hot water for tea.

TAMARIND PUREE

PLACE the tamarind pulp in a small bowl and pour the boiling water over it. Cover and let it cool completely. Massage to loosen the pulp. Let it sit for another 10 to 15 minutes before massaging the pulp again. Repeat the process several times, until the liquid turns into a thick sauce with the consistency of applesauce. Spoon out any solids such as seeds, casements, or pieces of shell. Store the tamarind puree in an airtight container in the refrigerator, where it will keep for up to a week.

MAKES ABOUT 1 CUP

One 3-inch square tamarind pulp

1½ cups boiling water

*L*ike many cultures, Thais consider chicken broth to be a highly nutritious food. Given to the sick, young, and elderly as a healing remedy, chicken broth is also used as an ingredient in many recipes or as a base when making soup or porridge. Chicken broth is good for all home elements. ⁓⁓⧂ Although there is no match for homemade chicken broth, for convenience substitute low-sodium, low-fat canned or boxed chicken broth. Taste before using, then adjust seasonings called for in the recipes accordingly.

CHICKEN BROTH

PUT the chicken in a large pot and cover with water. Bring to a boil. Remove from the heat and strain the chicken through a strainer. Discard the water. This step will get rid of the scum and other solids, resulting in a clear broth with a clean taste. Wash the saucepan before returning the chicken to it. Add the 10 cups water and the remaining ingredients. Bring to a boil, then reduce the heat to low, cover, and let simmer for at least 1 hour.

REMOVE from the heat and let cool before straining the broth. Save the chicken for another recipe. Transfer the broth to a tightly covered container and refrigerate overnight. The fat will congeal on the surface of the broth and can be scooped off. Chicken broth will keep, refrigerated, for 3 to 4 days, or in the freezer for 2 to 3 months. To freeze, measure the broth in 2- to 4-cup portions into plastic zip-top bags, set them on a baking sheet, and place in the freezer until frozen. Now you can store them stacked on one another. Make sure to date your bags.

MAKES ABOUT 10 CUPS

One 3½- to 4-pound chicken

10 cups water

1 teaspoon salt

2 tablespoons dry vermouth or Chinese cooking wine

One 9-inch daikon, peeled and cut into several pieces

1 onion, peeled

2 star anise

5 to 6 thin slices fresh ginger

Vegetable broth, which is lighter and less fatty than chicken broth but still highly nutritious, can be used in place of the latter. Follow this basic recipe, then experiment using other seasonal vegetables to make your own version. Store-bought vegetable broth tends to be salty with a musty aroma, so making your own is a real taste bonus, if you can. Vegetable broth is good for all home element types.

VEGETABLE BROTH

COMBINE the celery, carrots, onion, daikon, cabbage, cilantro, and water in a large pot over high heat and bring to a boil. Add the remaining ingredients, reduce the heat to low, cover, and let the broth simmer for at least 30 and up to 45 minutes.

REMOVE from the heat and let it cool before straining the broth. Transfer to a tightly covered container. Vegetable broth will keep in the refrigerator for 4 to 5 days or in the freezer for several months. To freeze, measure the broth in 2- to 4-cup portions into zip-top plastic bags, set them on a baking sheet, and place in the freezer until frozen. Now you can store them stacked on one another. Make sure to date your bags.

MAKES ABOUT 10 CUPS

3 stalks celery, quartered lengthwise

2 carrots, halved lengthwise

1 brown onion, peeled and quartered

1 cup peeled daikon cut into chunks

2 cups sliced napa cabbage

½ cup fresh cilantro leaves and stems, chopped

10 cups water

10 thin slices fresh ginger

6 cloves garlic, with skins left on

4 star anise

10 cloves

1 teaspoon salt

1 teaspoon sesame oil (optional)

Fish is the most common and important protein source in traditional Thai dishes. Rendering the taste of the river and sea, fish broth is appropriate for all seasons and home elements.

FISH BROTH

PUT the fish heads and bones in a large saucepan and cover with water. Bring to a boil, then pour into a cheesecloth-lined strainer set in the sink. Clean the saucepan before returning the fish heads and bones to it. This step will rid the broth of unwanted scum, resulting in a clear broth with a clean taste. Add the 7 cups water and the remaining ingredients. Bring to a boil, then reduce the heat to medium-low, cover, and simmer for at least 30 and up to 45 minutes. Turn off the heat and let cool. Strain through a fine-mesh strainer or one lined with cheesecloth and discard the solids. Transfer the broth to a tightly covered container. It will keep in the refrigerator for 2 to 3 days or in the freezer for a month. To freeze, measure the broth in 2- to 4-cup portions into zip-top plastic bags, set them on a baking sheet, and place in the freezer until frozen. Now you can store them stacked on one another. Make sure to date your bags.

MAKES ABOUT 6 CUPS

Heads and bones from 2 white-fleshed fish such as red snapper, catfish, or sea bass (don't use an oily, dark-fleshed fish such as mackerel or salmon)

7 cups water

1 bunch fresh cilantro

6 cloves garlic, with skins left on

10 thin slices fresh ginger

3 *krachai* (Chinese keys or lesser galangal; optional)

2 stalks lemongrass, tough outer layers removed, tender inner stalk cut into several pieces and slightly pounded

1 carrot, quartered lengthwise

6 shallots, peeled

½ teaspoon salt

1 teaspoon white peppercorns

1 teaspoon coriander seeds

Rice cooked in a covered saucepan on the stove requires constant tending so that it doesn't boil over or dry out. If you cook a lot of rice, invest in an electric rice cooker.

RICE

PLACE the rice in a strainer and rinse in cool water 2 to 3 times, until the water runs clear. Put the rice in a saucepan and add the 2 cups water. Bring to a boil, then immediately reduce the heat to medium. Continue to cook until the water disappears below the surface of the rice and there are craters in the rice. Turn the heat down as low as possible, cover the pan, and cook for another 10 to 12 minutes. When the top layer is moist and the grains are soft and tender, the rice is cooked. If the grains on the top layer are still hard and not completely cooked, add 1 to 2 tablespoons of water, cover, and cook for another minute or two.

FLUFF the grains with a fork or wooden spoon, cover, and let the rice rest for 10 minutes before serving.

Electric Rice Cooker

Rinse the rice as instructed above, then place the rice and water in a rice cooker. Cook the rice according to the manufacturer's directions. When the timer goes off, stir the rice with a fork or wooden spoon. Cover and let it rest for 10 minutes before serving.

Brown and Red Long-Grain Rice

Brown and red long-grain rice both have the bran left intact, which makes these grains more nutritious than white rice. The cooking process is somewhat different than that for white polished rice.

Both brown and red rice must be soaked in water for at least 2 hours or, preferably, overnight before cooking. The ratio of rice and water depends on when the rice was harvested. The longer rice grains are stored, the harder they are and the more water that's needed. When I cook brown or red rice, I add 2⅓ cups instead of 2 cups of water per 1 cup of rice. Aside from that, the directions for cooking the rice are the same as for white polished rice.

MAKES 4 TO 6 SERVINGS

1 cups long-grain rice, preferably Thai jasmine

2 cups water

Rice flour lacks gluten, while its starch content is believed to improve glucose regulation and moderate weight fluctuation. Rice flour makes light and airy pancakes. It is also a balancer for all home elements. Adjust the fruit mix to meet individual element needs as well as those of the weather and the changing seasons.

RICE AND BANANA PANCAKES WITH SEASONAL FRUIT MIX

COMBINE the fruit mix ingredients, except for the mint, in a medium bowl. Mix and let stand for 5 minutes before adding the mint. Mix to combine. Set aside.

COMBINE the rice flour, sugar, baking powder, and salt in a small bowl. In a large bowl, beat the melted butter and egg yolks together. Add the buttermilk and low-fat milk and mix well. Pour in the dry ingredients and stir until just combined. Add the banana and mix lightly.

IN a medium bowl, beat the egg whites until foamy, then them fold into the batter. Mix only enough to hold the ingredients together. Do not overmix. Let the batter sit for 15 minutes.

HEAT a skillet or griddle over high heat for 5 minutes. Lightly oil the surface with the butter or vegetable oil spray. Pour ¼ cup batter onto the griddle to form 3-inch cakes. Reduce the heat to medium-high. When bubbles appear on the surface, flip the cakes over and cook until the cakes feel springy and are golden on both sides. Serve hot with the fruit mix and warm maple syrup poured over them.

Seasonal Fruit Mix Variations

EARTH: Also add banana and more mango as well as coarsely chopped walnuts or toasted almonds.

WATER: Also add fresh raspberries, blackberries, and/or sliced strawberries or more mango.

WIND AND FIRE: Also add 1 cup seeded and cubed sweet summer melons mixed with 1 tablespoon minced fresh peppermint.

MAKES ABOUT 15 PANCAKES

SEASONAL FRUIT MIX

1 small ripe mango, peeled, cut off the seed, and diced

1 small ripe papaya, peeled, seeded, and diced

1 tablespoon honey

1 teaspoon minced candied ginger

Leaves from 4 fresh mint sprigs, cut into strands

RICE AND BANANA PANCAKES

1 cup fine rice flour

1 tablespoon sugar

1 teaspoon baking powder

½ teaspoon salt

1 tablespoon unsalted butter, melted and cooled

2 large eggs, separated

1 cup buttermilk

½ cup low-fat milk

1 large very ripe banana, peeled and mashed

1 tablespoon unsalted butter or nonstick vegetable oil spray

¾ cup maple syrup, or more to taste, warmed

y friend Carol, a master baker, helped me work out this recipe. It is absolutely scrumptious, with a custard-like texture and whiffs of orange zest. The combination of buttery, sweet, and sour tastes makes this recipe good for all elements. However, for Earth element people, instead of oat flour, which is not as agreeable to your constitution, substitute with buckwheat flour. You can also substitute the rice milk with soy or cow's milk. On a wet morning, add ¼ teaspoon cinnamon to the batter to appease the Wind element that brought us the rain.

APPLESAUCE PANCAKES

SIFT the flour, salt, and baking powder together in a small bowl. Add the orange zest and stir with a fork to mix.

COMBINE the egg whites in a medium bowl and beat until foamy. In a large bowl, beat the yolk and add the melted butter, rice milk, and orange juice. Mix well. Add the flour mixture and mix just enough to combine. Add the applesauce and mix again. Fold in the egg whites. Mix gently to combine. Let sit for at least 15 to 20 minutes for the flour to swell.

HEAT the griddle over high heat until very hot. Add ½ tablespoon of the frozen butter and spread evenly over the hot surface. Ladle enough batter onto the hot griddle to make pancakes 4 inches in diameter. Reduce the heat to medium-high. When air bubbles form holes on the surface of the pancake and the edges turn light brown, flip and cook on the other side. Repeat with the remaining butter and batter. Serve hot with maple syrup and your choice of topping.

1½ cups oat flour

¼ teaspoon salt

1 teaspoon baking powder

Grated zest of 1 orange

1 large egg, separated

1 large egg white

1 tablespoon unsalted butter, melted

½ cup rice milk

1 tablespoon orange juice

1 cup applesauce

1 tablespoon frozen unsalted butter

Maple syrup, warmed

TOPPINGS

EARTH: **sliced banana**

WATER: **berries and sliced orange**

WIND AND FIRE: **sliced pear**

PANCAKES

R ecently, Thai vendors have discovered how to make pancakes and sell them on the streets as a snack all day long. I love pancakes too, but for breakfast.

For the batter, I use white all-purpose flour during summer. On rainy or cold days, I switch to oat, whole-wheat, or buckwheat flour. One of my stepsons is sensitive to gluten, so when he visits, I make corn cakes.

I add mashed sweet overripe banana, applesauce, or blueberries to the batter, again depending on the weather or season. Most mornings, I use bananas. Blueberries are for summer when they are ripe, juicy, and sweet, with just enough tartness for balance. Applesauce is added to warm us on cold, wet, and gloomy mornings.

These are marvelous cakes when summer corn is sweet. It is a special treat for individuals who are sensitive to gluten. Topping them with ripe sweet-sour berries helps us balance the influence of the Water element, which influences the morning hours. A bit of mint tempers the heat of people with Wind or Fire as their home elements. Earth element people will relish the rich, buttery taste of corn. All in all, these make the perfect summer breakfast for all.

CORN CAKES WITH FRESH BERRIES

COMBINE the berries, honey, zest, and mint in a medium bowl. Mix lightly and set aside.

COMBINE the dry ingredients in a small bowl. In another small bowl, beat the egg white until foamy and set aside. In large bowl, whisk the egg yolk, then add the melted butter and beat until well blended.

PUT the buttermilk and corn in a blender and puree. Transfer to the bowl with the egg yolk and butter; whisk to combine. Add the dry ingredients and mix lightly to combine. Do not overmix. Fold the egg white into the mixture until there are no white streaks. Let the batter sit for 10 minutes.

HEAT a nonstick griddle over high heat for 5 minutes. Lightly grease the surface with the butter. Ladle enough batter onto the grill to form cakes 3 inches in diameter. Reduce the heat to medium-high. When bubbles appear on the surface, flip the cakes over and cook until they feel springy.

SERVE hot with the berry mixture, maple syrup, and turkey bacon, if using.

MAKES 14 TO 16 CAKES; ABOUT 3 SERVINGS

2 cups mixed fresh berries

1 tablespoon honey

Grated zest of 1 orange

7 to 10 fresh mint leaves, minced

1¼ cups fine cornmeal

¼ teaspoon salt

1 tablespoon sugar

¼ teaspoon ground cinnamon

½ teaspoon baking powder

1 large egg, separated

2 tablespoons unsalted butter, melted

1½ cups low-fat buttermilk

1 cup corn kernels cut fresh from the cob

1 tablespoon unsalted butter

Maple syrup, warmed

6 to 8 strips turkey bacon (optional), cooked and kept warm

*C*ompote is a wonderfully versatile preparation, both in how it can be served and in what it's made with. For serving, try it spooned over warm pancakes, with a drizzle of maple syrup on top. Or mix several spoonfuls of compote with a cup of plain yogurt and turn it into a mouthwatering treat. On a cold, rainy morning, it's a wonderful choice, served up with a couple of pieces of toast made from your choice of bread. It is a good base to which you can add or omit fruits and nuts most suitable to individual elements. ～⊷ Here are two different variations; each yields 3 cups.

FRUIT COMPOTE

FOR the Cranberry-Apple Compote, combine all the ingredients in a medium saucepan over medium heat and cook until the apples are soft, about 20 minutes.

FOR the Apple, Fig, and Pear Compote, combine the apples, figs, cranberries, orange zest and juice, and sugar in a medium saucepan over medium heat and cook until the apples are soft, about 20 minutes. Then add the pear, cinnamon, and nutmeg and cook until the pear is softened. Serve warm topped with the Grape-Nuts.

CRANBERRY-APPLE COMPOTE

¼ cup dried cranberries, soaked in 1 cup apple juice until softened (about 20 minutes)

2 apples, peeled, cored, and diced

½ cup sugar

1 cup water

APPLE, FIG, AND PEAR COMPOTE

2 apples, peeled, cored, and diced

½ cup dried figs

½ cup dried cranberries

Grated zest of 1 to 2 oranges

¼ cup orange juice

¾ cup sugar

1 pear, peeled, cored, and diced

¼ teaspoon ground cinnamon

¼ teaspoon freshly grated nutmeg

3 tablespoons Grape-Nuts cereal or wheat- or rice-based granola

m

y husband, Bob, who has Water with a cusp of Earth as his home elements, has low tolerance for fruit. I created this for him when our fig tree was heavy with fruit and fresh dried dates were on sale at the farmers' market, both of which are easy to digest. Combined with sweet pear, tart plum, and buttery, crunchy walnuts, this medley is not only a perfect treat for Water and Earth element people, it is also irresistible to Wind and Fire element people.

PEAR, PLUM, FIG, DATE, AND WALNUT TREAT

COMBINE all the ingredients, except for the walnuts and candied ginger, in a medium bowl. Just before serving, add the walnuts and candied ginger, mix, and serve.

Variations

EARTH: Add ½ cup dried Bing cherries.

WATER: Add sections from 2 tangerines or 1 orange.

WIND: Instead of walnuts, add toasted slivered almonds.

FIRE: Instead of plums, use nectarines or Pluots.

MAKES ABOUT 2 CUPS

3 pears, peeled, cored, and cut into chunks

4 plums, pitted and cut into chunks

6 fresh figs, quartered

1 teaspoon fresh lemon juice

1 cup chopped dates

½ cup chopped walnuts

1 tablespoon candied ginger, slivered

R egardless of our home elements, as the Wind element showers us with rain or the Earth element impacts us with cool air, we all need to stay in balance with them as well as with nature's Water element, which rules the morning hours. This recipe is a delicious balancing act.

CITRUS JOY

PEEL the oranges and grapefruit with a knife over a bowl to catch the juices. Section each to remove the pith, and put the segments in the bowl. Add the remaining ingredients and mix gently. Let sit for 5 to 10 minutes before serving.

Variations

EARTH: Add ¼ cup chopped walnuts.

WATER: Add ¼ cup toasted slivered almonds or pomegranate seeds.

WIND: Add ½ cup roasted shelled sunflower seeds.

FIRE: Add ¼ cup pomegranate seeds or 1 pear, peeled, cored, and sliced.

MAKES ABOUT 4 SERVINGS

2 navel or Valencia oranges

1 grapefruit

2 cups peeled, seeded, and sliced papaya

1 banana, peeled and sliced

1 tablespoon honey

¼ cup dried cherries

3 fresh mint leaves, cut into strands

Kai yud sai or "egg with stuffing" is a Thai-style omelet. Actually, it's a thin egg crepe wrapped around a filling. The edges are then folded and flipped over into a square and eaten with rice, but it's equally good on crispy wheat toast.

THAI-STYLE OMELET WITH TOMATO, CELERY, AND TOFU Kai Yud Sai

HEAT a medium skillet over high heat for 1 minute. Add the oil and heat for another minute. Add the garlic and stir-fry for 10 seconds. Add the ginger. Stir to mix, then add your selection of vegetables. Stir until they are cooked but still crunchy. Season with the salt, white pepper, and soy sauce. Remove from the heat.

BEAT the eggs, salt, pepper, and fish sauce together in a large bowl until frothy. Heat a 12-inch nonstick skillet over high heat for 1 to 2 minutes. Add 1 tablespoon of the oil and swirl around to coat the skillet. Pour half of the egg mixture into the skillet and swirl to spread it evenly over the bottom. When the top begins to congeal and the bottom is brown, loosen the edges and turn off the heat. Arrange half the filling in the center of the omelet. Sprinkle with 1 tablespoon of the cilantro. Fold the edges of the omelet over the filling to make a square. Carefully lift it from the skillet and flip it over and onto a serving plate. Repeat with the remaining ingredients. Serve hot with whole-wheat or multigrain toast.

Variations

EARTH: 2 asparagus spears, thinly sliced; 2 to 3 canned artichoke hearts, rinsed and finely chopped; ½ cup corn kernels; and ⅓ cup minced fresh Italian parsley

WATER: ¼ cup thinly sliced celery; 1 small ripe tomato, seeded and finely chopped; ½ cup finely chopped baked tofu; and 1 scallion, minced

WIND: ¼ cup thinly sliced celery; 1 small onion, minced; ⅓ cup finely chopped red or green bell pepper; ½ cup minced mushrooms; and ¼ cup fresh regular or Thai basil leaves, torn

FIRE: ½ cup minced mushrooms, ½ cup finely chopped broccoli florets, ½ cup finely chopped fennel bulb, and ⅓ cup minced fresh tarragon

MAKES 2 SERVINGS

FILLING

1 tablespoon canola, rice bran, sunflower, or safflower oil

1 teaspoon minced garlic

1 tablespoon peeled and minced fresh ginger

Your choice of vegetables (see variations below)

¼ teaspoon salt

½ teaspoon white pepper

1 tablespoon soy sauce

OMELET

4 large eggs, at room temperature

¼ teaspoon salt

½ teaspoon white pepper

1 teaspoon fish sauce (substitute with soy sauce for vegetarians)

2 tablespoons canola, rice bran, sunflower, or safflower oil

2 tablespoons chopped fresh cilantro

This smoothie is a breakfast drink suitable for all home elements when the weather is hot. For an afternoon snack, Wind and Water element people should substitute ⅓ cup peeled, seeded, and sliced cucumber for the honey.

BANANA-PAPAYA-MANGO RUMBA

PLACE all the ingredients, except for the mint, in a blender, but don't overstuff it. Cover tightly and blend at low to medium speed. If the fruit becomes jammed at the bottom, turn off the machine, uncover, and use a spatula to scrape down the sides of the blender. If the mixture is too thick, add a bit more orange juice. Cover and blend at medium speed until the mixture starts to churn and spin. Increase the speed to liquefy. Blend until smooth. Transfer to a glass, garnish with a mint sprig, and enjoy.

Variation

Substitute 2 cups pineapple chunks and 2 to 3 kiwis, peeled and sliced, for the papaya and mango.

MAKES 4 SERVINGS

1 ripe banana, peeled and sliced

2 cups peeled, seeded, and sliced papaya

1 cup peeled and sliced fresh mango

1 cup sliced frozen mango (or use 2 cups frozen and omit the fresh)

1 tablespoon honey

⅓ cup cold orange juice

4 fresh mint sprigs

Here's another smoothie suitable for all home elements during the warm seasons. As a midday snack for Water, Wind, and Fire element people, omit the honey and substitute apple juice for the milk.

MUMBO JUMBO MELON AND BANANA SMOOTHIE

PLACE all the ingredients in a blender, but don't overstuff it. Cover tightly and blend at low to medium speed. If the fruit becomes jammed at the bottom, turn off the machine, uncover, and use a spatula to scrape down the sides of the blender. If the mixture is too thick, add a bit more liquid, either orange juice or milk. Cover and blend at medium speed until the mixture starts to churn and spin. Increase the speed to liquefy. Blend until smooth. Transfer to a glass and enjoy.

MAKES 4 SERVINGS

1 cup each watermelon, cantaloupe, Crenshaw, or other melon chunks (3 cups total)

1 ripe banana, peeled and cut up

½ cup frozen mango chunks

1 tablespoon honey

½ cup cold orange juice

½ cup ice-cold low-fat milk or Almond Milk (page 21)

SMOOTHIES

When seasonal fruits are plentiful, slice and freeze them for making smoothies, or you can use store-bought frozen mango, peaches, and whatever else you can find. Combine the fresh and frozen fruits with the tastes and flavors best suited to your home element, the season, and the time of day.

To ensure the most intense flavor, start with cold ingredients where possible, so that you don't have to add ice. You'll see that some of my recipes call for a combination of fresh and frozen fruit for that very reason.

Hom mak means "very fragrant" in Thai, which perfectly describes this cinnamon-scented banana and pear smoothie. Serve it as a breakfast drink or for a midday snack for all home elements when it is cool or rainy.

BANANA AND PEAR Hom Mak

PLACE all the ingredients in a blender, but don't overstuff it. Cover tightly and blend at low to medium speed. If the fruit becomes jammed at the bottom, turn off the machine, uncover, and use a spatula to scrape down the sides of the blender. If the mixture is too thick, add a bit more soy milk. Cover and blend at medium speed until the mixture starts to churn and spin. Increase the speed to liquefy. Blend until smooth. Transfer to a glass and enjoy.

MAKES 4 SERVINGS

3 ripe bananas, peeled and cut up

2 cups peeled, cored, and sliced ripe pear

1 cup cold Soy Milk (page 24)
or Almond Milk (page 21)

2 tablespoons honey

¼ teaspoon ground cinnamon

½ cup crushed ice

This cool morning breakfast drink is ideal for Water element people. For Wind and Fire element people, add ⅓ cup minced fresh mint. For Earth element people, sweeten it with either an extra tablespoon of honey or use sweet melons instead of the papaya.

BERRY AND PAPAYA SMOOTHIE

PLACE all the ingredients in a blender, but don't overstuff it. Cover tightly and blend at low to medium speed. If the fruit becomes jammed at the bottom, turn off the machine, uncover, and use a spatula to scrape down the sides of the blender. If the mixture is too thick, add a bit more soy milk. Cover and blend at medium speed until the mixture starts to churn and spin. Increase the speed to liquefy. Blend until smooth. Transfer to a glass and enjoy.

MAKES 4 SERVINGS

2 cups mixed fresh or frozen berries, such as strawberries, blueberries, blackberries, and/or raspberries

1 cup peeled and seeded fresh papaya chunks

1 cup frozen papaya chunks

1 ripe banana, peeled and cut up

1 tablespoon honey

¼ cup Soy Milk (page 24) or Almond Milk (page 21)

This is best for Water element people, who need extra protection for their respiratory system.

BANANA AND PAPAYA SMOOTHIE WITH KUMQUAT, HONEY, AND GINGER PRESERVES

PLACE all the ingredients in a blender, but don't overstuff it. Cover tightly and blend at low to medium speed. If the fruit becomes jammed at the bottom, turn off the machine, uncover, and use a spatula to scrape down the sides of the blender. If the mixture is too thick, add a bit more apple juice. Cover and blend at medium speed until the mixture starts to churn and spin. Increase the speed to liquefy. Blend until smooth. Transfer to a glass and enjoy.

MAKES 4 SERVINGS

¼ cup Kumquat, Ginger, and Clove Preserves (page 100), minced

2 ripe bananas, peeled and cut up

2 cups peeled and seeded fresh papaya chunks

1 cup frozen papaya chunks

1 cup apple juice

The slightly bitter and astringent flavors kindle the inner heat of Fire element people in rainy and cold weather. Earth element people can add extra honey as a protective measure for joints and tendons. Water and Wind element people can dilute the pomegranate juice by substituting ½ cup of apple juice.

BANANA, PEAR, GRAPEFRUIT, AND POMEGRANATE SMOOTHIE

PLACE all the ingredients in a blender, but don't overstuff it. Cover tightly and blend at low to medium speed. If the fruit becomes jammed at the bottom, turn off the machine, uncover, and use a spatula to scrape down the sides of the blender. If the mixture is too thick, add a bit more soy milk. Cover and blend at medium speed until the mixture starts to churn and spin. Increase the speed to liquefy. Blend until smooth. Transfer to a glass and enjoy.

MAKES 4 SERVINGS

1 ripe banana, peeled and cut up

2 pears, peeled, cored, and cut into chunks

1 cup grapefruit sections

½ cup pomegranate juice

½ cup Soy Milk (page 24) or Almond Milk (page 21)

2 tablespoons honey

HERBAL DRINKS, JUICES, AND TEAS

The favorite beverage of Thai people of my generation is room-temperature water, at least 8 glasses a day. Herbal drinks, juices, and teas are booster beverages that can revitalize or restore our health and disposition, especially when the weather is fickle and extreme.

^Don't be turned off by the name of this beverage. This beautiful fan-shaped herb produces a rather unusual-looking dark olive green–colored juice. The flavor tastes like a combination of fresh spring celery and carrots. With a bit of sugar syrup, Asiatic Pennywort Drink is refreshing and cooling, with an almost instant calming effect, making it perfect for hot weather. It is also believed to relieve constipation and is suitable for all home elements. ⁓ᦉ During summer months, Asiatic pennywort herb is available in health food stores and Asian markets. It will keep in the refrigerator for 3 to 4 days.

ASIATIC PENNYWORT DRINK

IN a small saucepan over medium heat, combine the sugar and ½ cup of the water, stirring until the sugar is dissolved. Set aside.

IN a blender, combine 2 cups each of the water and pennywort. Blend at high speed until smooth. Carefully open the lid, add a handful more of the leaves, and blend until smooth. Continue doing this, adding more of the water as necessary to maintain a smooth puree, until all the leaves are used up.

LINE a fine-mesh strainer with cheesecloth. Pour the puree into the strainer. Pick up the cheesecloth and squeeze the liquid into a bowl. Save the pulp for another use (see below).

MIX the remaining water with the juice and add the sugar syrup. Stir to mix, cover, and refrigerate. Serve chilled or over ice cubes.

Asiatic Pennywort Pulp

The pulp left over from extracting the juice of Asiatic pennywort has long been used as a balm, massaged into the skin to reduce bruising and inflammation and to heal cuts and sores. The treatment is repeated several times a week during the first week immediately following the injury.

Put about 1 cup of the pulp in a piece of cheesecloth and warm for 10 to 15 seconds in the microwave. Massage gently around the affected area for at least 10 minutes. Repeat every 2 to 3 hours for a week or two, or until the pain and/or bruise lessens.

MAKES ABOUT 6 CUPS

½ **cup sugar**

7½ **cups water**

8 **cups fresh Asiatic pennywort leaves and stems, washed thoroughly**

Tamarind is often used to ease constipation. A glass of this juice a day will do the trick when needed. Clove is a warming spice that helps with digestion. This is a good drink for Water and Wind element people. For all elements, drink it when needed.

TAMARIND JUICE WITH CLOVES

COMBINE the sugar, cloves, and ½ cup of the water in a small saucepan over medium heat. Stir until the sugar is dissolved, then reduce the heat to low and let simmer for 5 minutes. Let cool a little, then strain into a pitcher to remove the cloves. Stir in the tamarind puree until well combined, then add the remaining 4 cups water. Stir well and serve over ice or refrigerate until cold. It will keep for a couple of days.

MAKES 4 CUPS

¾ cup sugar

6 cloves

4½ cups water

¾ cup Tamarind Puree (page 25)

W atermelon is refreshing and uplifting, especially during hot weather. It contains quantities of lycopene, an antioxidant, which may prevent prostate and skin cancer and reduce the risk of muscular degeneration. Also a diuretic, which is important for good kidney health, it's good for all home elements.

WATERMELON JUICE

COMBINE the sugar with ¼ cup of the water in a small saucepan over medium heat. Stir until the sugar is dissolved. Let cool completely.

COMBINE the remaining 1 cup water and 2 to 3 cups of the watermelon in a blender. Blend at high speed until smooth. Keep the motor running and carefully open the lid of the blender to add a cupful of the remaining watermelon at a time until it's all been added and the mixture is smooth. Transfer to a pitcher, add the sugar syrup, and mix well. Refrigerate until cold. Stir well to mix before serving chilled, over crushed ice if you like, garnished with a sprig of mint. This will keep in the refrigerator for a couple of days.

Sparkling Watermelon Juice

Add 1 cup sparkling water or Champagne and instead of sugar syrup, 2 tablespoons orange blossom syrup, and mix well.

MAKES ABOUT 7 CUPS

¼ **cup sugar**

1¼ **cups water**

8 **cups seeded and crushed watermelon**

7 **to 8 fresh mint sprigs**

Hot or cold chrysanthemum tea cools and calms the nerves. It is especially beneficial for Water and Fire element people, but suitable for all. Canned sweetened chrysanthemum tea and sweetened granulated chrysanthemum tea bags, as well as dried chrysanthemum blossoms, are available in Asian supermarkets and pharmacies and online.

CHRYSANTHEMUM TEA

PUT the chrysanthemum blossoms in a heat-resistant container. Pour the hot water over them. Cover and let it steep for 5 to 7 minutes. Strain the tea into another container or a teapot. If served hot, add a bit of sugar or honey to each serving. If to be served cold, add the sweetener to taste and stir well. Let the tea cool before refrigerating. It will keep for a couple of days.

MAKES ABOUT 6 CUPS

2 tablespoons dried chrysanthemum blossoms

6 cups boiling water

Sugar or honey to taste

Lemongrass tea is a diuretic, keeping the kidneys healthy and reducing hypertension, and is also good for soothing frayed nerves. Suitable for all home elements, it is particularly good for Water and Wind elements.

LEMONGRASS TEA

CUT the lemongrass into manageable lengths and pound slightly. Transfer to a large saucepan and add the water. Bring to a boil. Reduce the heat to medium-low and let the tea simmer for at least 30 minutes, until the color of the water turns slightly brown. Strain the tea into a heatproof container and add the sugar, stirring to dissolve. Serve hot or cold. It will keep for several days in the refrigerator; let it cool completely before refrigerating.

MAKES ABOUT 6 CUPS

10 to 12 stalks lemongrass, tough outer layers removed

8 cups water

¼ cup sugar or honey

*G*inger tea warms the respiratory system and is a comforting, nurturing drink when you have a cold. It also aids indigestion and calms the nerves. Suitable for all home elements, it is especially effective during rainy weather. If you don't want to use fresh ginger, individual ginger tea bags are sold in health food stores and sweetened ginger tea bags are available in Asian supermarkets and pharmacies.

GINGER TEA

PUT the ginger and water in a small saucepan and bring to a boil. Reduce the heat to medium-low and let the tea brew for 20 to 30 minutes. Strain the tea into teacups and add the honey. Stir to dissolve. Serve hot.

MAKES 2 CUPS

10 to 12 thin slices fresh ginger, slightly pounded

3 cups water

1 tablespoon honey

*O*n rainy or cold days, hot cocoa is comforting for breakfast or a mid-day snack. Instead of regular milk, try making it with almond milk or soy milk.

HOT COCOA WITH ALMOND MILK

PUT all the ingredients in a small saucepan, stir to mix, and heat over medium heat. Stir until it boils. Serve hot.

MAKES 1 SERVING

1 cup Almond Milk (page 21) or Soy Milk (page 24)

1 teaspoon sugar or honey

1 tablespoon unsweetened cocoa powder

1 to 2 drops almond extract (add only if using almond milk)

$\mathbf{m}$*ieng khum* is considered the perfect snack, appropriate for all seasons and all home element types. In a single bite, you experience *grom-grawm* (see page 52) and are rewarded with the nine essential natural tastes, flavors, and aromas that nurture our bodies' elements. *Mieng khum* sauce can be made ahead. It keeps very well for at least a couple of months in the refrigerator. Coconut matchsticks, the most laborious task of the process, can also be made ahead. After dry-roasting, store them in an airtight container at room temperature, where they stay crisp and fresh for several months.

ONE SAVORY BITE Mieng Khum

PREHEAT the oven to 500°F.

SPREAD the shrimp paste on the softened corn husk, roll it up, secure it with a toothpick, and roast it until it begins to char, about 5 minutes. Let cool. (If using red miso, skip this step.)

IN a mortar, pound the galangal, lemongrass, and shallot together into a paste. Add the roasted shrimp paste or red miso and mix well to combine. Transfer to a small saucepan and add the palm sugar and fish sauce. Stir to mix and heat over medium heat. When it begins to boil, reduce the heat to low and continue to stir. Stir in the dried shrimp and water. When the mixture begins to boil and the mixture thickens, stir in the coconut flakes. Transfer the mixture to a bowl and let cool. If making ahead, store in an airtight container in the refrigerator. When ready to use, take the amount needed and heat briefly to soften. If the sauce is too thick, stir in 1 tablespoon water and heat through.

USE a vegetable peeler to peel the coconut into thin, long ribbons. Stack several ribbons together and slice across into tiny matchsticks. Repeat with the remaining coconut ribbons. Put them in a large skillet and dry-roast over medium-high heat, stirring constantly to prevent burning and ensure even roasting. When the matchsticks turn golden, remove to a plate to cool completely. You can store them in an airtight container at room temperature for months.

THERE are two ways to serve mieng khum:

PUT all the ingredients, except the greens you choose, in small individual bowls, with the sauce in a slightly larger bowl. Put the bowls and the greens on a large platter. Instruct each guest to pick up a leaf and shape it into a cone. Fill it with one or two pieces of dried shrimp, peanuts, shallots, ginger, limes, and chiles (the diners can skip the chiles if they

MAKES 12 SERVINGS

SAUCE

2 teaspoons fermented shrimp paste or red miso

1 dried corn husk, softened in warm water and dried thoroughly

2 tablespoons minced galangal or peeled and minced fresh ginger

1 stalk lemongrass, tough outer layers and green stem removed, tender inner stalk minced

2 shallots, minced

1 cup palm sugar, dark brown sugar, or maple sugar

2 tablespoons fish sauce (substitute with light soy sauce for vegetarians)

2 tablespoons dried shrimp, soaked in warm water to soften, dried thoroughly, and pounded to pulverize (omit for vegetarians or if you can't find)

½ cup water

⅓ cup Dry-Roasted Coconut Flakes (page 101)

prefer less hotness). Top it off with a teaspoon of coconut matchsticks, then ladle a small spoonful, or less, of the sauce on top. Fold the cone over and eat in one bite.

OR, smear ½ teaspoon of the sauce in the center of each leaf and place them on a large serving platter, lining the platter with the leaves. Garnish the center of each leaf with 1 piece each of dried shrimp, peanut, shallot, ginger, and lime. Finish with ½ teaspoon, or more, of the coconut matchsticks. Put the chiles in a small bowl with a spoon in the center of the platter for the guests to help themselves. Instruct the guests to gather and wrap the leaf around with the fillings into a bundle. Eat in one bite.

CONDIMENTS

1 coconut, meat removed from the husk and outer dark parts peeled (page 22)

⅓ cup small dried shrimp (omit for vegetarians or if you can't find; substitute with smoked salted fish such as salmon or sturgeon, minced)

⅓ cup dry-roasted unsalted peanuts

1 to 2 shallots, cut into small dice

One 3-inch piece young ginger, peeled and cut into small dice (you can substitute regular ginger, but if you do, soak it in water to which you've added ¼ teaspoon salt for 5 to 6 minutes, then rinse, pat dry, and cube

1 to 2 limes, cut into small dice

3 to 4 fresh Thai or 1 to 2 fresh serrano chiles, thinly sliced

24 spinach, Chinese broccoli, broccoli raab, or young tender kale leaves

$\mathcal{A}$ gift from Southern Thailand, this rice salad bursts forth with a harmonious, vibrant, and intense blend of tastes, flavors, and aromas. In one single bite, you can taste the robust flavors of the earth, splashed with the briny taste of the ocean, swathed in the exuberant experience of dazzling sunshine.

FRAGRANT RICE SALAD

WASH the salt off the anchovies and put in a medium saucepan. Add the remaining dressing ingredients and cook over high heat. When it begins to boil, stir to mix, lower the heat to medium-low, and cook until you have a syrup that clings slightly to the back of the spoon, 15 to 20 minutes. Taste for a pleasing balance of saltiness and sweetness. Pour the dressing through a fine-mesh strainer. Discard the solids and let the dressing cool. If making ahead, store in an airtight container in the refrigerator, where it will keep for months. When ready to use, warm in a microwave to liquefy the dressing.

ARRANGE the salad ingredients, except for the slices of lime, in mounds on a large platter. When ready to serve, mix them together. Pour the dressing over everything and toss gently to combine. Add the juice of 2 slices of lime. Taste first before adding the juice from the third slice, if needed. Serve immediately.

MAKES 4 SERVINGS

DRESSING

¾ cup anchovies packed in salt (available in specialty food stores)

1 cup water

1 cup palm sugar, firmly packed dark brown sugar, or maple sugar

6 shallots, peeled and slightly pounded

2 stalks lemongrass, tough outer layers removed, tender inner stalk cut into bite-size pieces and slightly pounded

10 kaffir lime leaves, slightly torn, or 1 tablespoon slivered lime zest

15 thin slices galangal or fresh ginger, slightly pounded

SALAD

1 cup loosely packed cooked white, brown, or red rice (page 29)

1 tablespoon dried shrimp, softened in warm water, drained, patted dry, and pounded into a puree (substitute with smoked and salted fish, minced)

¼ cup Dry-Roasted Coconut Flakes (page 101)

½ teaspoon or more pure chile powder of your choice

½ cup bean sprouts, both ends removed

1 stalk lemongrass, tough outer layers removed, tender inner stalk thinly sliced across into rings

2 tender, young kaffir lime leaves, cut into slivers, or 1 tablespoon grated lime zest

⅓ cup peeled and shredded green mango or unpeeled tart green apple

⅓ cup thinly sliced green beans

2 to 3 slices lime

Originally created by the staff at the Thai Traditional Medicine Development Foundation of Bangkok, this salad combines 18 Thai herbs, spices, and greens, all selected to harmonize the nine natural tastes, flavors, and aromas that balance our body elements. The dressing blends together ingredients from two opposite elements—Earth and Wind—plus a sour note representing the Water element. ～⋙ Some of the greens in the original recipe are not available anywhere but Thailand, so I have substituted greens with similar tastes and flavors.

SWEET 18 SALAD Yum Sow Sip Phad

COMBINE the sugar, vinegar, and salt in a small saucepan over high heat. When the sugar and salt have dissolved, remove from the heat to cool. Stir in the cayenne, then the lime juice. If not using right away, store in an airtight container, where it will keep for several weeks.

IN a large salad bowl, toss together all the salad ingredients, except for the sesame seeds. Add the dressing and toss gently to mix. Sprinkle the sesame seeds on top and toss lightly again. Serve immediately.

MAKES 4 SERVINGS

DRESSING

⅓ cup sugar

2 tablespoons distilled white vinegar

½ teaspoon salt

½ teaspoon or more cayenne pepper

1 tablespoon fresh lime juice

SALAD

1 cup thinly slivered spinach

½ cup thinly sliced wing beans or green beans

6 to 7 arugula leaves, thinly sliced into long ribbons

2 to 3 sorrel leaves, thinly sliced into long ribbons

⅓ cup slivered Belgian endive

⅓ cup slivered frisée (6 to 7 sprigs)

⅓ cup slivered beet greens

⅓ cup slivered Asiatic pennywort or watercress leaves

½ cup shredded carrot

⅓ cup peeled and shredded green mango or unpeeled tart green apple

1 stalk lemongrass, tough outer layers removed, tender inner stalk thinly sliced across into rings

3 thin slices galangal or fresh ginger, slivered

¼ cup fresh Thai basil or peppermint leaves, slivered

1 tablespoon minced fresh dill

¼ cup fresh holy basil or peppermint leaves, slivered

Leaves from 7 to 8 sprigs fresh Italian parsley, slivered

2 tablespoons black or white sesame seeds, toasted in a small skillet over medium heat until fragrant

SALADS

The ideal Thai salad, a culinary experience filled with expected and unexpected textures and tastes, is an indulgent blending of meats, cooked and fresh vegetables, sweet-tart fruits, and a crispy-crunchy garnish. Thai salads exemplify the notion of *grom-grawm*, which means pleasing the eye and teasing the palate while healthfully nurturing our body elements.

Included here are two examples that glorify the Thai notion of grom-grawm, while fulfilling the philosophy of the basic four elements. Each uses ingredients that balance the nine natural tastes, flavors, and aromas. Their harmonious blend makes each a perfect dish for all of us, whatever our home element. Also included are the recipes for Northeastern Thai Salad and Cucumber Relish, which you can tailor-make to nurture the particular needs of your home element.

Following the salads is a selection of dressings. Each of them is balanced and perfect for all home elements, although some are more suited for specific home elements. A few have bold flavors and pair well with hearty salads made with combinations of meat or poultry, greens, and fruit. The lighter dressings are a good match for mixed vegetable salads and those containing poultry and/or seafood.

Although there are many versions of this spicy-sour salad, the one from northeastern Thailand is popular throughout Thailand. Northeasterners, who live in the dry, arid climate, tend to stretch their limited resources by dressing their *som-tum* with bland green papaya strands pounded with loads of fresh, fiery hot chiles, salted baby crab, and lime juice. This recipe is more in tune with the Bangkok style. Bangkokians love their *som-tum* with "exotic" ingredients, including shredded carrots and strawberries. They also tone down the flavors, balancing the spiciness with the sweetness of palm sugar. The peanuts are a Bangkok addition. *Som-tum* is best suited for Earth, Water, and Wind element people. For Fire element people, lessen the heat by adding fewer chiles and wrap the salad in lettuce or cabbage leaves for a cooling crunch.

NORTHEASTERN THAI SALAD Som-Tum

PUT the garlic in a mortar and pound into a paste. Add the chiles and pound to bruise. Add the palm sugar and pound to combine. (If your mortar is small, transfer the mixture to a metal bowl, using it in place of the mortar.) Add the fruit and pound with the pestle to bruise. Use a spoon to mix and blend the ingredients together. Sprinkle with the fish sauce and lime juice. Mix with a spoon and pound lightly to incorporate it well. Add the peanuts, if using, and mix to combine. Line a platter with lettuce leaves and top with the salad mixture. Serve with cooked rice.

Suggested *som-tum* combinations

1 cup peeled, seeded, and shredded green papaya; ⅓ cup shredded carrot; 4 to 6 cherry tomatoes, sliced; and ⅓ cup peeled green mango or unpeeled tart green apple cut into matchsticks *or*

¾ cup peeled, seeded, and shredded green papaya, ⅓ cup thinly sliced strawberries, and ⅓ cup pineapple cut into small pieces or peeled green mango or unpeeled tart green apple cut into matchsticks *or*

¾ cup peeled, seeded, and shredded green papaya; ⅓ cup peeled jicama cut into matchsticks; ⅓ cup shredded carrot; and 3 to 4 cherry tomatoes, sliced, or ⅓ cup peeled green mango or unpeeled tart green apple cut into matchsticks

MAKES 1 SERVING

1 clove garlic, peeled

2 to 3 fresh Thai or 1 fresh serrano chile(s)

1 teaspoon palm sugar, dark brown sugar, or maple sugar

1½ cups shredded or thinly sliced fruits and/or vegetables of your choice (see below for suggested combinations)

1½ tablespoons fish sauce

1 tablespoon fresh lime juice

1 tablespoon slightly crushed dry-roasted unsalted peanuts (optional)

3 to 4 lettuce or cabbage leaves

Cucumber relish is served as an accompaniment to spicy or richly flavored dishes such as curries or deep-fried fish or meat. The basic recipe combines sliced cucumber (cool/refreshing for Fire and Wind elements) with salt (Earth element), sugar (Earth element), and vinegar (Water element), making it perfect for all home elements.

CUCUMBER RELISH Ajaad

COMBINE all the ingredients in a medium bowl and let rest for 5 to 10 minutes before serving.

Variations

Add one or more of the following ingredients to the main recipe.

EARTH: 1 tablespoon freshly grated coconut, 1 teaspoon toasted sesame seeds, 1 tablespoon coarsely chopped dry-roasted unsalted peanuts

WATER AND FIRE: 1 tablespoon peeled and minced fresh ginger, 1 teaspoon slivered fresh turmeric or parsnip, 2 tablespoons coarsely chopped fresh cilantro, 1 tablespoon slivered fresh mint

WIND: 1 clove garlic, thinly sliced; 1 tablespoon peeled and slivered fresh ginger; 1 shallot, thinly sliced; 1 teaspoon minced fresh chile; 1 teaspoon slivered fresh turmeric or parsnip; 2 tablespoons coarsely chopped fresh cilantro; 1 tablespoon slivered fresh mint

FOR ALL HOME ELEMENTS: Select an ingredient from each of the elements' variations and add to the main recipe.

2 cups peeled and seeded cucumber thinly sliced on the diagonal

½ teaspoon salt

2 tablespoons sugar

1 tablespoon distilled white vinegar

B lack sesame seeds are a good source of essential fatty acids, and are also known to have twice as much calcium as regular white sesame seeds. They are also good for the kidneys and liver. The dressing's combination of Earth element's creamy sesame and sweet honey with Water element's sour tamarind and Wind's punchy-spicy taste of garlic, ginger, and pepper is a good match for salads made with bitter greens or grilled meat.

BLACK SESAME DRESSING

PUT the sesame seeds in a mortar and grind with a pestle into powder. Transfer to a blender, add the remaining ingredients, and blend until smooth. Adjust the taste for a balance of sweet, sour, slightly spicy, and salty. Refrigerate until ready to use. It will keep for a day, though the lime juice might lose its sourness. Before using, taste and adjust.

Salad suggestions (each makes 3 to 4 servings; use ¼ cup of dressing, or to taste)

EARTH: One 12-ounce carton firm tofu, cut lengthwise into ¾-inch-thick slices, or ½ pound pork tenderloin, marinated with 1 tablespoon soy sauce and ½ teaspoon sesame oil, grilled and thinly sliced; 1 cup thinly sliced fennel bulb; and ½ cup thinly sliced crisp, tart apple

WATER: ½ pound peeled and deveined shrimp marinated with a pinch of salt, ½ teaspoon hot paprika, and 1 tablespoon safflower oil and grilled; 3 oranges, peeled and thinly sliced; 1 cup tightly packed watercress; and ¼ cup slivered almonds, toasted in a small skillet over medium heat until lightly golden

WIND: 2 handfuls asparagus, lightly coated with 1 teaspoon sesame oil, 1 teaspoon salt, and grated zest of 1 lemon and grilled; and 1 ripe avocado, cut in half lengthwise, peeled, pitted, and cut into long, thin slices

FIRE: 2 parsnips and 2 beets, both lighted coated with 1 tablespoon rice bran or safflower oil, roasted in a 375°F oven for 45 minutes, peeled, and cut into bite-size pieces; 5 to 6 escarole leaves, sliced across into bite-size pieces; and 1 large chicken breast, rubbed with 1 tablespoon rice bran or safflower oil and ½ teaspoon salt, broiled or roasted, cooled, and cubed

MAKES ABOUT ½ CUP

1½ tablespoons black sesame seeds, toasted in a small skillet over medium heat until fragrant

1 teaspoon salt

1 clove garlic, minced

2 to 3 thin slices peeled fresh ginger, minced

1 teaspoon paprika

1 teaspoon cayenne pepper

1½ tablespoons honey

¼ cup apple juice

3 tablespoons fresh lime juice

Wind element's shallots, garlic, and chiles turn smoky after being broiled or dry-roasted, adding another layer of rich, buttery flavor to this salad dressing. Earth element's sweet-tasting brown sugar and apple juice tempers the heat from the chiles. Water element's sour tamarind gives the dressing the right balance. This dressing accentuates the fresh, crispy textures of vegetables, heightens sweet and tangy fruits, and harmonizes with the varied tastes of meat, poultry, or seafood. Its fully realized flavors are great for all home elements.

APPLE-TAMARIND DRESSING

COMBINE all the ingredients in a jar with a lid and shake well to mix. Add to the salad just before serving. It will keep in the refrigerator for a couple of days.

Salad suggestions (each makes 4 servings; use ¼ cup of the dressing, or to taste)

EARTH: ½ to ⅔ pound ground beef, chicken, or turkey seasoned with ¼ cup bread crumbs, 1 tablespoon chopped fresh Italian parsley, ½ teaspoon salt, and ⅛ teaspoon freshly ground black pepper mixed and formed into patties and grilled. When cool, break up into manageable pieces and mix with 3 romaine lettuce leaves torn into bite-size pieces; 12 cherry tomatoes, halved; 3 shallots, thinly sliced; and ½ cup crumbled baked potato chips

WATER: Six ½-inch-thick fresh pineapple rings, lightly oiled with safflower oil, grilled, and cut into bite-size pieces; ½ cup fresh mint leaves, torn; 2 Belgian endive, thinly sliced across; and ½ cup crumbled feta cheese

WIND: 1 cucumber, peeled, seeded, and thinly sliced; 2 to 3 radishes, thinly sliced; 1 stalk celery, thinly sliced; 2 nectarines, sliced into thin wedges; and ⅓ cup fresh mint leaves, torn

FIRE: 1½ cups bite-size pieces smoked fish such as salmon or whitefish, skin and bones removed; 1½ cups loosely packed watercress; and 3 radishes, thinly sliced

MAKES ABOUT ¾ CUP

2 shallots, broiled for 10 minutes, peeled, and minced (1 teaspoon)

2 cloves garlic, broiled for 10 minutes, peeled, and minced (1 teaspoon)

2 dried de arbol chiles or chiles Japones, dry-roasted in a small skillet over medium-high heat until charred, then ground in a coffee grinder

1½ tablespoons light brown sugar

1 teaspoon salt

1 tablespoon fish sauce

¼ cup apple juice

¼ cup Tamarind Puree (page 25)

¼ cup Almond Milk (page 21)

This spicy dressing will perk up bland-flavor greens or seafood. It complements bitter greens or astringent-flavor vegetables. If you need a little picker-upper on a rainy or cool wintry day, when the Wind and Earth elements tax your energy, make a salad with your favorite vegetables and/or fruits combined with chicken or shrimp. Drizzle this dressing over it. Regardless of your home element, your appetite will be stirred, giving just the lift you need.

ROASTED CHILE OIL DRESSING

COMBINE all the ingredients and stir well to mix. It will keep for a day, refrigerated, in an airtight container. Shake well before using.

Salad suggestions (each makes 4 servings; use ¼ cup of the dressing, or to taste)

EARTH: ½ pound medium shrimp, peeled, deveined, rubbed with 1 teaspoon grated lemon zest and 1 tablespoon olive oil, and broiled; 1 cup frisée; 6 figs, quartered; and 1 tablespoon coarsely chopped fresh tarragon

WATER: 3 cups cauliflower florets, tossed with 1 tablespoon olive oil and ½ teaspoon salt and roasted in a 400°F oven for 25 to 30 minutes; 2 tablespoons minced fresh Italian parsley; ½ pound medium shrimp, peeled, deveined, boiled until just cooked through, and cooled; and ½ cup pomegranate seeds

WIND: 2 cups peeled, seeded, and cubed papaya; ½ pound medium shrimp, peeled, deveined, and broiled until pink and firm, 3 to 5 minutes, cooled, and sliced in half lengthwise; ½ cup fresh basil leaves, torn; and 2 tablespoons Dry-Roasted Coconut Flakes (page 101)

FIRE: A handful of asparagus, tossed with 1 tablespoon safflower oil and ½ teaspoon salt, grilled, and cut into bite-size pieces; 1 cup arugula, torn into bite-size pieces; 1 cup smoked salmon (not lox) or tuna, broken into small pieces; and ½ cup dried cherries

MAKES ¾ CUP

1 tablespoon Roasted Chile Oil (page 65)

⅓ cup Coconut Cream (page 22)
or Almond Milk (page 21)

¼ teaspoon salt

1 tablespoon sugar

1 tablespoon fish sauce

¼ cup fresh lime juice

Water element people are partial to this dressing. Others will be drawn to its clean, sparkling taste, reviving memories of sunny, warm days. With sweet honey and spicy mustard, horseradish, and paprika, the dressing is balanced and good for all home elements.

CITRUS DRESSING

COMBINE all the ingredients in an airtight container and shake until well combined. It will keep, refrigerated, for a couple of days. Taste before using, as the lime juice might lose its sourness in the refrigerator. Add more to balance the flavors.

Salad suggestions (each makes 4 servings; use ¼ cup of dressing, or more to taste)

EARTH: 8 fresh baby artichoke hearts, thinly sliced and mixed with 1 teaspoon fresh lemon juice; 12 stalks asparagus, tossed with 1 tablespoon olive oil and ½ teaspoon salt, broiled, and cut into bite-size pieces; and ½ pound sea bass fillets, marinated with 1 tablespoon olive oil and 1 tablespoon minced fresh sage, grilled, cooled, and cut into bite-size pieces

WATER: 1 cup each watermelon and cantaloupe chunks; 1 chicken breast, grilled and cut into small cubes; and 1 ripe peach, peeled, pitted, and cubed

WIND: 1 cup peeled jicama cut into matchsticks; 1 cup peeled and cubed ripe mango or peach; 1 plum, cut into thin wedges; ½ cup fresh mint leaves, torn; and 2 tablespoons shelled roasted sunflower seeds

FIRE: 2 cups tightly packed frisée torn into bite-size pieces; 2 hard-boiled eggs, peeled and quartered; 4 radishes, thinly sliced; ½ cup thinly sliced tart apple; and ½ cup black or green olives, halved and pitted

MAKES ABOUT ½ CUP

1 teaspoon Dijon mustard

½ teaspoon prepared horseradish

1 tablespoon honey

¼ teaspoon salt

¼ teaspoon paprika

1 tablespoon fish sauce

⅓ cup fresh orange juice

1 tablespoon fresh lime juice

This is a fabulous dressing for rainy and cool days to help our bodies stay in balance with the dominant Wind element (wet climate) and Earth element (cold climate). Water and Wind element people will have a hard time resisting salads made with this dressing. For all home elements, it is a curative balm for chest colds.

KUMQUAT, GINGER, AND CLOVE PRESERVE DRESSING

COMBINE all the ingredients in an airtight container and shake vigorously to mix well. It will keep, refrigerated, for a couple of days.

Salad suggestions (each makes 4 servings; use ¼ cup of dressing, or more to taste)

EARTH: 1 cup thinly sliced fennel bulb; 1 ripe avocado, peeled, pitted, and cubed; 1½ cups tightly packed watercress; and ½ pound pork tenderloin, rubbed with ⅛ teaspoon each salt and pepper and 1 teaspoon olive oil, roasted in a 400°F oven for 20 to 25 minutes, cooled, and sliced

WATER: 2 cups peeled and cubed pumpkin tossed with 1 tablespoon safflower oil, ½ teaspoon salt, and 1 tablespoon minced fresh sage, roasted in a 350°F oven until tender, 10 to 15 minutes, and cooled; ½ cup dry-roasted unsalted cashews; ⅓ cup dried cherries; and 1 whole smoked trout, skin removed and broken into bite-size pieces

WIND: 1 cup cubed ham; 3 cups tightly packed torn frisée; 2 shallots, thinly sliced; and ⅓ cup slivered almonds, toasted in a small skillet over medium heat until lightly golden

FIRE: 2 cups tightly packed baby spinach leaves; 1 teaspoon minced fresh tarragon; 2 Napa cabbage leaves with stem, thinly sliced across; 2 shallots, thinly sliced; and 1 cup sliced smoked turkey

MAKES ½ CUP

1 tablespoon minced Kumquat, Ginger, and Clove Preserves (page 100)

1 teaspoon hot mustard powder

1 teaspoon paprika

½ teaspoon salt

1 tablespoon honey

⅓ cup fresh orange juice

1 teaspoon balsamic vinegar

This dressing can be used on either simple tossed greens or a seafood salad. The ingredients combine tastes, flavors, and aromas from all four elements, making the dressing suitable for all. Because of the warming ginger, paprika, and cayenne, it is best for rainy or cool days.

MISO-GINGER DRESSING

COMBINE all the ingredients in an airtight container and whisk to mix. Set aside or refrigerate until ready to use. It will keep, refrigerated, for a week.

Salad suggestions (each makes 4 servings; use all the dressing)

EARTH: ½ pound salmon fillet, marinated with 1 tablespoon peeled and minced fresh ginger, ½ teaspoon salt, ⅛ teaspoon white pepper, and 1 teaspoon sesame oil, broiled until just cooked through, cooled, and flaked into bite-size pieces; 2½ cups tightly packed mixed salad greens; and 2 tablespoons white or black sesame seeds, toasted in a small skillet over medium heat until fragrant

WATER: Same as for Earth, but also add 3 oranges, peeled and sectioned

WIND: Same as for Earth, but substitute the mixed salad greens with watercress.

FIRE: Same as for Earth, but substitute the sesame seeds with ¼ cup slivered pickled ginger.

MAKES ⅓ CUP

1 teaspoon red miso

1 teaspoon peeled and minced fresh ginger

½ teaspoon salt

½ teaspoon paprika

¼ teaspoon or more cayenne pepper

1 tablespoon honey

2 tablespoons distilled white vinegar

½ teaspoon sesame oil

*T*his fruity-spicy dressing adds a surprising touch to chicken salad or a delicate seafood salad.

KIWI-GINGER DRESSING

PUT all the ingredients in a blender and puree. Refrigerate until ready to serve. It will keep for a day.

Salad suggestions (each makes 4 servings; use ¼ cup of dressing, or more to taste)

EARTH: 1 large skinless, boneless chicken breast, rubbed with ½ teaspoon salt and 1 tablespoon olive oil, roasted in a 350°F oven until just cooked through, 15 to 18 minutes, cooled, and cubed; ½ cup thinly sliced celery; and 1 cup crumbled crispy instant ramen noodles (use only the noodles, not the seasoning packet)

WATER: 1 cup each thinly sliced cabbage and iceberg lettuce; ¼ cup thinly sliced onion; 1 skinless, boneless chicken breast, rubbed with ½ teaspoon salt and 1 teaspoon rice bran or olive oil, broiled until just cooked through, cooled, and cubed; ¼ pound medium shrimp, peeled, deveined, rubbed with 1 teaspoon rice bran or olive oil, broiled, cooled, and sliced in half lengthwise; and ¼ cup coarsely chopped fresh cilantro

WIND: 1 cup peeled jicama cut into matchsticks; 1 large or 2 small ripe peaches, peeled, pitted, and cut into thin wedges; 1 cup cubed smoked turkey; and ½ cup fresh mint leaves, torn

FIRE: 1 pound large scallops, marinated with the grated zest of 1 lemon, ¼ teaspoon salt, ⅛ teaspoon paprika, 1 tablespoon safflower oil, and grilled or broiled until just cooked through; 1 cup peeled jicama cut into matchsticks; and 1 cup mixed salad greens

MAKES ABOUT ¾ CUP

1 tablespoon peeled and minced fresh ginger

1 teaspoon salt

½ teaspoon cayenne pepper

¼ teaspoon ground cumin

1 very ripe kiwi, peeled and sliced

1 tablespoon honey

½ cup pineapple juice

1½ tablespoons fresh lime juice

1 tablespoon rice bran, soybean, safflower, or sunflower oil

MINT-CILANTRO DRESSING

mint and cilantro both possess a seemingly magical sensor, able to match our bodies' needs. On a cold day, they warm us, whereas on a hot day, they cool and refresh us. This twosome makes this dressing a healing balm, especially for Fire and Wind element people. For Earth and Water element people, it shields them against the Wind element on wet days, and fans them with a cool breeze on hot days when the Fire element dominates.

COMBINE the garlic, salt, sugar, fish sauce, and vinegar in a small saucepan and heat over low heat, stirring until the salt and sugar are dissolved. Let cool completely, then add the chile and lime juice. Mix well, then stir in the cilantro and mint. This will keep for a day, refrigerated, in an airtight container.

Salad suggestions (each makes 4 servings; use all the dressing)

EARTH: 1 pound salmon fillet marinated with 1 tablespoon minced garlic, ¼ teaspoon salt, juice of 1 lime, and 1 tablespoon olive oil, broiled until just cooked through, cooled, and broken into bite-size pieces; 1 cucumber, peeled, seeded, and thinly sliced; 6 cherry tomatoes, halved; 3 to 4 iceberg lettuce leaves, thinly sliced into ribbons; and ¼ cup coarsely chopped dry-roasted unsalted peanuts

WATER: Same as for Earth, but substitute 6 to 7 arugula leaves for the lettuce.

WIND: Same as for Earth, but substitute ½ cup peeled jicama cut into matchsticks for the tomatoes and toasted slivered almonds for the peanuts.

FIRE: Same as for Earth, but substitute dry-roasted unsalted pistachios for the peanuts.

MAKES ⅓ cup

4 cloves garlic, roasted in a 350°F oven until soft, 10 to 15 minutes, and peeled

¼ teaspoon salt

3 tablespoons sugar

1 tablespoon fish sauce

2 tablespoons distilled white vinegar

1 fresh Thai or serrano chile, minced

3 tablespoons fresh lime juice

1 tablespoon minced fresh cilantro

1 tablespoon minced fresh mint

BASIC STIR-FRY

ORGANIZATION is the key to a successful stir-fry dish. Prepare all of ingredients and arrange them on a tray in the order in which they will be cooked. Place the tray near the stove.

STIR-FRYING is a fast cooking process done over very high heat with the food constantly stirred and moved around in the hot wok or skillet. Once the dish is done, it should be served right away. If you wish to make stir-fry dishes for the next day's lunch, cook the vegetables just until their colors brighten. Before eating, microwave for 1 to 2 minutes, until heated through.

BEGIN by heating a large skillet over high heat. After a minute, add the cooking oil. Wait for another minute for the oil to get hot before adding the seasoning paste, minced garlic, and/or minced ginger. Stir-fry quickly for another minute, until its aroma is released. Add the protein of your choice, if using, and stir-fry. If the pan seems dry, add a tablespoon or two of water, broth, or wine. When the meat is partially cooked, add seasonings such as salt, pepper, soy sauce, fish sauce, or fresh chiles. Stir-fry to mix well before adding vegetables with hard textures such as broccoli stems, cauliflower florets, and/or carrots. Continue to stir-fry until the color brightens. If the pan seems dry, add another tablespoon or two of liquid. Continue to stir-fry, then add vegetables with delicate textures such as mustard green leaves, spinach, and/or bean sprouts. Continue to stir-fry until the vegetables are cooked but still firm. If the recipe calls for aromatic herbs such as basil or mint, add them now. Stir to mix and, when the herbs turn limp, transfer to a serving plate and serve hot.

IF using eggs, before beginning the stir-fry, beat the eggs lightly with ¼ teaspoon salt and 1 tablespoon fresh lime juice to combine. Heat the skillet for a minute. Add 1 tablespoon oil and swirl to coat the skillet. Add the egg and swirl to spread thinly over the bottom of the skillet. When the egg browns slightly underneath and the top surface is set, flip and cook the other side until it too is brown. Transfer to a plate to cool, slice into long strips, and add to the stir-fry after the meat and vegetables are cooked and before adding fresh herbs.

Suggested stir-fries for Earth home element
(each makes 4 servings)

1 tablespoon canola or corn oil; 1 tablespoon Basic Stir-Fry Seasoning (page 64); about 6 ounces beef or chicken, thinly sliced; ½ cup seeded and thinly sliced red bell pepper; 2 cups green beans thinly sliced on the diagonal and blanched in boiling water for 1 minute; and 1 tablespoon soy or fish sauce.

1 tablespoon canola or corn oil; 1 tablespoon Bean Paste Stir-Fry Seasoning (page 66); 6 to 8 ounces chicken, pork, or beef, thinly sliced, or a little over ¼ pound medium shrimp, peeled, deveined, and sliced in half across, or 1 cup cubed firm tofu; 1 tablespoon white wine; 6 to 8 cups sliced bok choy, stems sliced on the diagonal about ½ inch wide, leaves sliced across into strips about 2 inches wide; 1 tablespoon soy sauce; and ¼ teaspoon white pepper.

Suggested stir-fries for Water home element
(each makes 4 servings)

1 tablespoon canola, corn, or sunflower oil; 1 tablespoon Basic Stir-Fry Seasoning (page 64); one 12-ounce carton firm tofu, cubed; 2 cups sugar snap peas; 1 tablespoon white wine; and 1 tablespoon soy or fish sauce.

1 tablespoon canola or corn oil; 1 tablespoon Bean Paste Stir-Fry Seasoning (page 66); 6 to 8 ounces chicken, pork, or beef, thinly sliced, or a little over ¼ pound medium shrimp, peeled, deveined, and sliced in half across, or 1 cup cubed firm tofu; 1 tablespoon white wine; 1 medium onion, thinly sliced; 1 cup peeled, seeded, and thinly sliced cucumber; 1 medium tomato, cut into wedges; 1 tablespoon soy sauce; and ¼ teaspoon white pepper.

Suggested stir-fries for Wind home element
(each makes 4 servings)

2 tablespoons soybean oil; 1 tablespoon Basic Stir-Fry Seasoning (page 64); ½ cup thinly sliced celery; 2 cups bean sprouts; 1 cup fresh basil leaves, torn; 1 tablespoon soy sauce; ⅛ teaspoon white pepper; and 4 large slightly beaten eggs added over vegetables while cooking for omelet.

1 tablespoon canola or corn oil; 1 tablespoon Bean Paste Stir-Fry Seasoning (page 66); 6 to 8 ounces chicken, pork, or beef, thinly sliced, or a little over ¼ pound medium shrimp, peeled, deveined, and sliced in half across, or 1 cup cubed firm tofu; 1 tablespoon white wine; 6 to 8 cups sliced bok choy, stems sliced on the diagonal about ½ inch wide, leaves sliced across into strips about 2 inches wide; 1 to 2 fresh serrano chiles, seeded or unseeded, depending on how much heat you can tolerate, thinly sliced across; 1 tablespoon soy sauce; ¼ teaspoon white pepper; and ½ cup fresh mint or basil leaves, torn.

1 tablespoon canola or corn oil; 1 tablespoon Bean Paste Stir-Fry Seasoning (page 66); 6 to 8 ounces chicken, pork, or beef, thinly sliced, or a little over ¼ pound medium shrimp, peeled, deveined, and sliced in half across, or 1 cup cubed firm tofu; 1 tablespoon white wine; 1 medium onion, thinly sliced; 1 cup peeled, seeded, and thinly sliced cucumber; 1 medium tomato,

cut into wedges; 1 to 2 fresh serrano chiles, seeded or unseeded, depending on how much heat you can tolerate, thinly sliced across; 1 tablespoon soy sauce; ¼ teaspoon white pepper; and ½ cup fresh mint or basil leaves, torn.

Suggested stir-fries for Fire home element

1 tablespoon safflower oil; 1 tablespoon Basic Stir-Fry Seasoning (below); ¼ pound medium shrimp, peeled, deveined, and cut in half across; 1 tablespoon peeled and slivered fresh ginger; 2 cups tightly packed green beans thinly sliced on the diagonal and blanched in boiling water for 1 minute; and 1 tablespoon soy or fish sauce.

1 tablespoon canola or corn oil; 1 tablespoon Bean Paste Stir-Fry Seasoning (page 66); 6 to 8 ounces chicken, pork, or beef, thinly sliced, or a little over ¼ pound medium shrimp, peeled, deveined, and sliced in half across, or 1 cup cubed firm tofu; 1 tablespoon white wine; 2 cups thinly sliced broccoli florets and stems, or 2 cups bean sprouts, or 2 cups thinly sliced cauliflower florets, or 1 cucumber, peeled, seeded, and thinly sliced; 1 tablespoon soy sauce; and ¼ teaspoon white pepper.

Stir-fries for all home elements

1 tablespoon rice bran, safflower, or soybean oil; 1 tablespoon Basic Stir-Fry Seasoning (below); 6 to 8 ounces chicken, beef, or pork, thinly sliced, or ¼ pound medium shrimp, peeled and deveined, or 8 ounces firm tofu, cubed; 2 tablespoons soy sauce; 1 cup thinly sliced onion; 1 cup thinly sliced broccoli florets, blanched in boiling water for 1 minute; 2 tablespoons white wine; 1 cup bean sprouts; and 2½ cups cooked egg noodles (page 87) or thin (not angel hair) rice noodles (page 86). Serve with Fresh Chiles in Vinegar (page 84).

1 tablespoon oil of your choice; 1 tablespoon Bean Paste Stir-Fry Seasoning (page 66); ½ cup each thinly sliced chicken and medium shrimp, peeled and deveined; 1 cup thinly sliced cabbage; ½ cup each thinly sliced carrots and celery; 2½ cups cooked egg noodles (page 87); 1 tablespoon soy sauce; 1 tablespoon oyster sauce; garnished with ½ cup coarsely chopped fresh cilantro and ⅛ teaspoon white pepper. Serve with Tabasco or sriracha sauce.

This seasoning paste can also be used to season soup or marinate chicken and meat for grilling. It combines ingredients of Earth and Wind elements, creating a perfect balance for all the elements.

BASIC STIR-FRY SEASONING

PUT the salt and garlic in a mortar and pound into a paste. Add the remaining ingredients, one at a time, and only after each has been incorporated into the paste with the pestle. It will keep in an airtight container for several weeks.

MAKES ½ CUP

½ **teaspoon salt**

1 **tablespoon minced garlic**

1 **teaspoon white peppercorns, dry-roasted and ground (page 70)**

½ **teaspoon coriander seeds, dry-roasted and ground (page 70)**

1 **tablespoon minced fresh cilantro stems**

1 **tablespoon peeled and minced fresh ginger**

1 **tablespoon minced shallot**

oasted chile oil is used as seasoning for hot-and-sour soup and in stir-fries and salad dressings, but it's also delicious on toast, and very tasty mixed with warm cooked rice. You can use store-bought chile oil imported from Thailand, but it is sweeter and oilier than homemade. Taste it before using and adjust the seasonings called for in the recipes accordingly. Also, read the ingredients on the label, especially if you are allergic to shrimp. ~~§> Roasted chile oil is good for all home elements, though Fire element people should eat it in moderation, especially in hot weather.

ROASTED CHILE OIL Nam Phrik Pow

PREHEAT the oven to 500°F.

SPREAD the shrimp paste on the corn husk, roll it up, and secure with a toothpick. Place on a small baking sheet and roast in the oven until the outer layer of the husk chars slightly, 2 to 3 minutes. Remove from the oven and let cool. (If using the red miso, skip this step.)

PUT the oil in a large saucepan over high heat. When the oil is hot, about 1 to 2 minutes, sprinkle 1 teaspoon of the salt into the oil. Reduce the heat to low, add the garlic, and stir constantly until it is golden. Remove the garlic from the oil using a wire mesh strainer and transfer to a strainer lined with paper towels. Repeat the same process, one at a time, with the shallots, ginger, chiles, and dried shrimp. (If using grilled chicken meat, it does not have to be deep-fried.) Transfer all but 2 tablespoons of the oil to a container (you can reuse it in other recipes).

SCRAPE the roasted shrimp paste into a food processor (or add the red miso) and add the remaining 1 tablespoon salt, the garlic, shallots, ginger, chiles, dried shrimp (or chicken), palm sugar, fish sauce, and tamarind puree. Cover and blend at high speed until smooth. If the mixture is coarse, add 1 tablespoon of the frying oil and blend to puree.

HEAT the reserved 2 tablespoons oil in the saucepan over medium-low heat for 1 minute. Add the puree and stir until well combined and aromatic, 1 to 2 minutes. Let cool to room temperature. Store in an airtight container in the refrigerator for several months.

Roasted Chile Oil Stir-Fry (makes 4 servings)

1 tablespoon your choice of oil; 1 tablespoon minced garlic; 2 shallots, thinly sliced; 1 cup thinly sliced chicken, beef, pork, or squid, or medium shrimp, peeled and deveined; 1 tablespoon or more Roasted Chile Oil; and vegetables suitable to your home element(s):

1 tablespoon fermented shrimp paste or red miso

1 dry corn husk (optional if using red miso), soaked in water to cover until softened (15 to 20 minutes) and dried thoroughly

3 cups vegetable oil

1 teaspoon plus 1 tablespoon salt

¼ cup coarsely chopped garlic

1 cup thinly sliced shallots

⅓ cup peeled and thinly sliced fresh ginger

1 cup dried de arbol chiles or chiles Japones

¼ cup dried shrimp, softened in warm water (2 to 3 minutes) and dried thoroughly, or minced grilled chicken

¼ cup palm sugar or firmly packed dark brown sugar

3 tablespoons fish sauce

½ cup Tamarind Puree (page 25)

EARTH: 2 cups green beans thinly sliced on the diagonal and blanched in boiling water for 1 minute, or thinly sliced Brussels sprouts, and ½ cup fresh basil leaves, torn

WATER: 2 cups thinly sliced mushrooms and 1 cup thinly sliced bamboo shoots

WIND: 1 medium onion, thinly sliced into half-moons; 1 small or medium green bell pepper, seeded and thinly sliced into strips; 1 fresh serrano chile, slivered; and ½ cup fresh basil leaves, torn

FIRE: 1 medium onion, thinly sliced into half-moons; 2 cups thinly sliced cauliflower florets; and ½ cup fresh mint leaves, torn

*C*ontaining ingredients of Earth and Wind elements, this seasoning is balanced and can be used for all home element types.

BEAN PASTE STIR-FRY SEASONING

PUT the garlic and salt in a mortar and pound into a paste, leaving some of the garlic skins intact. Add the peppercorns and ginger and pound into a paste. Add the chiles, if using, and pound enough to bruise. Add the bean paste and sesame oil. Mix to blend. Store in an airtight container in the refrigerator for up to several weeks.

MAKES ¼ CUP

3 cloves garlic, with skins left on

½ teaspoon salt

1 teaspoon white peppercorns, roasted and ground (page 70)

1 tablespoon peeled and minced fresh ginger

2 to 3 fresh Thai or 1 to 2 fresh serrano chiles (optional), minced

3 tablespoons bean paste

½ teaspoon sesame oil

According to legend, this combination of healing herbs and spices is said to be potent enough to jolt one out of a hangover. It's also believed that its intoxicating aroma of garlic, chiles, galangal, and lemongrass will protect all home elements from the damp air. ～⊗ *Kee mao* seasoning can be used to season stir-fried rice or noodles. Although it is made with ingredients of Earth and Wind, it is appropriate for all home element types, though Fire element people should use fewer chiles, especially during hot weather.

DRUNKEN SEASONING Kee Mao

PUT the salt and garlic in a mortar and pound into a paste. Add the remaining ingredients one at a time, adding the next only after the previous one has been incorporated into the paste. Store in an airtight container in the refrigerator for several weeks.

Drunken Stir-Fry (makes 4 servings)

1 tablespoon your choice of oil; 1 tablespoon Drunken Seasoning; 1 cup thinly sliced chicken, pork, beef, or squid or medium shrimp, peeled and deveined; 2 cups vegetables suitable to your home element (see below); ¼ teaspoon salt; 1 tablespoon fish sauce; ½ teaspoon sugar; ½ cup fresh basil leaves, torn;

EARTH: 1 cup green beans, thinly sliced on the diagonal and blanched in boiling water for 1 minute, and 2 Belgian endive, thinly sliced lengthwise

WATER: 1 cup thinly sliced mushrooms and 1 cup thinly sliced bamboo shoots

WIND: 1 medium onion, cut into thin wedges; 1 fresh serrano chile, slivered; and 1 cup thinly sliced okra

FIRE: 1 cup thinly sliced mushrooms and 1 cup thinly sliced broccoli florets, blanched in boiling water for 1 minute

Drunken Stir-Fried Noodles (makes 1 serving)

1 tablespoon oil of your choice; 1 teaspoon minced garlic; 1 teaspoon or more Drunken Seasoning; ½ cup your choice of thinly sliced chicken or medium shrimp, peeled and deveined; ½ cup vegetables suitable for your home element (see below); 1 tablespoon fish sauce; 1 teaspoon oyster sauce; 1 cup tightly packed softened pad thai noodles or wide rice noodles (page 86); 1 to 2 tablespoons water; and ¼ cup fresh basil leaves, torn;

EARTH: Green beans, thinly sliced on the diagonal and blanched in boiling water for 1 minute

WATER: Mustard greens or kale, sliced into bite-size pieces

WIND: Thinly sliced onion and/or broccoli florets blanched in boiling water for 1 minute

FIRE: Thinly sliced bamboo shoots and/or mushrooms

MAKES ABOUT ⅓ CUP

1 teaspoon salt

4 cloves garlic, minced

15 to 20 dried de arbol chiles or chiles Japones, softened in hot water to cover, dried thoroughly, and minced

1 stalk lemongrass, tough outer layers removed, tender inner stalk minced

6 thin slices galangal or fresh ginger, minced

Grated zest of 1 kaffir or regular lime

2 shallots, minced

*T*hai Curry Chile Paste (page 72) is made with ingredients from opposite elements, making it perfectly balanced for all. If making this stir-fry ahead for the next day's lunch, undercook the vegetables slightly. When ready to eat, microwave for 1 to 2 minutes, until heated through. Serve with hot rice.

CURRY STIR-FRY

HEAT a large nonstick skillet over high heat for 1 minute. Add the oil and wait for another 10 to 12 seconds, then add the chile paste. Stir for 1 minute, then add the coconut milk and stir to blend and to dissolve the chile paste. Add the salt, fish sauce, and sugar and stir to mix. Add the meat and stir-fry until it is partially cooked, then add the vegetables. Stir-fry until the vegetables are cooked but still firm, then add the chiles, if using, and basil and stir until the basil is limp. Add the lime leaves, stir well, and serve immediately.

Vegetable choices

EARTH: Green beans, thinly sliced on the diagonal; russet potato, peeled and cut into matchsticks; or Japanese eggplant, thinly sliced into rounds, sprinkled with 1 teaspoon salt for 10 minutes, rinsed, and patted dry

WATER, WIND, AND FIRE: Thinly sliced broccoli or cauliflower florets and stems, green beans thinly sliced on the diagonal, and/or thinly sliced bamboo shoots, onions, or mushrooms

MAKE 4 SERVINGS

1 tablespoon vegetable oil of your choice

1½ to 2 tablespoons Thai Curry Chile Paste (page 72)

½ cup Coconut Milk (page 22) or Almond Milk (page 21)

½ teaspoon salt

1 tablespoon fish sauce or soy sauce

1 teaspoon sugar

2 cups thinly sliced chicken, pork, or beef or cubed firm tofu, or medium shrimp, peeled and deveined (for vegetarians, choose tofu or increase the amount of vegetables to 4 cups)

1½ to 2 cups sliced or cut-up vegetables best suited to your home element (see below)

1 to 2 fresh Thai or serrano chiles (optional), slivered

½ cup fresh Thai basil or peppermint leaves, torn

1 teaspoon slivered kaffir lime leaves or grated lime zest

Fried rice is best prepared one serving at a time. It's easier to cook and it also allows you to customize the dish to your diners. You can increase the amounts below to yield more servings, but only cook one portion at a time. Don't worry—this goes together so fast that you're not going to really increase your overall cooking time by much, and the difference in taste and texture will make it well worth it. ⧼⧽ Fried rice should balance saltiness with a slightly sweet taste that is perfumed with garlic and ginger, making it an excellent dish for all home element types. Add more or less of the ingredients suggested below to suit your own home element.

FRIED RICE

HEAT a medium skillet over high heat for 1 minute. Add the oil, wait for 10 to 12 seconds, then add the garlic and ginger. Stir to mix for 1 minute, then add the meat of your choice and stir until just cooked through. Add the rice and stir to mix. If the mixture appears dry, add 1 tablespoon water and continue to stir-fry. Add the vegetables. Stir to mix and, when the vegetables are partially cooked, season with soy sauce and ketchup. Stir to mix. (For Earth element, if using raisins and pine nuts, add them now; see the variation below.) Add the egg and stir to combine. Add the pepper and mix well. Transfer to a plate and garnish with the cilantro. Serve with the accompaniments in little bowls, for your diners to add to their plates themselves.

Drunken Fried Rice

Substitute 1 teaspoon or more Drunken Seasoning (page 67) for the garlic. Instead of the cilantro, substitute peppermint leaves. Omit the white pepper.

Spicy Fried Rice

Add 1 teaspoon or more Roasted Chile Oil (page 65) along with the garlic and ginger. Substitute mint for the cilantro. Omit the white pepper.

FRIED RICE FOR EARTH HOME ELEMENT: Add 1 tablespoon each raisins and toasted pine nuts, or ½ cup asparagus or green beans thinly sliced on the diagonal.

FRIED RICE FOR WATER HOME ELEMENT: Add ½ cup thinly sliced broccoli florets or ½ cup thinly sliced fresh pineapple and ¼ cup torn fresh basil.

FRIED RICE FOR WIND HOME ELEMENT: Add an additional half an onion, cubed, or ½ cup tightly packed baby spinach.

FRIED RICE FOR FIRE HOME ELEMENT: Add ¼ cup thinly sliced mushrooms or cabbage.

MAKES 1 SERVING

1 tablespoon vegetable oil of your choice

1 clove garlic, minced

1 teaspoon peeled and minced fresh ginger

½ cup crabmeat, small shrimp, thinly sliced beef, pork, lamb, or chicken, or diced firm tofu

1½ cups cooked rice (it's best if it's cold leftover rice), fluffed to loosen the grains

½ cup mixed cubed onion, celery, carrot, and peas or other vegetables of your choice

1 tablespoon soy sauce or fish sauce

1 tablespoon ketchup

1 egg, scrambled and cut into bite-size pieces

½ teaspoon freshly ground white pepper

⅓ cup coarsely chopped fresh cilantro

ACCOMPANIMENTS

Chili powder of your choice

1 to 2 slices lime

6 to 7 slices cucumber

1 scallion, chopped

THAI CURRIES

nstead of the word *curry*, which is synonymous with Indian cooking, Thais use the word *gaeng* for these types of dishes, stew-like preparations or soups, which are the heart of Thai cooking. All spicy Thai *gaeng* use a chile paste as the primary seasoning. These pastes combine fresh medicinal herbs and dried spices with the tastes, flavors, and aromas of two opposing elements (Earth and Wind).

Curry pastes are traditionally made, even today, using a mortar and pestle. To do this most effectively, mince the fresh ingredients and dry-roast and grind the spices first to make for easy pounding. Place the mortar on a dish towel on the counter, preferably about 9 inches below your waist. Use one hand to cradle and secure the mortar, the other to hold the pestle near the top of the mortar. To pound, bring the pestle down into the center of the bowl in a measured, even rhythm. Use a spoon between poundings to scrape down the paste as it creeps up the side of the mortar.

Beginning with the first two ingredients listed in the recipe, pound them into a paste in the mortar. Add the remaining ingredients one at a time and only after the previous one has been incorporated into the paste. Transfer the paste to an airtight container and refrigerate. It will keep for a month.

HOW TO DRY-ROAST SPICES: Place the spices in a small skillet over high heat. Shake the pan constantly back and forth over the burner until the spice is fragrant and lightly browned. Remove from the heat and transfer to a plate to cool completely.

HOW TO GRIND SPICES: Place the roasted spices in the mortar and grind with the pestle in a circular motion, pressing the spices hard against the inner wall of the mortar until they turn to powder. Or, place the roasted spices in an electric coffee grinder or spice grinder. Cover tightly and grind until they turn to powder. Let the powder settle before opening the lid. Clean the grinder by putting 2 to 3 tablespoons of sugar in it and grinding for a couple of seconds. Discard the sugar and wipe clean.

aeng koa is one of the most ancient curries, developed after chiles were brought to Thailand in the sixteenth century by the Portuguese. The ingredients blend the tastes and flavors of opposite elements—earth and wind—to create a perfect balance, not only in taste, but also for health. *Gaeng koa* is a lighter curry using less coconut cream and more coconut cream and milk combined. The paste can also be used as seasoning for stir-fried dishes and savory custard.

THAI CURRY Gaeng Koa

POUND the salt and garlic together in a mortar until they form a paste. Add the remaining chile paste ingredients one at a time, adding the next only after the previous one has been incorporated into the paste. The paste will keep in an airtight container, refrigerated, for up to a month.

COMBINE the coconut cream and chile paste in a medium saucepan over medium-high heat and heat until the oil separates out and the oil bubbles take on the color of the chile paste, stirring frequently. Add the coconut cream and milk combined and almond milk and stir to mix. When the mixture comes to a boil, add the salt, fish sauce, palm sugar, lemongrass, chiles, and lime leaves and stir to combine. When it boils again, reduce the heat to medium-low and simmer for 10 to 15 minutes. (If making the curry broth ahead, let cool completely at this point and refrigerate. It will keep overnight. Bring to a boil before adding the meat and vegetables.)

ADD the main ingredients to the simmering broth. Once they are cooked, add the slivered lime leaves and stir until limp. Serve immediately.

Variation

For a different twist, make this with 2 cups small shrimp and scallops, 1 pound large mussels or ½ pound smaller ones, and 1½ cups sliced tart fruit such as apricots, tart plums, or grapes.

MAKES 4 SERVINGS

THAI CURRY CHILE PASTE

1 teaspoon salt

5 cloves garlic, minced (2 tablespoons)

15 dried de arbol chiles or chiles Japones, soaked in hot water to soften, dried thoroughly, and minced

1 stalk lemongrass, tough outer layers and green stem removed, tender inner stalk minced

7 thin slices galangal or fresh ginger

1 tablespoon minced smoked salmon (not lox; optional)

1 shallot, minced

1 teaspoon fermented shrimp paste or red miso

CURRY BROTH

1 cup Coconut Cream (page 22)

1 cup Coconut Cream and Milk combined (page 22)

1 cup Almond Milk (page 21; or you can use 2 cups almond milk and eliminate the coconut cream and milk combined)

1 teaspoon salt

2 tablespoons fish sauce (for vegetarians, use light soy sauce)

2 teaspoons palm sugar, dark
brown sugar, or maple sugar

1 stalk lemongrass, tough outer
layers removed, tender inner stalk cut
lengthwise and slightly pounded

6 to 7 fresh Thai or 3 to 4 fresh
serrano chiles, slightly crushed

6 to 7 kaffir lime leaves, slightly
crushed, or grated zest of 1 lime

MAIN INGREDIENTS

About 2 cups bite-size pieces beef, chicken,
or firm-fleshed fish fillet such as catfish,
red snapper, or sea bass, dried thoroughly

2 cups mixed firm-textured vegetables
such as onions cut into chunks; green
beans cut into 2-inch lengths on the
diagonal; mushrooms, halved; cauliflower
florets; and/or bamboo shoots

TO FINISH

2 kaffir lime leaves, slivered, or
zest of 1 lime, cut into slivers

*T*his curry takes its name from the city of Panang, in Malaysia, located near the southern Thai border, which centuries ago was a part of Thailand. Traditional cooking from Panang is similar to Malaysian and Indonesian cooking, generously seasoned with spices such as cinnamon, cumin, nutmeg, and mace. Panang curry paste is rich, aromatic, and warming.

PANANG CURRY Panang

POUND the salt and garlic together in a mortar until they form a paste. Add the remaining chile paste ingredients one at a time, adding the next only after the previous one has been incorporated into the paste. The paste will keep in an airtight container, refrigerated, for up to a month.

COMBINE the coconut cream and chile paste in a medium saucepan over medium-high heat and heat until the oil separates out and the oil bubbles take on the color of the chile paste, stirring frequently. Add the coconut cream and milk combined and almond milk and stir to mix. When the mixture comes to a boil, add the salt, fish sauce, palm sugar, lemongrass, chiles, and lime leaves and stir to combine. When it boils once again, reduce the heat to medium-low and simmer for 10 to 15 minutes. (If making the curry broth ahead, let cool completely at this point and refrigerate. It will keep overnight. Bring to a boil before adding the meat and vegetables.)

ADD the main ingredients to the simmering broth. Once they are cooked, add the slivered lime leaves and stir until limp. Serve immediately.

MAKES 4 SERVINGS

PANANG CURRY CHILE PASTE

1 teaspoon salt

5 cloves garlic, minced (2 tablespoons)

12 dried de arbol chiles or chiles Japones, soaked in hot water to soften, dried thoroughly, and minced

1 teaspoon coriander seeds, dry-roasted and ground (page 70)

½ teaspoon cumin seeds, dry-roasted and ground (page 70)

1 stalk lemongrass, tough outer layers and green stem removed, tender inner stalk minced

7 thin slices galangal or fresh ginger, minced

1 shallot, minced (1 tablespoon)

1 teaspoon fermented shrimp paste or red miso

1 tablespoon dry-roasted unsalted peanuts or slivered almonds, ground

CURRY BROTH

1 cup Coconut Cream (page 22)

1 cup Coconut Cream and Milk combined (page 22)

1 cup Almond Milk (page 21; or, you can use 2 cups almond milk and eliminate the coconut cream and milk combined)

1 teaspoon salt

2 tablespoons fish sauce (for vegetarians, use light soy sauce)

2 teaspoons palm sugar, dark brown sugar, or maple sugar

1 stalk lemongrass, tough outer layers removed, tender inner stalk cut lengthwise and slightly pounded

6 to 7 fresh Thai or 3 to 4 fresh serrano chiles, slightly crushed

6 to 7 kaffir lime leaves, slightly crushed, or zest of 1 lime, slivered

MAIN INGREDIENTS

4 cups thinly sliced beef, pork, chicken, halibut, or cubed firm tofu, or whole medium shrimp, peeled and deveined, dried thoroughly (if also adding vegetables, reduce the amount of protein to 2 cups)

2 cups mixed firm-textured vegetables, such as sliced bamboo shoots, onions, carrots, or mushrooms, and/or green beans cut into 2-inch lengths on the diagonal (optional)

TO FINISH

2 kaffir lime leaves, slivered, or zest of 1 lime, slivered

Red curry paste is the most versatile of all curry pastes. It is used not only for making curry and other stew-like dishes, but also as a seasoning for stir-fries, savory custards, and fish or shrimp cakes. The literal translation of the Thai name is "hot or spicy curry." This is because it is made with a handful of fiery dried red chiles. If you're thinking of reducing the amount of chiles to tone down the heat of the dish, please don't, as it will alter the taste balance of the dish. Instead, I suggest reducing the amount of paste called for in the recipe. Another alternative is to add a bit of sugar while cooking to counteract the heat.

RED CURRY Gaeng Ped

POUND the salt and garlic together in a mortar until they form a paste. Add the remaining chile paste ingredients one at a time, adding the next only after the previous one has been incorporated into the paste. The paste will keep in an airtight container, refrigerated, for up to a month.

COMBINE the coconut cream and chile paste in a medium saucepan over medium-high heat and heat until the oil separates out and the oil bubbles take on the color of the chile paste, stirring frequently. Add the coconut cream and milk combined and stir to mix. When the mixture comes to a boil, add the salt, fish sauce, palm sugar, lemongrass, chiles, and lime leaves and stir to combine. When it boils again, reduce the heat to medium-low and simmer for 10 to 15 minutes. (If making the curry broth ahead, let cool completely at this point and refrigerate. It will keep overnight. Bring to a boil before adding the meat and vegetables.)

ADD the main ingredients to the simmering broth. Once they are cooked, add the basil and stir until limp. Serve immediately.

MAKES 4 SERVINGS

RED CURRY CHILE PASTE

1 teaspoon salt

5 cloves garlic, minced (2 tablespoons)

20 dried de arbol chiles or chiles Japones, soaked in hot water to soften, dried thoroughly, and minced

1 teaspoon white peppercorns, dry-roasted and ground (page 70)

1 teaspoon coriander seeds, dry-roasted and ground (page 70)

1 teaspoon cumin seeds, dry-roasted and ground (page 70)

1 tablespoon minced fresh cilantro roots and stems

1 stalk lemongrass, tough outer layers removed, tender inner stalk minced

1 tablespoon minced galangal or fresh ginger

1 teaspoon minced kaffir or regular lime zest

1 shallot, minced (1 tablespoon)

1 teaspoon fermented shrimp paste or red miso

CURRY BROTH

1 cup Coconut Cream (page 22)

2 cups Coconut Cream and Milk combined (page 22)

1 teaspoon salt

2 tablespoons fish sauce (for vegetarians, use light soy sauce)

2 teaspoons palm sugar, dark brown sugar, or maple sugar

1 stalk lemongrass, tough outer layers removed, tender inner stalk cut lengthwise and slightly pounded

6 to 7 fresh Thai or 3 to 4 fresh serrano chiles, slightly crushed

6 to 7 kaffir lime leaves, slightly crushed, or zest of 1 lime, cut into slivers

MAIN INGREDIENTS

2 cups cubed chicken, beef, or pork, dried thoroughly

2 cups seasonal vegetables, including green beans cut into 2-inch lengths on the diagonal; sliced mushrooms and/or bamboo shoots; cauliflower florets; and/or bite-size chunks of potatoes, pumpkin, and/or sweet potatoes (for vegetarians, increase the amount of vegetables to 4 cups)

TO FINISH

½ cup fresh Thai basil or peppermint leaves

ew-generation Thais interpret the words *khio* (green) and *wan* (sweet) as a curry that should be sweetened with loads of sugar. Traditional green curry, however, is not sweet, but savory, rich, and very spicy. The heat comes from the unripe green chiles used to make the paste and several more that are added to the curry while it's being cooked. To temper and balance the fiery flavor, rich coconut cream and, at the most, a couple teaspoons of palm sugar are added. Green curry paste can be used as a seasoning for stir-fried dishes; many modern Thai cooks use it particularly to prepare stir-fried noodles.

GREEN CURRY Gaeng Khio Wan

POUND the salt and garlic together in a mortar until they form a paste. Add the remaining chile paste ingredients one at a time, adding the next only after the previous one has been incorporated into the paste. The paste will keep in an airtight container, refrigerated, for up to a month.

COMBINE 1 cup of the coconut cream and the chile paste in a medium saucepan over medium-high heat and heat until the oil separates out and the oil bubbles take on the color of the chile paste, stirring frequently. Add the remaining 1 cup coconut cream, plus the coconut cream and milk combined, and stir to mix. When the mixture comes to a boil, add the salt, fish sauce, palm sugar, lemongrass, chiles, and lime leaves and stir to combine. When it boils again, reduce the heat to medium-low and simmer for 10 to 15 minutes. (If making the curry broth ahead, let cool completely at this point and refrigerate. It will keep overnight. Bring to a boil before adding the meat and vegetables.)

ADD the main ingredients to the simmering broth. Once they are cooked, add the basil and stir until limp. Serve immediately.

MAKES 4 SERVINGS

GREEN CURRY CHILE PASTE

1 teaspoon salt

5 cloves garlic, minced (2 tablespoons)

20 fresh green Thai or 9 fresh serrano chiles, minced

1 teaspoon white peppercorns, dry-roasted and ground (page 70)

1 tablespoon coriander seeds, dry-roasted and ground (page 70)

1 teaspoon cumin seeds, dry-roasted and ground (page 70)

1 tablespoon minced fresh cilantro roots and stems

1 stalk lemongrass, tough outer layers removed, tender inner stalk minced

1 tablespoon minced galangal or peeled fresh ginger

1 teaspoon minced kaffir or regular lime zest

1 teaspoon minced fresh or pure ground dried turmeric (for rainy weather only)

1 shallot, minced (1 tablespoon)

1 teaspoon fermented shrimp paste or red miso

CURRY PASTES: FRESHLY MADE VS. STORE-BOUGHT

In every small or large traditional Thai market, there is at least one stall that sells mounds of fresh curry pastes in hues of red, brown, and green. They lure customers in with their intense smell of herbs and spices intermingled with pungent chiles and fermented shrimp paste. Although the strong tradition prevails among serious Thai cooks that one should make one's own curry paste, there are growing numbers of those whose lives have taken on a fast pace. These are the shoppers who, when they decide to make curry, may buy ready-made paste. They develop fierce loyalty to and voice strong opinions in support of favorite vendors whom they have come to trust and rely upon for top-quality curry pastes.

And so it seems that you too have to decide which of the two camps you wish to join. I am a traditionalist who loves and doesn't mind making everything from scratch. I have also learned to accept that shortcuts in cooking are a fact of life when many of us lead busy lives.

There are several brands of ready-made curry pastes from Thailand. I am familiar with three: Mae Ploy, Mae Anong, and Mae Sri. These are reliable and good-tasting curry pastes available in Asian supermarkets and online. Since Thai foods have gained huge popularity in recent years, more and more ready-made products for preparing Thai foods, including curry pastes, are available in major supermarkets and specialty markets. Read the label to make sure that the product is packaged with little or no preservatives. Then give it a try and form your own judgment.

CURRY BROTH

2 cups Coconut Cream (page 22)

1 cup Coconut Cream and Milk combined (page 22)

1 teaspoon salt

2 tablespoons fish sauce (for vegetarians, use light soy sauce)

2 teaspoons palm sugar, dark brown sugar, or maple sugar

1 stalk lemongrass, tough outer layers removed, tender inner stalk cut lengthwise and slightly pounded

6 to 7 fresh Thai or 3 to 4 fresh serrano chiles, slightly crushed

6 to 7 kaffir lime leaves, slightly crushed, or zest of 1 lime, cut into slivers

MAIN INGREDIENTS

2 cups bite-size chicken, beef, pork, or roast duck, dried thoroughly

2 cups combination of thinly sliced onion; green beans cut into 2-inch lengths on the diagonal; sliced bamboo shoots; quartered Thai eggplants or sliced regular eggplants; and/or pineapple chunks (for vegetarians, increase the amount of vegetables to 4 cups)

TO FINISH

½ cup fresh Thai basil or peppermint leaves

This curry is a good example of Thai cooks' ability to borrow and alter other countries' recipes to suit their personal taste. Yellow curry originated in India, where the use of golden orange turmeric powder is more prevalent. It is one of the few Thai curries in which root vegetables such as potato, sweet potato, parsnip, and winter squashes such as pumpkin can be used. The roasting of the garlic, shallots, and ginger endows the curry with a warm, smoky perfume. ~~⬙~~ Yellow curry paste can also be used as a seasoning for stir-fried dishes and noodle dishes.

YELLOW CURRY Gaeng Gari

POUND the salt and garlic together in a mortar until they form a paste. Add the remaining chile paste ingredients one at a time, adding the next only after the previous one has been incorporated into the paste. The paste will keep in an airtight container, refrigerated, for up to a month.

COMBINE the coconut cream and chile paste in a medium saucepan over medium-high heat and heat until the oil separates out and the oil bubbles take on the color of the chile paste, stirring frequently. Add the coconut cream and milk combined and stir to mix. When the mixture comes to a boil, add the salt, fish sauce, palm sugar, lemongrass, chiles, and lime leaves and stir to combine. When it boils again, reduce the heat to medium-low and simmer for 10 to 15 minutes. (If making the curry broth ahead, let cool completely at this point and refrigerate. It will keep overnight. Bring to a boil before adding the meat and vegetables.)

ADD the main ingredients to the simmering broth. Once they are cooked, serve immediately.

MAKES 4 SERVINGS

YELLOW CURRY CHILE PASTE

1 teaspoon salt

8 cloves garlic, roasted in a 375°F oven until soft (10 to 12 minutes), then peeled (2 tablespoons)

10 dried de arbol chiles or chiles Japones, dry-roasted in a skillet over high heat until blackened and charred (5 to 7 minutes), then minced

1 teaspoon white peppercorns, dry-roasted and ground (page 70)

1 teaspoon coriander seeds, dry-roasted and ground (page 70)

1 teaspoon cumin seeds, dry-roasted and ground (page 70)

One 1-inch chunk fresh ginger, roasted in a 375°F oven for 15 minutes, then peeled and minced

4 shallots, roasted in a 375°F oven for 15 minutes, then peeled

1 tablespoon Madras curry powder

1 teaspoon fermented shrimp paste or red miso

CURRY BROTH

1 cup Coconut Cream (page 22)

2 cups Coconut Cream and Milk combined (page 22)

1 teaspoon salt

2 tablespoons fish sauce (for vegetarians, use light soy sauce)

2 teaspoons palm sugar, dark brown sugar, or maple sugar

1 stalk lemongrass, tough outer layers removed, tender inner stalk cut lengthwise and slightly pounded

6 to 7 fresh Thai or 3 to 4 fresh serrano chiles, slightly crushed

6 to 7 kaffir lime leaves, slightly crushed, or zest of 1 lime, cut into slivers

MAIN INGREDIENTS

2 cups bite-size pieces firm fish fillets (such as sea bass, snapper, or catfish), beef, pork, or chicken, dried thoroughly

2 cups mixed vegetables, such as sliced bamboo shoots and/or bite-size chunks of peeled potato, sweet potato, parsnip, and/or summer and winter squashes

This particular curry has a strong ginger flavor, derived from the galangal, which is a type of ginger. Thus its Thai name literally translates as *phrik* (chile) and *king* (ginger.) Traditionally, the paste is used to prepare a curry of beef, pork, and shrimp curry with a gravy-like sauce instead of with a more stew- or soup-like consistency. Sometimes, as here, green beans are included.

PHRIK KING CURRY

POUND the salt and garlic together in a mortar until they form a paste. Add the remaining chile paste ingredients one at a time, adding the next only after the previous one has been incorporated into the paste. The paste will keep in an airtight container, refrigerated, for up to a month.

COMBINE the coconut cream and chile paste in a medium saucepan over medium-high heat and heat until the oil separates out and the oil bubbles take on the color of the chile paste, stirring frequently. Add the coconut cream and milk combined and stir to mix. When the mixture comes to a boil, add the salt, fish sauce, palm sugar, lemongrass, chiles, and lime leaves and stir to combine. When it boils again, reduce the heat to medium-low and simmer for 10 to 15 minutes. (If making the curry broth ahead, let cool completely at this point and refrigerate. It will keep overnight. Bring to a boil before adding the meat and vegetables.)

ADD the main ingredients to the simmering broth. Once they are cooked, add the basil and stir until limp. Serve immediately.

MAKES 4 SERVINGS

PHRIK KING CHILE PASTE

1 teaspoon salt

5 cloves garlic, minced (2 tablespoons)

20 dried de arbol chiles or chiles Japones, soaked in hot water to soften, dried thoroughly, and minced

½ teaspoon white peppercorns, dry-roasted and ground (page 70)

½ teaspoon coriander seeds, dry-roasted and ground (page 70)

1 tablespoon minced fresh coriander roots and stems

1 stalk lemongrass, tough outer layers removed, tender inner stalk minced

6 thin slices galangal or peeled fresh ginger, minced

1 tablespoon minced kaffir or regular lime zest

¼ cup dried shrimp, soaked in hot water to soften

CURRY BROTH

1 cup Coconut Cream (page 22)

1 cup Coconut Cream and Milk combined (page 22)

1 teaspoon salt

2 tablespoons fish sauce (for vegetarians, use light soy sauce)

2 teaspoons palm sugar, dark brown sugar, or maple sugar

1 stalk lemongrass, tough outer layers removed, tender inner stalk cut lengthwise and slightly pounded

6 to 7 fresh Thai or 3 to 4 fresh serrano chiles, slightly crushed

6 to 7 kaffir lime leaves, slightly crushed, or zest of 1 lime, cut into slivers

MAIN INGREDIENTS

2½ cups thinly sliced beef or pork, dried thoroughly

1 pound large shrimp, peeled and dried thoroughly

1½ cups julienned green beans (for vegetarians, increase the green beans to 2 cups and add 1 cup shelled and peeled fresh fava beans and 1 cup canned hominy, rinsed and patted dry)

TO FINISH

½ cup fresh Thai basil or peppermint leaves

One of the best culinary fusions between southern Chinese and Thai cooking is noodle soup. There are countless versions of this marvelous invention, all built on the same foundation. No matter what time of day or season of the year, you will find Thais slurping noodle soup at street stands. ⁓⊗ Noodle soup is a healthy, simple one-dish meal, perfect for all people no matter their home element. Arrange the ingredients in the order they are to be cooked. Although this recipe is for one serving, you can increase the amount to accommodate several people. You can cook one order at a time to customize each bowl to the diner's preference. ⁓⊗ Serving noodle soup is a lesson in democracy. Place condiments and garnishes such as fish sauce, soy sauce, sugar, chili powder, Tabasco, Fresh Chiles in Vinegar (recipe follows), hoisin sauce, and crushed dry-roasted peanuts on the table so people can enjoy their soup as they prefer it. ⁓⊗ *Tienjin* preserved vegetable is salted cabbage flakes that look like wet cornflakes. It is packaged in a small, round ceramic or plastic jar and sold in Asian supermarkets. Rinse off the salt and dry thoroughly before using.

NOODLE SOUP Kuey Teow Namm

PUT the broth in a medium saucepan and bring to a boil. Lower the heat to a simmer.

FILL a large saucepan three-quarters full with water and bring to a boil. Add the bean sprouts and mustard greens and parboil them until their colors brighten, 10 to 12 seconds. Use a strainer to remove them from the boiling water, shake off the excess liquid, and place in your serving bowl.

COOK the noodles in the boiling water until cooked or heated through, 10 to 12 seconds. Transfer to the bowl with the vegetables, first shaking the noodles to remove excess water. Add the meat to the boiling water and transfer to the bowl when just cooked through. Season the cooked ingredients with the salt, sugar, fish sauce, chili powder (for spicy flavor), *tienjin* preserved vegetable, celery, and white pepper. Ladle the broth over the noodles. (If using canned, taste and adjust the seasonings accordingly.) Garnish with the fried garlic and cilantro. Serve hot with the accompaniments mentioned above.

MAKES 1 SERVING

1½ cups homemade (page 26 or 27) or canned low-sodium, low-fat chicken or vegetable broth

⅓ cup or more fresh bean sprouts

½ cup or more sliced mustard greens

1 cup tightly packed noodles of your choice (fresh wide rice noodles; cooked Chinese egg noodles; or thin or regular rice vermicelli, softened, page 86)

⅓ cup thinly sliced chicken, pork, or beef; medium shrimp, peeled and deveined; crabmeat, picked over for shells; cubed firm tofu; or fish, pork, or beef balls (available in the refrigerated section of Asian supermarkets)

½ teaspoon salt

¼ teaspoon sugar

1 tablespoon fish sauce (for vegetarians, substitute soy sauce)

½ teaspoon or more chili powder, or 1 to 2 tablespoons Roasted Chile Paste (page 90; optional)

1 teaspoon *tienjin* preserved vegetable or capers, rinsed and dried thoroughly

1 tablespoon minced celery

¼ teaspoon freshly ground white pepper

1 teaspoon fried garlic (page 100)

1 tablespoon coarsely chopped fresh cilantro

This is one of the condiments offered by noodle shops and vendors in Thailand. A little bit of it is all you need to add another layer of sour and spicy taste to salty and/or sweet seasonings in most noodle dishes, including the stir-fried noodle variations under Basic Stir-Fry (page 63) and Noodle Soup (page 82). It is acceptable for all elements. However, the chief beneficiaries of this condiment are Water and Wind element people.

FRESH CHILES IN VINEGAR

COMBINE all the ingredients in a glass jar with a tight lid. Shake well to combine. Refrigerate. They will keep for several weeks.

MAKES 1 CUP

6 to 8 fresh serrano chiles, thinly sliced

½ teaspoon salt

¾ cup distilled white vinegar

OODLES OF NOODLES

Until recently, the Asian food section in supermarkets was so small that to buy even the most common Asian ingredient, such as a bottle of soy sauce, you would have to be ready to go on a treasure hunt. The closest thing to real Asian-style noodles available were the Chung King crispy noodles packaged with ready-to-heat chop suey mixture. No more. With the popularity of Asian foods, supermarkets today have expanded their Asian food sections at least tenfold. Specialty food markets devote several shelves to Asian spices, condiments, canned goods, rices, and noodles. Online outlets offer even more variety. In cities with large Asian settlements, megasized Asian supermarkets occupying several street blocks have sprouted up. The dried noodles section usually takes up an entire aisle, while freshly made noodles are stocked in their own large refrigerated section.

It is not unusual for the same kind of noodles, made by different companies from several countries, to be sold under different names and descriptions. It is a mind-boggling experience, even for expert Asian shoppers.

Here is a list of noodles used in recipes in the book. Included is a brief description and how to prepare them.

PAD THAI NOODLES

These are also sold as Chantaburi Noodles, Ban Pho, or Sen Lek. These dried noodles are flat and about ⅛ inch wide, resembling fettuccine. The strands are brittle, off-white in color, folded over a couple of times into a tight bundle, and packaged in cellophane. They are used to make pad thai and the Vietnamese noodle soup called pho. The wider strand, or sen yai, is about ¼ inch wide and similar to Italian dried egg noodles. It is used for noodle soups and stir-fried noodles.

Asian supermarkets also sell both types of pad thai noodles fresh. The fresh thin noodles are coiled up into a tight bundle the size of a medium-size fist and packaged in airtight plastic wrap. They are stocked either on a nonrefrigerated shelf next to fresh wide rice noodles, or sometimes in the refrigerated section. The wide noodle is pure white and coated with oil. The strands are uniformly cut from folded rice noodle sheets and laid flat as is, in plastic wrap. They are never refrigerated because the oil used in their preparation will congeal and harden the noodle. If you buy the fresh noodles and cannot use them the same day, go ahead and refrigerate them. For thin rice noodles, take them out of the refrigerator several hours before you intend to prepare them to allow them to come to room temperature. For wide noodles, microwave them for 30 to 40 seconds to soften, then loosen the strands into ribbons before cooking.

To prepare the dried rice noodles for cooking, soak them in very warm water until the strands are pliable, 25 to 30 minutes. Wider rice noodles might take a bit longer to soften. Rinse with cool water to rid them of excess starch and dry thoroughly. Leave them in a strainer and cover with a dish towel until ready to use.

If using them in a stir-fry, fresh rice noodles don't need prior preparation. Whether using fresh or dried noodles, add a couple of tablespoons of water to the pan several times while cooking to further soften and cook them.

If using them in a noodle soup, put the softened noodles in a fine-mesh strainer and lower them into the boiling water over medium-high heat until the strands are soft and cooked, 1 to

2 minutes. Discard as much excess water as you can before putting them into the serving bowl. Ladle the broth over them.

RICE VERMICELLI

Also sold as may-fun, mai fun, or rice sticks, this type of dried rice noodle comes in two sizes. One resembles angel hair pasta and is used as a filling in rice paper wrappers. The other is a bit thicker, like spaghetti noodles. Both are off-white in color. The thicker strands are used for stir-fried noodles, cool rice noodles, and crispy noodles, and in noodle soups. Both kinds are sold folded over a couple of times, bundled, and packaged in cellophane. They are made in Taiwan, China, Vietnam, and Thailand.

Cook the thinner noodles in boiling water over high heat until they turn soft and are cooked through, 2 to 3 minutes. Transfer them to a strainer in the sink and run cool water over them until the strands are cool and the water drains clear. Drain thoroughly. Leave in the strainer and cover with a dish towel to keep moist.

If using in a stir-fry, soak the wider noodles in hot water until they are pliable and the strands have turned whiter and softer. Drain them through a strainer in the sink. Run cool water over them to get rid of the starch. Dry thoroughly and keep them in a strainer. Cover with a dish towel until ready to use.

If using for a cold noodle preparation, soak the wider noodles in cool water until they are pliable and the strands have turned whiter and softer. Drain, then cook in boiling water over medium-high heat for 3 to 4 minutes. Drain, then run cool water over them to get rid of the starch. Dry thoroughly and cover with a dish towel until ready to use.

If using for crispy deep-fried noodles, soak the wider noodles in cool water until the strands are pliable. Dry thoroughly. Add a small handful to hot oil over medium-high heat. Within an instant, the strands will puff and curl into light white clouds of noodles. Remove to a strainer lined with layers of paper towels.

If using in a noodle soup, soak the wider noodles in cool water until the strands are pliable. Drain in a fine-mesh strainer, then lower the strainer into boiling water until the strands are soft and cooked, 1 to 2 minutes. Shake off the excess water, put them in a serving bowl, then add the broth.

GLASS NOODLES

Also sold as bean threads, mung bean noodles, and cellophane noodles, this type of noodle is made from mung beans. It is very brittle and rather sinewy and wiry like fishing line. The seemingly endless strands are tightly bundled into one large bundle, tied with a couple of strings, and packaged in cellophane. To extract the portion you need, put the bundle in a large paper bag and cut off the amount you need. Fortunately, sometimes you can find them sold in smaller bundles, with 8 to 12 pieces wrapped together in a package. It is difficult to tell by looking at them if glass noodles are made entirely of mung beans. If they aren't, they will completely disintegrate into the water when you cook them, while the real ones will become transparent. They are made in Taiwan, China, Vietnam, and Thailand.

If using in a soup or stir-fry, soak glass noodles in cool water until pliable, then drain, cut them into manageable lengths, and cook according to the recipe.

If using in a salad, soak the noodles until pliable, drain, then cook in boiling water until they turn translucent, 10 to 12 seconds. Drain and rinse with cool water until the noodles cool off. Extract excess water and cut into manageable lengths.

EGG NOODLES

Also sold as yellow longevity egg noodle, Shanghai noodle, or imitation noodle, they are made with wheat flour, salt, and eggs, and sold dried or fresh. The dried noodle strand is thinner than a spaghetti noodle, brittle, and bright yellow. Some are tightly wrapped in small 2½-inch bundles and sold 6 to 8 together in a package. Others are either tightly or loosely folded over a couple of times, both laid flat and packaged in cellophane. Fresh egg noodles are sold in the refrigerated section where wonton skins are stocked. They come in many sizes, from thin to fat, and are beige, light yellow, or green (spinach). Most are packaged with 4 to 8 small one-serving bundles in a plastic container. Some are sold as one large portion, enough for 4 to 6 servings.

Both dried and fresh noodles need to be cooked in boiling water over medium-high heat for 2 to 4 minutes, until they are slightly al dente. If using dried noodles, when the strands begin to soften, loosen the tightly wrapped bundles for even cooking. Drain the noodles in a strainer set in the sink. For noodle soup, transfer them to a bowl and ladle the broth over. For stir-fried noodles, rinse with cool water to rid them of excess starch. Shake the strainer to discard excess water, transfer to a bowl, and add 1 to 2 tablespoons sesame oil to the noodles. Mix well, then use according to the recipe.

SOBA NOODLES

This type of noodle is made with wheat flour, thus the strand is a whitish color. Some are made with buckwheat, which turns the strands grayish. Recently, spinach and even green tea leaves have been added to the flour, turning the strands green. Soba resembles very thin fettuccine, cut into about 8-inch lengths. Most are wrapped into thin 1-inch bundles and secured with either plastic or paper bands and sold in a group of 4 to 6 in plastic wrap. Some are sold loosely packed in plastic wrap. Until rice vermicelli for making cool rice vermicelli became available, I used soba noodles as a substitute. For further information on soba noodles, refer to page 110.

If using in a soup or stir-fry, or to serve as cool soba, cook in boiling water over high heat until soft and pliable, 2 to 3 minutes. Drain through a strainer in the sink. For soup, portion the noodles into individual bowls and ladle the hot broth over. For a stir-fry or to serve as cool soba, rinse the noodles with cool water to rid them of starch until the draining water runs clear. Shake the strainer to discard excess water. For a stir-fry, transfer to a bowl and add a teaspoon or more of sesame oil, mix, and use according to the recipe. For cool soba, transfer to individual serving plates.

*T*om yum is best served as a part of a dinner menu on a rainy, damp, or cold evening because sour taste balances the double influence of the Water element, which rules the evening hours and the weather. Although the soup is made with a balance of spicy, salty, sour, and slightly sweet tastes, serve it with accompaniments including fish sauce, minced chiles, and lime slices to allow guests to flavor it as desired.

HOT AND SOUR SOUP WITH ROASTED CHILE OIL Tom Yum

BRING the broth to a boil in a large saucepan. (If using canned broth, taste and adjust the seasonings accordingly.) Add the lemongrass, galangal, lime leaves, and chiles. Reduce the heat to low, cover, and simmer for 15 minutes. Turn off the heat. Strain the broth and discard the solids. Return the broth to the pan and bring to a boil over medium heat. Reduce the heat to low and season with the chile oil, salt, fish sauce, and palm sugar. Cook for another 10 minutes. Increase the heat to medium and add the vegetables. Cook, stirring, for 5 to 7 minutes. Add the fish and/or shellfish or tofu and cook just until cooked or heated through. Turn off the heat. Combine the lime juice and cilantro in a large serving bowl. Ladle the soup into the bowl. Stir and mix and serve hot in soup bowls with cooked rice.

MAKES 4 SERVINGS

4 cups homemade (page 26) or canned low-sodium, low-fat chicken broth or Fish Broth (page 28)

2 stalks lemongrass, tough outer layers removed, tender inner stalk cut into bite-size pieces and slightly pounded

6 to 7 thin slices galangal or fresh ginger

7 kaffir lime leaves, slightly crushed, or zest of 1 lime, cut into slivers

7 to 8 fresh Thai or 2 to 3 fresh serrano chiles, slightly pounded

1 tablespoon Roasted Chile Oil (page 65)

½ teaspoon salt

3 tablespoons fish sauce

1 tablespoon palm sugar or light brown sugar

MAIN INGREDIENTS

1 cup mixed sliced mushrooms, onions, and/or winter and/or summer squash

2 cups bite-size pieces fish fillets such as red snapper, catfish, trout, or sea bass; crabmeat; medium shrimp, shelled and deveined; scallops; and/or squid, bodies cut into rings (for vegetarians, increase vegetables to 3 cups and add 1 cup cubed firm tofu)

TO FINISH

Juice of 1 lime (about 3 tablespoons)

¼ cup chopped fresh cilantro

*T*his version of *tom yum* has a fruitier, more savory taste because of the addition of tamarind puree, making it an excellent variation for Water and Wind element people. The roasted chile paste is also tasty stirred into a noodle soup or stir-fry. It will keep for several weeks in the refrigerator.

HOT AND SOUR SOUP WITH ROASTED CHILE PASTE AND TAMARIND

COMBINE the salt and chiles in a mortar and pound into a paste. Add the garlic and shallots and pound until incorporated.

BRING the fish broth to a boil in a large saucepan. Add the lemongrass, lime leaves, chiles, chile paste, salt, fish sauce, and palm sugar, reduce the heat to low, cover, and let simmer for 20 minutes. Increase the heat to medium, add the vegetables, and cook until tender, 5 to 7 minutes. Add the fish and cook just until cooked through. Stir in the tamarind puree, then add the combined parsley, and mint, and the scallions. When the broth comes to a boil, turn off the heat. Ladle into individual serving bowls and serve hot with hot white, brown, or red rice.

MAKES 4 SERVINGS

ROASTED CHILE PASTE (MAKES ⅓ CUP)

1 teaspoon salt

15 to 20 dried de arbol chiles or chiles Japones, dry-roasted in a skillet over medium heat, shaking the skillet, until blackened (7 minutes), minced

7 cloves garlic, roasted in a 450°F oven until soft (15 minutes), peeled, and minced

5 shallots, roasted in a 450°F oven until soft (15 minutes), peeled, and minced

SOUP

4 cups Fish Broth (page 28)

2 stalks lemongrass, tough outer layers removed, tender inner stalk cut into bite-size pieces

5 to 6 kaffir lime leaves, slightly crushed, or zest of 1 lime, cut into slivers

6 to 7 fresh Thai or 1 to 2 fresh serrano chiles, slightly crushed

1½ teaspoons salt

3 to 4 tablespoons fish sauce, to your taste

1 tablespoon palm sugar, dark brown sugar, or maple sugar

MAIN INGREDIENTS

1 cup combination of sliced bamboo shoots; torn arugula leaves; squash blossoms; sliced summer squash; small, thin slices of Chinese winter melon; peeled, seeded, and thinly sliced cucumber; thinly sliced okra; and/or sliced leek whites

2 cups bite-size pieces firm, slightly oily fish fillets, such as mackerel, swordfish, or lingcod

TO FINISH

½ cup Tamarind Puree (page 25)

½ cup coarsely chopped fresh Italian parsley and peppermint combined

¼ cup coarsely chopped scallions

$\mathcal{E}$arth and Wind element people adore this soup because of Earth element's rich, creamy texture infused with herbs and spices that are the taste and flavor of Wind element. It's best served for lunch on rainy, damp, and cold days, when Wind and Earth elements dominate. For Water and Wind elements, use all coconut milk instead of coconut cream and coconut milk combined or, better yet, use all almond milk. Since almond milk lacks the floral essence of coconut milk, add 2 to 3 drops of coconut extract. To intensify the essence of the broth, add more galangal, kaffir lime leaves, and lemongrass. For the Fire element person, use the almond milk version to protect against possible inflammation of the circulatory system. ⁓⧉ Whatever version you make, particularly if you add tart fruit, add just enough lime juice to balance the taste of creamy, spicy, salty, sweet, and sour. Serve with additional chopped fresh chiles and lime juice.

COCONUT CREAM SOUP Tom Ka

BRING the broth to a boil in a large saucepan. (If using canned broth, taste and adjust the seasonings accordingly.) Add the garlic galangal, lemongrass, lime leaves, chiles, and shallots. Cover, reduce the heat to low, and simmer for 30 minutes. Strain the broth and discard the solids. Return the broth to the saucepan and set over low heat. Add the salt, sugar, and fish sauce and taste for a pleasing balance of spicy and salty. Add the coconut cream and milk combined. When the broth begins to simmer, add the main ingredients. Increase the heat to medium. When they are cooked, turn off the heat.

PUT the lime juice, cilantro, and scallion, if using, in a large serving bowl. Ladle the hot soup into the bowl and stir to mix. Ladle into individual serving bowls and serve with hot white, brown, or red rice.

MAKES 4 SERVINGS

2 cups homemade (page 26 or 27) or canned low-sodium, low-fat chicken or vegetable broth

2 cloves garlic, peeled

7 to 8 thin slices galangal or fresh ginger

1 stalk lemongrass, tough outer layers removed, tender inner stalk cut into bite-size pieces and slightly pounded

12 kaffir lime leaves, slightly crushed, or zest of 1 lime, cut into slivers

5 to 6 fresh Thai or 2 to 3 fresh serrano chiles, slightly pounded

3 shallots, cut in half

1 teaspoon salt

1 teaspoon sugar

¼ cup fish sauce

2 cups Coconut Cream and Milk combined (page 22) or Almond Milk (page 21)

MAIN INGREDIENTS

2 cups bite-size pieces chicken or snapper, sea bass, or trout fillets (for vegetarians, increase the vegetables to 3 cups and use a variety of mushrooms and squash)

1 cup straw mushrooms or bite-size chunks peeled pumpkin

TO FINISH

2 to 3 tablespoons fresh lime juice

¼ cup chopped fresh cilantro

1 scallion (optional), minced

aeng som is best served as a part of the dinner menu to balance the Water element, which rules the dinner hours. Although it can be eaten all year round, it's most beneficial during rainy, damp, and cool weather. For the Earth element person, palm sugar can be added to sweeten the broth, while Water and Wind element people might want to add more tamarind juice. For the Fire element person, the balance of taste, flavor, and aroma in the recipe is just right.

SAVORY SOUR SOUP Gaeng Som

COMBINE the salt and chiles in a mortar and pound into a paste. Add the remaining chile paste ingredients one at a time, adding the next only after the previous one has been incorporated into the paste.

BRING the water to a boil in a large saucepan. Add the chile paste, fish sauce, palm sugar, and tamarind puree. Taste and adjust for a pleasing balance of salty, sour, slightly sweet, and spicy. Add the main ingredients and cook over high heat for 5 minutes. Lower the heat to medium and cook for another 5 minutes. Serve with hot white, brown, or red rice.

MAKES 4 SERVINGS

GAENG SOM CHILE PASTE

½ teaspoon salt

12 dried de arbol chiles or chiles Japones, soaked in warm water to soften, dried thoroughly, and minced

5 cloves garlic, minced

2 shallots, minced

1 teaspoon fermented shrimp paste or red miso

1 tablespoon minced smoked trout (optional)

SOUP

4 cups water

3 tablespoons fish sauce

3 tablespoons palm sugar, dark brown sugar, or maple sugar

½ cup Tamarind Puree (page 25)

MAIN INGREDIENTS

1 cup each of 3 kinds of seasonal vegetables with different textures, such as sliced okra; summer and winter squashes; melons; eggplants; bamboo shoots; mushrooms; tomatoes; squash blossoms; torn arugula, spinach, and/or beet greens; and/or cauliflower florets and sliced stems

½ pound delicately textured fish fillets such as trout or freshwater bass, cut into bite-size pieces (optional; if adding this, make sure the total volume of fish and vegetables doesn't exceed 3 cups)

aeng liang is a Thai soup served when the rainy weather begins to wane, giving way to the cool season. Thais believe that our respiratory system is vulnerable during this transition. *Gaeng liang* combines garlic and white peppercorns to prevent and relieve cold symptoms. Cool/refreshing vegetables are added to soothe sore throats. The soup is also served to nursing mothers to increase milk flow. Good for all home elements, it's especially nourishing to Water, Wind, and Fire element people.

GAENG LIANG

HEAT the oil in a small saucepan over high heat until it begins to smoke, 2 to 3 minutes. Add the smoked trout and fry until crispy, 2 to 3 minutes. Using a slotted spoon, remove the pieces of trout from the oil to a plate lined with paper towels to cool. Transfer to a mortar and pound into a pulp. Add the garlic and pepper and pound into a paste. Add the shrimp paste and mix well.

BRING the broth to a boil in a large saucepan. (If using canned broth, taste and adjust the seasonings accordingly.) Stir in the chile paste and fish sauce. Add the vegetables and cook on high heat for 5 minutes. Lower the heat to medium and cook for another 5 minutes. Stir in the basil. Ladle the soup into individual soup bowls and serve with hot white, brown, or red rice.

MAKES 4 SERVINGS

GAENG LIANG CHILE PASTE

1 cup vegetable oil of your choice

⅓ cup flaked smoked trout

5 cloves garlic, minced

1 teaspoon white peppercorns, dry-roasted and ground (page 70)

1 teaspoon fermented shrimp paste or red miso

SOUP

4 cups homemade (page 26) or canned low-sodium, low-fat chicken broth

1 tablespoon fish sauce

3 to 4 kinds of vegetables to make a total of 4 cups: bite-size chunks pumpkin; squash blossoms; peeled and thinly sliced summer Chinese melon; peeled and thinly sliced cucumber; thinly sliced okra; baby corn; green beans thinly sliced on the diagonal; and sliced mushrooms

⅔ cup fresh Thai basil or peppermint leaves

94

ot, spicy, buttery, and cool/refreshing tastes and flavors balance our body's elements during seasonal changes. This northern Thai dish is best for Water and Wind element people or for all elements as a healing soup to relieve a cold. Traditionally, it is cooked with a combination of seasonal greens called *pak roh,* or fence vegetables found growing wild along fences.

GAENG KHAE

COMBINE the salt and garlic in a mortar and pound into a paste. Add the remaining chile paste ingredients one at a time, adding the next only after the previous one has been incorporated into the paste.

BRING the broth to a boil in a large saucepan over high heat. (If using canned broth, taste and adjust the seasonings accordingly.) Stir in the chile paste, salt, and fish sauce. Add the main ingredients. When the broth comes back to a boil, continue to boil for 5 minutes. Reduce the heat to medium-low and simmer until the meat is just cooked through and the vegetables are still slightly firm, about 5 minutes. Add the arugula, basil, and parsley and stir to mix. When the herbs turn limp, turn off the heat. Ladle into individual soup bowls and serve with hot white, brown, or red rice.

GAENG KHAE CHILE PASTE

½ teaspoon salt

8 cloves garlic, minced

15 dried de arbol chiles or chiles Japones, soaked in hot water to soften, dried thoroughly, and minced

2 stalks lemongrass, tough outer layers removed, tender inner stalk minced

2 shallots, minced

1 teaspoon fermented fish or shrimp paste or red miso

SOUP

4 cups homemade (page 26) or canned low-sodium, low-fat chicken broth

½ teaspoon salt

2 tablespoons fish sauce

MAIN INGREDIENTS

1 cup bite-size chunks chicken, stir-fried in hot oil for 1 to 2 minutes before adding to the broth

3 cups mixed seasonal vegetables: thinly sliced Thai and/or Japanese eggplants, bamboo shoots, green beans cut into bite-size pieces, mushrooms cut in half, thinly sliced okra, and/or bite-size chunks of peeled seeded green papaya, summer melons, spinach, beet greens, radish or turnip greens, and/or Swiss chard

TO FINISH

1 cup coarsely chopped arugula

¼ cup fresh holy or Thai basil or peppermint leaves

¼ cup coarsely chopped fresh Italian parsley

*E*very region in Thailand has its own version of this thick, hearty soup, served to nurture one's health during abrupt and sudden turns of weather. During the cool season, southern Thais substitute pork and beef for the fish and fish broth to strengthen the body structure. *Gaeng awm* is appropriate for all home elements, although Water and Wind element people are likely to be even more partial to it.

GAENG AWM

COMBINE the salt and shallots in a mortar and pound into a paste. Add the chiles and pound into a paste. Add the softened rice and pound into a paste.

COMBINE the condiment ingredients in a small bowl and set aside.

BRING the broth to a boil in a large saucepan. Stir in the chile paste, lemongrass, salt, and fish sauce. Reduce the heat to medium-low and let it simmer for 10 minutes. Add the eggplant and chiles and cook until tender before adding the main ingredients. When they are cooked, about 10 minutes, add the arugula, if using, basil, and scallions. When they turn limp, stir in the dill. Ladle into individual soup bowls and serve with hot white, brown, or red rice, with the condiment on the side.

MAKES 4 SERVINGS

GAENG AWM CHILE PASTE

½ teaspoon salt

3 shallots, minced

8 fresh Thai or 4 fresh serrano chiles, minced

2 tablespoons Thai jasmine long-grain glutinous rice, soaked in room temperature water for 30 minutes to soften (you can buy this in specialty food markets or online; for this recipe, you can also use Japanese short-grain glutinous rice)

CONDIMENT

⅓ cup fish sauce

3 to 4 fresh Thai or 1 to 2 fresh serrano chiles, minced

1 clove garlic, thinly sliced

SOUP

4 cups Fish Broth (page 28)

1 stalk lemongrass, tough outer layers removed, tender inner stalk cut into bite-size pieces and slightly pounded

1 teaspoon salt

3 tablespoons fish sauce

1 cup quartered Thai eggplant or 1 Japanese eggplant, cut into 1-inch-thick rounds

3 to 4 fresh Thai or 1 to 2 fresh serrano chiles, slightly pounded

MAIN INGREDIENTS

2 cups bite-size catfish fillets, or medium shrimp, peeled and deveined (for vegetarians, increase the vegetables to 5 cups)

3 cups mixed seasonal greens such as chopped Swiss chard, spinach, and/or beet greens; bite-size chunks peeled summer Chinese melon; thinly sliced bitter melons, salted for 10 minutes, rinsed, and dried thoroughly; thinly sliced okra; and/or green beans cut into bite-size pieces

TO FINISH

1 cup coarsely chopped arugula (optional)

⅓ cup fresh holy or Thai basil or peppermint leaves, slightly crushed

2 scallions, thinly sliced

⅓ cup chopped fresh dill

Rice keeps all the body's elements in balance and is good all year round. Thais believe that rice increases one's energy level while soothing anxiety and lowering stress. They love rice porridge for breakfast or as a late evening snack. It is considered especially nurturing for the very young and the elderly, and it speeds recovery during illnesses. ⁓§ Instead of toast, serve plain rice porridge with a scrambled egg and sausage. Or, use it as a base for a variety of recipes listed in the individual home element chapters. Short-grain glutinous rice is often called Japanese rice and can be bought in supermarkets, specialty food markets, and Asian markets, or online.

RICE PORRIDGE WITH BROWN OR WHITE RICE

COMBINE all the ingredients in a large saucepan over high heat. When the liquid begins to boil, stir to mix well. Cover, turn the heat to low, and let simmer for 30 to 35 minutes (10 to 12 minutes longer for brown rice), stirring occasionally. When done, the porridge should be smooth and silky, like a thin pudding, with some whole rice kernels still intact. Serve hot.

Gingered Rice Porridge

Cut the recipe in half and, instead of water, use homemade (page 26) or canned low-sodium, low-fat chicken broth and add 6 to 7 slices fresh ginger. I have made this recipe for friends undergoing chemotherapy who were unable to eat or keep food down. A tablespoon or two at each serving helped restore their strength.

MAKES 5 CUPS

6 cups water (7 cups for brown rice)

½ teaspoon salt

¼ cup brown or white long-grain jasmine rice

2 tablespoons short-grain white glutinous or Japanese rice

COMFORT FOODS

There is a Chinese word, *pu,* which roughly translates as "extra healthful supplement." The Thais use this concept to describe a revitalizing, restorative, or strengthening process for one's health during changing climates or after an illness. Here are some of my favorite recipes that I make and share with family and friends.

Silken tofu has a custard-like texture and, when combined with warm ginger syrup, it can be enjoyed by all home elements, especially during cold and/or rainy weather. Serve it over cooked fruits such as baked apples or pears, or eat it like pudding.

SILKEN TOFU WITH GINGER SYRUP

COMBINE the ginger, sugar, and water in a small saucepan over medium heat. When the liquid comes to a boil and the sugar has dissolved, reduce the heat to low and simmer for 10 to 15 minutes.

STRAIN the syrup into a heatproof container and let cool before refrigerating. It will keep for at least a week. (The cooked ginger pieces, laced with the sugary syrup, are a delicious snack. Store in a container with a lid and refrigerate. They will keep for several weeks. Heat in the microwave for 20 seconds to warm.)

FOR a single serving, spoon about 1 cup of the tofu into a microwave-safe bowl. Top it with 3 tablespoons of the ginger syrup. Cover and microwave for 50 seconds. Serve warm.

MAKES 2 TO 3 SERVINGS

10 thin slices fresh ginger, slightly pounded

½ cup sugar

½ cup water

One 19-ounce package silken tofu

umquat soothes the throat and relieves coughing and nasal congestion. Ginger nourishes all home elements, warms the respiratory system, and balances the Wind element when it's cold and wet outside. Clove is an analgesic and relieves cold symptoms. Adding honey eases coughing and balances the body's elements. All together, this medicinal preserve is a must to keep on hand as a preventative and healing remedy for colds. A spoonful in your daily mug of hot tea during the winter is revitalizing.

KUMQUAT, GINGER, AND CLOVE PRESERVES

COMBINE all the ingredients in a large, heavy-bottomed saucepan over high heat. As soon as the honey liquefies and comes to a boil, reduce the heat to medium-low. Stir occasionally until the kumquats become soft and their color brightens, about 30 minutes. Remove from the heat and transfer to a clean jar with a tight lid. Cover and let cool before storing in the refrigerator, where it will keep for several months.

MAKES 2 PINTS

4 cups kumquats

2 cups honey

20 thin slices fresh ginger

15 to 20 cloves

tablespoon or two of these garnishes is all you need to perk up noodle dishes and salads.

BASIC FRIED GARNISH

HEAT the oil in a large saucepan over high heat for about 4 minutes. Do not overheat the oil, or the ingredients will burn. Test the oil by putting a wooden chopstick or the handle of a wooden spoon into the oil. When bubbles begin to form around the wood, it is ready. Sprinkle the salt over the oil and reduce the heat to medium-low. (Salt is believed to help maintain an even temperature for frying and enhances crispness.) Add what you're frying. Stir constantly to ensure even cooking. When the ingredient turns golden, remove it from the oil using a strainer and let it drain on several layers of paper towels. Use immediately, or you can let cool completely and store in an airtight container in the refrigerator for up to 2 weeks.

MAKES ABOUT 1 CUP

4 cups vegetable oil of your choice

½ teaspoon salt

2 cups coarsely chopped garlic; thinly sliced shallots; tender inner stalk of lemongrass sliced thinly across into rings and pounded to separate and loosen the fibers; whole kaffir lime leaves; or dried chiles, softened in warm water and dried thoroughly

Sprinkle dry-roasted coconut flakes on salads, baked or fresh fruits, and ice cream.

DRY-ROASTED COCONUT FLAKES

PUT the coconut pulp in a large skillet over medium-high heat. Stir frequently (to ensure even roasting) until the pulp turns golden. Let cool completely before storing in an airtight container at room temperature, where it will keep for at least a month.

MAKES 2 CUPS

2 cups coconut pulp (page 23)

Freshly grated coconut is used primarily as a garnish for Thai desserts. Invest in a Japanese grater. This inexpensive kitchen tool is a small oblong plastic box with several interchangeable grating surfaces. The fine metal grater, used to grate daikon for sushi, produces fluffy cloud-like coconut flakes.

GRATED FRESH COCONUT

FOLLOW the instructions for how to extract the meat from the husk on page 22. Peel the outer dark peel from the pieces of meat with a vegetable peeler. Using a Japanese grater, fit the fine metal grater to the box and grate the coconut into thin strands. Grated coconut with 1 fresh Thai chile added will keep in an airtight container in the refrigerator for 2 to 3 days and in the freezer for up to a month.

MAKES ABOUT 3 CUPS

1 coconut

GARNISHES

Garnishes provide the surprising and contrasting touches so central to Thai dishes. They tend to be Wind element ingredients, with pungent flavors and cool/refreshing aromas. They are generally deep-fried in oil, which gives them the rich, buttery flavor of the Earth element. Just a tablespoonful of any garnish per serving is all that is needed to achieve the perfect blend of opposite elements, suitable for all home elements.

CHAPTER THREE

My friend, Uncle Non, lived with his family in a traditional Thai house. Its main support was a solid teak post planted deep in the ground that ascended up through the middle of the house, ending at the roof's base. Every night, Uncle Non burned incense in a dish next to the post and then splashed a couple of shots of whiskey on the post and drank the rest. Uncle Non said that the post was where the spirit of the house lived, watching over the structure and his family.

Din in the Thai language means "earth, land, ground, or soil." In Thai folk medicine, *din,* like Uncle Non's house, is the basic physical structure, the tangible, solid parts of the human body. Earth represents and dominates the body's flesh, bones, and connective tissues, which includes the ligaments, muscles, and tendons. If your home element is Earth, these areas are your strength and your weakness and you must be alert to any changes that might signal a shift away from their good health, as well as the health of your heart and digestive system. Traditional Thai healers would advise that, like Uncle Non's teak pole, you must be the spirit of the house, honoring and protecting your physical "home."

If Earth is your home element, you are most likely gifted with a robust, sturdy, and compact body but you need to be vigilant about your weight, as it can fluctuate. Your voice is full and deep. You are blessed with firm, supple skin and hair that is thick and glossy.

As an Earth element person, you are self-confident and hold your convictions strongly, though sometimes you can be overly sensitive; at work you are self-directed, steady, reliable, and patient.

According to Thai traditional healers, Earth element types require a long, uninterrupted night's sleep for peak performance. Catnaps are out of the question. But even when tired, you will opt for an energetic workout. You love to travel, gravitating to the ocean, which soothes your mind and spirit. Although you are able to acclimate to different climates, warm and temperate weather rejuvenates you, whereas a cold and damp climate can weigh you down, making you feel drained and lethargic.

With Earth as your home element, you are more open to change than others, and once you make up your mind to do something, you do it. Change is an enjoyable challenge for the self-directed and confident Earth element person. So join hands with nature. Tune into the treasures of your inner being. Honor and keep your physical body fit and strong and your innate, glorious spirit alive and radiant.

EARTH

FOOD FOR HEALTH

I have long observed my friend Mali's eating habits, which are perfectly in sync with the Earth element person she is. She watches her weight because it seesaws up and down, the result, in many cases, of eating when she's bored, nervous, or anxious, which in turn makes her feel guilty, which in turn leads to more anxiety and more eating.

When she is in control of her eating habits, Mali eats light meals at scheduled times and cooks a healthy dinner with an abundance of seasonal greens. She carries bottled water with her at all times. As an Earth element person, good hydration is essential to her health, as water cleanses the intestines, allowing nutrients to pass into the body.

Thai healers would say that the Earth element is like the structure of one's house, requiring strong and healthy soil to keep it intact. Regular maintenance keeps the house from falling apart. The idea of "soil and regular maintenance" serves as a road map for Earth element people. As for diet, an Earth element person will want to seek out seasonal fruits and vegetables with astringent, buttery, sweet, and salty characteristics, as they contain healing qualities necessary to protect and maintain vital body structure: skin, bones, muscles, and connective tissues. Astringent-flavor vegetables such as artichokes, asparagus, cauliflower, and Swiss chard keep body tissues healthy, are good for the digestive system, and balance other body elements, while rich, buttery, and creamy flavors such as potato, coconut, pumpkin, and avocado provide important nutrients that nourish tendons, muscles, and connective tissues. Coffee and tea, which are astringent, are less damaging to Earth element people, and drinking alcohol in moderation is fine. Sweet-tasting foods also nurture the muscles and the heart. Some Earth element people crave sweets when tired, irritable, or thirsty; according to traditional healers, sweet-tasting foods tend to relieve these symptoms. Many Earth element people can't set the table without the salt shaker within ready reach. That's your body letting you know that you need salt for the good health of your muscles, tendons, and connective tissues. Just be careful not to overindulge.

HOT WEATHER RECIPES

Earth element people thrive in summer, basking in the light and relishing the warmth. You let your guard down, flow easily with life, and feast on the fresh fruits and vegetables that complement your body's needs. Balance your diet with seasonal fruits and vegetables with the taste, flavor, and aroma of your home element as well as nature's Fire element, which dominates the hot weather. This means cooking and eating foods with ingredients combining Fire element's bland flavor, bitter taste, and cool/refreshing flavor together with your Earth element's astringent flavor, sweet and salty taste, and buttery flavor. Be prudent in hot weather when it comes to your taste for sweetness, as it increases body heat if taken in excess. If you succumb to temptation, balance your indulgence with astringent-flavor vegetables, which will lower your body temperature.

Earth element people are drawn to the sun like iron to a magnet. Wouldn't you rather be like a cool, shaded oasis rather than dry, parched, and scorched desert sands? Use protective sunblock for your skin and wear a hat. Drink plenty of water when spending time in the sun. Add a bit more salty taste to your diet. It will replenish depleted salts and water in your body.

Hot weather beckons Earth element people toward the water. Even if you are busy, take a break for walks along the water, wherever you may live. Relax and be joyful.

BREAKFAST

For Earth element people, starting the day with a light breakfast will curb your temptation to snack. In addition to combining the tastes, flavors, and aromas of your home element together with the hot climate dominated by the Fire element, include sour, bland, and/or bitter taste in your breakfast. The latter is to balance the Water element, which dominates the morning hours. Limit your intake of coffee and tea to no more than two cups. A 4- to 6-ounce glass of a sweet/sour-tasting fruit juice such as orange or apple-cranberry, sweet/astringent grape, or sour/bitter grapefruit juice will balance your body's elements with that of nature's Water element. Be careful, though, as too much sour taste on a hot day can make you feel bloated and overheated. As an alternative, sip a cool/refreshing, sweet smoothie like Banana-Papaya-Mango Rumba on page 38, adding either soy or almond milk or nonfat yogurt to satisfy your Earth need for rich, buttery flavors.

Combining sweet-tasting fruits with some tangy ones in a morning fruit salad, or on top of your cereal, will also satisfy your Earth home element's need for sweet taste and Water element's requirement for sour taste. Cool/refreshing foods, such as sweet summer melon, with a touch of a pungent herb like mint added will balance nature's Fire element, which dominates hot weather. You can satisfy your home element's needs for foods with sweet, buttery flavor with pancakes or cereal. Try Rice and Banana Pancakes with Seasonal Fruit Mix (page 31). They are light and delicious.

LUNCH

On hot summer days, as nature's Fire element rules the weather and the noon hours, Earth element people might think of having spicy food for lunch to perspire and cool off, but traditional healers recommend the opposite. They warn that while the slight euphoria caused by the endorphins kicked up after eating hot chiles might feel good, in the end, you will be left feeling bloated and drained. This is because too many chiles can be hard on the digestive and vascular systems, especially when the weather is hot. Better choices are cold noodles or a noodle soup made with cool/refreshing-, bland-, and bitter-tasting vegetables to keep you in balance with the hot weather's Fire element (such as Noodle Soup, page 82). Soothe the Fire element by adding pungent flavors like ginger, galangal, garlic, shallots, and lemongrass, which are also good for digestion, an important consideration for Earth element people. Above all, eat bitter-tasting as well as bland-flavor vegetables, which specifically appease nature's Fire element and are the best protection for your earthy disposition. Check out the Earth element variations under Basic Stir-Fry (page 63). In addition, both water spinach and regular spinach, broccoli, Napa cabbage or bok choy, green beans, snap peas, and even the rather exotic bitter melon are delicious when stir-fried. You can make a stir-fry from a combination of them or choose one or two to stir-fry with thinly sliced chicken, medium shrimp, or cubed firm tofu. Spike them with minced fresh ginger, or garlic and thinly sliced shallots.

For salads, refer to the suggested salad ideas for each of the salad dressing recipes on pages 55 to 62, especially Black Sesame Dressing (page 55). You can also shower the parched soil of your Earth element with a summer salad, combining buttery, pungent, and cool/refreshing tastes to keep nature's Fire element in balance with your home element.

Here are a few more tasty combinations:

- Toss together shredded leftover grilled chicken, mixed greens, and the tender inner green portion of 1 stalk lemongrass, thinly sliced across and separated into rings, with Black Sesame Dressing (page 55) and garnish with fried shallots (page 100).

- Toss together thinly sliced baked tofu, the kernels from an ear of grilled corn, peeled and cubed mango, and mixed greens with Black Sesame Dressing (page 55).

- The next time you have your grill going, grill the ingredients for this salad for a lunch that will go together in minutes. Toss together grilled medium shrimp, grilled asparagus that you've sliced diagonally into 2-inch lengths, sliced grilled portobello mushrooms, and peeled and sliced kiwi with Black Sesame Dressing (page 55).

Although Earth element people fare well when the weather is hot, it is still important to keep your body's Fire element in check with nature's elements, preventing you from possible summer chills and fevers.

For beverages, indulge in sweet, refreshing fruit juices such as sugar cane juice (sold canned in Asian supermarkets), fresh Watermelon Juice (page 45), or coconut juice (also available in Asian markets, some major supermarkets, and selected specialty food markets), as well as hot and cold revitalizing herb teas such as Chrysanthemum Tea (page 46) or rose-hip tea.

For a midday snack, when the Wind element dominates, cool and refreshing fruits such as watermelon, honeydew, ripe papaya, and/or mango will curb your natural urge to munch and, at the same time, soothe your home element against nature's Wind element, which rules the late afternoon. Iced herbal teas such as orange blossom, peach, or mint, with a touch of honey and sprig of fresh mint added, will also stave off the urge to snack.

DINNER

Dinner served outdoors on a warm summer evening is as good as life gets. Prepare a salad or two, spiked with a tangy dressing to balance nature's Water element, which returns to dominate the dinner hours. Keep in mind to combine ingredients with Earth element tastes and flavors to take care of your home element together with those for the Fire element, which dominates the hot weather. Remember that good health is the result of following the rule of keeping a balance between your home element and nature's elements. Even your craving for a fat, juicy hamburger, for instance, can be met with this rule in mind. Mix lots of chopped parsley and tarragon into the hamburger mixture before forming patties. For a finishing touch, tuck in between the buns and on top of the meat a juicy tomato slice (Water element), and thin slices of crispy cucumber and several pieces of lettuce (Fire element).

A stir-fried dish made with bitter and other seasonal vegetables laced with spices, or an ice-cold soup prepared from fresh fruit to steady the summer season's Fire element, will fan and refresh your body as surely as a cool breeze. Summer salads combining salad greens and summer fruits add delicious nutrients to keep Earth element people feeling and looking good.

For beverages, cool herbal teas such as chamomile or mint, mixed with orange juice or cranberry-apple juice, served over crushed ice and garnished with bruised fresh peppermint leaves, are a balmy cure for a hot evening.

TASTE	VEGETABLES	FRUITS	HERBS/SPICES	GRAINS	
ASTRINGENT		Unripe banana, quince, medlar			
ASTRINGENT/BITTER	Tea				
ASTRINGENT/BLAND	Artichoke, beet greens, cauliflower, Swiss chard, green beans, yard-long beans, wing beans	Unripe guava			
ASTRINGENT/SPICY			Marjoram, turmeric		
ASTRINGENT/SOUR	Rhubarb	Cranberry			
ASTRINGENT/COOL/ REFRESHING	Lotus root, pea shoots				
BUTTERY				Millet	
BUTTERY/ASTRINGENT				Buckwheat, rye	
BUTTERY/BITTER					
BUTTERY/BLAND	Mushrooms, potatoes, taro	Unripe papaya			
BUTTERY/COOL/REFRESHING				Rice	
BUTTERY/SWEET	Acorn, butternut, kabocha, and spaghetti squash; pumpkin; parsnip; shell peas; sugar snap peas; sweet potato	Avocado, banana, coconut		Barley	
SALTY	Seaweed				
SALTY/ASTRINGENT	Celery, lovage (Chinese celery), spinach				
SWEET	Beet; carrot; corn; green, yellow, and red bell peppers	Date, fig, jujube date, mango, nectarine, ripe papaya, Fuyu persimmon			
SWEET/ASTRINGENT	Asparagus, cabbage	Apple, blackberry, blueberry, gooseberry, grape, kiwi, peach, pear, Hachiya persimmon, plum, pomegranate, raspberry, ripe guava, strawberry			
SWEET/COOL/REFRESHING	Fennel, sugarcane, water chestnut	Canary, Crenshaw, cantaloupe, and honeydew melons; watermelon; jicama; loquat			
SWEET/SOUR	Tomato	Apricot, cherry, orange, passion fruit, pineapple, Pluot, pomelo, star fruit, tangerine, tangelo, tamarind			
AROMA					
BITTER/PUNGENT					
SWEET/FLORAL/WARMING					
SWEET/WOODY/WARMING					

SEEDS/NUTS	BEANS/LEGUMES	COOKING OILS	ESSENTIAL OILS	SEASONINGS
	Coffee			
Sunflower seeds, pumpkin seeds	Black-eyed peas, kidney beans, lentils, lima beans, soybeans	Canola, corn, olive, mustard, safflower, sunflower		
Walnuts	Chickpeas			
Black and white sesame seeds	Cocoa beans, fava beans			
Cashews, peanuts	Azuki beans			
				Bean paste, fish sauce, fermented shrimp paste, miso, salt, soy sauce
				Agave syrup, corn syrup, fructose, honey, maple syrup, molasses, palm sugar, white sugar
			Cedar, juniper berry	
			Jasmine, patchouli, rose otto, rosewood, rose absolute, ylang-ylang	
			Sandalwood	

Soba noodles are made with buckwheat, which is perfect for Earth element people, who have sensitive digestive tracts. There are many grades of soba, depending on where the wheat was grown, how it was milled, the quality of water used to make the dough, and how the noodles were rolled and cut. Most Japanese supermarkets carry different varieties of dried soba and it is hard to know which one to buy. I would ask the proprietor to recommend one he or she likes best. Soba noodles can also be bought at some major supermarkets, specialty food markets, or online. Like dried pasta, soba keeps well in your pantry for months. Soba is packaged in different quantities, from one large bundle to several small individual bundles wrapped together. A tightly held together bundle about 1 inch in diameter is enough for one serving. ⁓⧉ Soba noodles can be served hot in broth as a noodle soup or as they are here, in a cold salad. It is so easy to make, you can prepare it the night before for lunch the next day.

COLD SOBA NOODLES

BRING a pot of water to a boil. Add the soba and cook until the strands are soft, 2 to 3 minutes. Drain and rinse under cool running water to get rid of the starch. Drain well. Transfer to a plate, then to the refrigerator to chill. (If making for the next day's lunch, put the noodles, together with the daikon, carrot, and cucumber, in a container with a lid and refrigerate. Wrap the seaweed in plastic wrap.)

HEAT the soup until it boils. Transfer to a serving bowl. (If making for the next day's lunch, transfer the amount needed from the bottle into a container with a lid. Refrigerate until ready to eat. Microwave until hot, about 1 minute.)

PUT the daikon, carrot, cucumber, and seaweed on top of the noodles. Put the scallion into the warm soup. Put the wasabi, if using, on a small plate. Smear a bit of wasabi on the noodles and pick up this mouthful of noodles together with bits of the vegetables and seaweed with a fork or chopsticks, dip all into the soup, and enjoy.

MAKES 1 SERVING

1 tightly held together bundle about 1 inch in diameter dried soba noodles

1 cup soup base for cold soba noodles (available ready for boiling in 17-ounce bottles in some supermarkets, specialty food markets, Asian markets, and online)

¼ cup grated daikon or 4 radishes, cut into matchsticks

¼ cup thinly sliced carrot

¼ cup peeled, seeded, and thinly sliced cucumber

1 to 2 tablespoons shredded dried seaweed

1 scallion, minced

1 teaspoon wasabi paste (optional)

Sweet and light tart mango fulfills both Earth and Water elements' needs. Mixed greens double the efforts in keeping your home element in tune with nature's elements.

GRILLED SHRIMP AND MANGO SALAD

HEAT the grill to medium-high.

PEEL the mangos and cut the flesh off the seed. Spray the slices lightly with vegetable oil spray and put on the grill. Cook until slightly charred, turning them once, about 7 minutes total. Put the shrimp on the grill and cook until firm and pink, turning them once, about 5 minutes total. Let cool. Cut the mango into long, thin slices.

PLACE the mixed salad greens on a serving platter. Arrange the mango slices and shrimp on top. Drizzle the dressing over and garnish with the fried shallots. Serve.

MAKES 4 SERVINGS

2 mangos

Vegetable oil spray

½ pound medium shrimp, peeled and deveined

2 cups mixed salad greens

½ cup or more Apple-Tamarind Dressing (page 56)

1 tablespoon fried shallots (page 100)

This is a symphony of tastes and color to delight any Earth element person on balmy summer nights.

GRILLED SCALLOP, BEET, AND CORN SALAD

HEAT the grill to high.

WRAP the beets in aluminum foil and put on the grill. Turn occasionally to ensure even cooking and cook until fork-tender, 25 to 30 minutes. Grill the corn until the kernels are slightly charred, about 7 minutes. Spray vegetable oil spray on the scallops and grill until the outer surfaces are firm and slightly charred, 4 to 5 minutes.

PEEL and slice the beets into small chunks. Put in a large salad bowl. Slice the corn kernels off the cob and add to the bowl. Add the salad greens and jicama. Toss lightly and add all but 1 tablespoon of the dressing. Toss again and put on serving plates. Slice each scallop in half and put on top of the greens. Drizzle the remaining 1 tablespoon dressing over the top of each plate and serve.

MAKES 4 SERVINGS

1 to 2 beets (1 cup, chopped)

1 ear corn, husk stripped off

Vegetable oil spray

1 pound large scallops

2 cups mixed salad greens

1 cup peeled jicama cut into matchsticks

¼ cup or more Apple-Tamarind Dressing (page 56)

Sweet and crunchy snap peas are Mother Nature's pride and joy and your home element's summer treat. Make a salad with slightly sweet baby zucchini and bland-tasting enoki mushrooms. This salad befits your home element's needs and answers Fire and Water elements' call.

SNAP PEA, BABY ZUCCHINI, ENOKI MUSHROOM, AND CHICKEN OR TOFU SALAD

HEAT the grill to high.

COMBINE the olive oil, soy sauce, and ginger in a medium bowl. Add the chicken breast or tofu strips. Toss to coat, then let marinate for at least 15 minutes or up to 1 hour.

IF using chicken, grill the chicken over medium heat until it is firm and cooked through, 7 to 10 minutes. Turn frequently to prevent burning. Let cool before slicing into thin strips. If using tofu, grill until the outer surface is slightly charred, 3 to 4 minutes. Let cool, then slice into chunks.

BRING a pot of water to a boil. Add the snap peas and salt to the boiling water. Boil until the color brightens, 1 to 2 minutes. Drain and rinse under cool running water. Transfer to a large bowl. Thinly slice the zucchinis on the diagonal and add to the bowl. Add the mushrooms and toss gently together. Add the chicken or tofu and drizzle the dressing over them. Toss gently to mix and transfer to individual serving plates.

MAKES 4 SERVINGS

1 teaspoon olive oil

1 tablespoon soy sauce

1 teaspoon peeled and minced fresh ginger

1 chicken breast, or one 12-ounce carton firm tofu, drained and cut into 1-inch-thick strips

1 cup sugar snap peas

¼ teaspoon salt

8 baby zucchinis

1 cup enoki mushrooms or thinly sliced white mushrooms

¼ cup or more Apple-Tamarind Dressing (page 56)

*L*ate spring and summer is asparagus season. The taste of fresh asparagus reminds us of clear and cloudless warm days. Asparagus aids digestion and relieves bloating, and is a vegetable that is good for Earth element people.

GRILLED SHRIMP, ASPARAGUS, AND MUSHROOM SALAD

PREPARE a grill. While waiting for the grill to get hot, mix the sesame oil and salt together in a mixing bowl. Toss the shrimp and asparagus in the mixture. Place on the grill over medium heat and grill until the shrimp turn pink and firm and the color of the asparagus brightens. Remove to a plate to cool. Lightly spray the mushrooms with vegetable oil spray and grill until they are tender but firm. Remove to a plate to cool.

MAKES 4 SERVINGS

2 tablespoons sesame oil

1 teaspoon salt

1 pound medium-size shrimp, peeled and dried thoroughly

8 asparagus spears

Vegetable oil spray

2 portobello mushroom caps

¼ cup Black Sesame Dressing (page 55)

2 kiwis, peeled and sliced

my friends and family members who dislike curry in general changed their minds when they tasted this curry. It is light, with surprising tastes and contrasts, compared to the more common curry. This is because of the almond milk and apricots. This particular recipe can be made ahead as early as the night before and assembled quickly by adding the shrimp minutes before serving for an elegant summer dinner.

GAENG KOA WITH SHRIMP AND APRICOTS

COMBINE the coconut cream and chile paste in a medium saucepan over medium-high heat. Stir and cook until the oil separates out and the oil bubbles take on the color of the chile paste. Add the almond milk and stir to mix. When the mixture comes to a boil, add the salt, fish sauce, palm sugar, lemongrass, chiles, and crushed lime leaves. Stir to mix, then add the apricots. Reduce the heat to medium-low and cook for 10 minutes. Add the shrimp and stir to mix. When the shrimp are firm and turn pink, 3 to 5 minutes, turn off the heat. Transfer to individual serving bowls, garnish with the slivered lime leaf, and serve with white, brown, or red rice.

Variation

Instead of apricots and shrimp, make this with chicken, bland/astringent-flavor green beans, and bland/slightly sweet summer squash on especially hot summer nights when the Fire element cranks up the heat. Add 2 cups thinly sliced chicken breast and 1 cup each sliced green beans and summer squash. Mix well, cover, and cook over medium-low heat until the chicken is cooked through and the vegetables are crisp-tender, about 7 minutes.

MAKES 4 TO 6 SERVINGS

1 cup Coconut Cream (page 22)

⅓ cup or more *Gaeng Koa* Chile Paste (page 72)

2 cups Almond Milk (page 21)

1 teaspoon salt

2 tablespoons fish sauce

2 teaspoons palm sugar, light brown sugar, or maple sugar

1 stalk lemongrass, tough outer hard layers removed, tender inner stalk cut into 2- to 3-inch lengths and slightly pounded

6 to 7 fresh Thai or 3 to 4 fresh serrano chiles, slightly crushed

6 to 7 kaffir lime leaves, slightly crushed, or zest of 1 lime, cut into slivers

1½ cups pitted and sliced fresh apricots

½ pound medium shrimp (about 2 cups), peeled and deveined

1 kaffir lime leaf, slivered, or 1 teaspoon slivered lime zest

The variety of melons used is what makes this cooling soup taste so good, but if you have just one kind of melon, it will certainly work.

COOL MELON SOUP WITH FRESH MINT

PUT all the ingredients, except for the almonds, in a blender. Cover and blend at high speed until the mixture is a smooth puree. You can serve immediately, garnished with the almonds and mint, or refrigerate until ready to serve.

MAKES 4 SERVINGS

1 cup cantaloupe chunks

1 cup Crenshaw melon chunks

1 cup honeydew melon chunks

1 cup frozen honeydew melon chunks

½ cup crushed ice

1 teaspoon peeled and minced fresh ginger

1 teaspoon minced carrot

1 tablespoon honey

2 tablespoons chopped fresh mint

¼ cup slivered almonds, toasted in a small skillet over medium heat until lightly golden

¼ cup torn fresh mint leaves

Young fresh coconut looks like a white cylinder with a pointed top. Available in major supermarkets, specialty markets like Whole Foods and Trader Joe's, and Asian markets, its juice has a floral scent and tastes refreshingly sweet. The meat is soft and gelatin-like.

MANGO SORBET WITH YOUNG COCONUT RIBBONS

COMBINE the sugar, water and gelatin in a small saucepan and cook over medium-low heat until the sugar and gelatin dissolve. Set aside to cool.

PUT the mangos, lemon juice, and sugar syrup in a blender to puree. Transfer to an ice-cream maker and follow the manufacturer's instructions. Transfer to a container with a lid and freeze for about 30 minutes before serving.

USING a heavy knife, hack off the pointed top of the young coconut. Drain the juice for drinking. Use a spoon to scoop out the meat, and slice it into thin ribbons . (If making ahead, refrigerate until ready to use.)

WHEN ready to serve the sorbet, scoop a couple of spoonfuls into each individual serving bowl and generously garnish with the coconut ribbons.

MAKES 4 SERVINGS

½ cup sugar

¼ cup water

1 teaspoon Knox unflavored gelatin

4 cups peeled and sliced very ripe mangos

1 teaspoon fresh lemon juice

1 young coconut

RAINY WEATHER RECIPES

Wet, cool rain brought in by nature's Wind element might feel good at first, but for some of us, with sensitive tendons, joints, and muscles, aches and pains eventually begin to take hold. Follow the precautions taken by traditional healers during the monsoon season: Cook vegetables with sweet and salty tastes, along with buttery and pungent flavors to nourish the body's Earth element. Make a rich, savory soup with coconut cream, or prepare buttery-flavor dishes such as fried fish with a sweet and tangy sauce. Combinations of these tastes and flavors are believed to strengthen joints and muscles. To protect the chest against colds and other respiratory infections that nature's Wind element can bring on cold, damp days, season dishes with piquant herbs and spices such as ginger, galangal, shallots, onions, garlic, chives, and lemongrass. Chiles, in particular, will aid blood circulation. This type of season-sensitive cooking is the perfect blueprint for Earth element people. What a treat to be able to feast on food you love that also happens to be good for you.

BREAKFAST

A rich, flavorful breakfast is both a great energy builder and a comfort food for gloomy, damp mornings. A touch of sour-tangy taste to neutralize the influence of nature's Water element, which rules the breakfast hours, and Wind element's spicy taste and/or cool/refreshing flavor keeps your chest warm against the dampness. Drink a glass of carrot juice with some finely minced candied ginger added or a glass of grapefruit juice, or create your own tasty concoction, blending together your choice of parsley, mint, cilantro, celery, and/or fresh ginger with pineapple, apple, and/or carrot.

As nature's Wind element blows in the rain, your body needs extra protection. A smoothie such as Banana and Pear *Hom Mak* (page 40), with its rich, buttery, sweet tastes, is a good way to strengthen your Earth element's sensitive physical structure and shake off stiff and achy joints. You could also enjoy multigrain toast or a bagel spread with low-fat or nonfat cream cheese, pancakes made with buckwheat (page 32) served with a fruit compote (page 34), or Silken Tofu with Ginger Syrup (page 99).

An assortment of fresh seasonal fruit will make breakfast a sunny affair on dreary days. Mix and match your favorite fruits and garnish with sunflower seeds, almond slivers, fresh mint, and/or candied ginger.

LUNCH

To stay warm and cozy on rainy days, eat lightly, just enough to satisfy. Overeating may weigh you down, causing you to feel tired and sluggish.

Cook with lots of basil, mint, shallots, and chives to keep you in balance with nature's Wind element and to steady nature's Fire element (which dominates the time of day). Like an umbrella, they will protect you against the wet, moist air.

Salads blend the fresh, cool taste of nature and lighten our spirits on damp, rainy days. Mix and match fresh bitter salad greens with bland-flavor vegetables and combine them with crispy, tart fruits. Bitter and bland flavors will help your home element stay in balance with nature's Fire element, while sour taste strengthens the respiratory system against rain.

Here are two combinations I like:

- Blanch broccoli florets in boiling water for 1 to 2 minutes, then slice and combine with shredded grilled chicken and Black Sesame Dressing (page 55). Garnish with fried garlic and fried shallots (page 100).

- Combine equal amounts of arugula and watercress and toss with thinly sliced apple and smoked trout you've broken into bite-size pieces. Garnish with fried lemongrass and crumbled fried kaffir lime leaves (page 100) and toss with Black Sesame Dressing (page 55).

Besides nurturing your Earth element's physical structure on rainy days, creamy, rich, flavorful soups laced with the Wind element's herbal remedies will cloak you in comfort and warmth. Try Coconut Cream Soup (page 91), adding 1 cup slivered tart plums after the coconut cream has been added and simmering until softened. Then stir in 1 cup quartered mushrooms and 2 cups bite-size pieces of catfish, red snapper, or halibut fillets and finish as directed. Or make one of the curries on pages 72 to 81, using seasonal vegetables together with your choice of meat, poultry, and/or seafood. One-dish meals like Drunken Fried Rice (see variation on page 69), the stir-fried noodle variations of Basic Stir-Fry (page 63), or Noodle Soup (page 82) will also make a quick and healthful lunch.

For beverages, warming and pungent teas such as Lemongrass Tea (page 46) or Ginger Tea (page 47) will ease digestion. For a midday snack, when the Wind Element reigns, indulge in applesauce, or handfuls of walnuts or pumpkin seeds, to provide a pick-me-up between meals.

DINNER

For some of us, rain-soaked evenings call for extra protective measures. To guard against the wet and dampness brought on by nature's Wind element, combined with the return of dominant Water element ruling the dinner hours, dinner for Earth element people should include sour-tasting foods to nurture and protect the respiratory system. Citrus combined with warming ginger, galangal, shallots, and garlic will guard and shield you. As you choose among ingredients, combine the tastes, flavors, and aromas of your home element with those of nature's elements, whether you do it within one single dish or a combination of dishes you are serving.

Warm and soothing soups and stir-fries seasoned with spices and perky sour tastes will blanket you against the damp. Try the recipes below or *Gaeng Awm* on page 96, using 1 cup sliced Swiss chard (both the leaves and the stems), 2 cups spinach (remove any heavy stems), and 2 cups medium shrimp, peeled and deveined, as the main ingredients.

Salads are another good choice, combining the sweet, buttery, and salty tastes of your home element with the sour taste of the evening hours' Water element and the spicy, cool/refreshing flavor of the weather's Wind element.

Drinking warm orange blossom or jasmine tea will cheer and soothe the rainy day blues; a cup of warm ginger or hibiscus tea will ease your digestion.

The province of Samut Prakarn is a short drive out of Bangkok heading toward the Gulf of Siam. Sitting near a bridge by the main road is a restaurant started by a Chinese-Thai cook some 55 years ago. Her most famous dish is this stir-fried crab with Madras curry. I spent a couple of days watching teenage cooks, taught by the owner, wielding heavy woks over a blazing fire. As they sprinkled spicy seasonings over the crab, the hot, peppery fumes cleared my sinuses and warmed the chest. This dish will protect Earth element people against any gust of rain brought on by nature's Wind element.

STIR-FRIED CRAB WITH MADRAS CURRY

COMBINE the chile oil, oyster sauce, and vermouth in a small bowl. Set aside.

SEPARATE the crab legs and claws at the joints. Pull apart the carcass from the hard shell. Drape a dish towel over the legs and claws. Use a mallet to pound and crack the shells. Cut the carcass into bite-size pieces. If you like the soft tomalley in the shell, save it.

HEAT a wok or large nonstick skillet over high heat for 1 to 2 minutes. Add the canola oil and let heat for 1 minute. Add the ginger, onion, celery, and jalapeño and stir-fry until the onion softens, about 5 minutes. Add the curry, stir to combine, then add the crab, except for the shell with the tomalley, and stir vigorously. Stir in the chile oil mixture and almond milk. Cover and let cook for about 5 minutes. Check if the crab is heated through. If not, add about 2 tablespoons water, and stir. Add the shell with the tomalley, if using, cover, and let cook for another 2 to 3 minutes.

WHEN ready to serve, transfer the crab to a serving platter. Add the egg to the skillet and stir until it is cooked. Spoon on top of the crab. Garnish with the cilantro and serve with hot white, brown, or red rice.

MAKES 4 SERVINGS

1 tablespoon Roasted Chile Oil (page 65)

2 tablespoons oyster sauce

¼ cup dry vermouth

One 1½-pound Dungeness crab

2 tablespoons canola or corn oil

3 to 4 thin slices fresh ginger

1 large yellow onion, cut in half, then thinly sliced into half-moons

½ cup chopped Chinese or regular celery

1 fresh red jalapeño, thinly sliced lengthwise

1 teaspoon Madras curry powder

¾ cup Almond Milk (page 21)

1 large egg, slightly beaten

¼ cup coarsely chopped fresh cilantro

*T*his is an irresistible noodle dish even for those of us who have an aversion to broccoli. Its bland flavor commends itself to the noodle's perfectly balanced seasoning of salty-sweet-sour.

NOODLES WITH CHINESE BROCCOLI AND PORK OR CHICKEN Phad Se Ewe

IN a small bowl, combine the sugar, cayenne, both soy sauces, and the vinegar. Mix well to dissolve the sugar. Set aside.

HEAT a medium nonstick skillet over high heat for 1 to 2 minutes. Add the oil and heat for 1 minute. Add the stir-fry seasoning and stir for 1 minute. Add the meat and stir; when it is partially cooked, add the noodles and keep stirring. Sprinkle a bit of water over the noodles and continue to stir.

WHEN the noodles soften, add the sugar–soy sauce mixture and stir to combine. Continue to stir-fry for another minute, then add the broccoli and stir-fry until it is cooked but still firm, 1 to 2 minutes.

PUSH the mixture to one side of the skillet. Add the remaining oil and crack the egg onto the empty space. Scramble the egg and, as it begins to congeal, fold it in the noodles. Stir to mix. Transfer to a serving plate and serve hot with Fresh Chiles in Vinegar.

MAKES 1 SERVING

1 teaspoon sugar

¼ teaspoon cayenne pepper (optional)

1 teaspoon dark soy sauce

1 teaspoon regular soy sauce

1 tablespoon distilled white vinegar

2 tablespoons canola or corn oil

1 tablespoon Basic Stir-Fry Seasoning (page 64)

¼ cup thinly sliced pork or chicken, small shrimp, or cubed baked tofu

2 cups fresh wide rice noodles (page 85)

1 cup Chinese broccoli, or mustard greens stems sliced on the diagonal and leaves sliced 2 to 3 inches wide, or regular broccoli florets, thinly sliced

1 large egg

Fresh Chiles in Vinegar (page 84)

Rocket is the name used by Thais for arugula. In recent years, it has become all the rage for Bangkokians, who have taken to eating Western-style salads for health reasons. Its spicy and slightly bitter tastes are most agreeable to the Thai palate and pair well with bold-flavored ingredients such as in this salad.

SMOKED SALMON, MUSHROOM, AND ARUGULA SALAD

HEAT the grill to medium-high.

MIX the mushrooms with the salt in a medium bowl. Coat them with vegetable oil spray and mix again. Place a fine-mesh rack over the grill rack, then spread the mushrooms over the rack and grill until they are slightly soft and charred. When cool enough to touch, slice each mushroom in half and put in a large bowl.

PUT the pine nuts in a small skillet over high heat. Shaking the skillet over the burner, toast the nuts until they're slightly golden. Let cool completely.

ADD the smoked salmon, arugula, and lime zest to the bowl with the mushrooms. Add the dressing and toss to coat everything evenly with it. Transfer to a serving platter, garnish with the pine nuts, and serve.

MAKES 4 SERVINGS

1½ cups brown or white mushrooms

Pinch of salt

Vegetable oil spray

¼ cup pine nuts

2 cups bite-size pieces smoked salmon (not lox)

2 cups arugula, torn into bite-size pieces

1 tablespoon grated lime zest

¼ cup Apple-Tamarind Dressing (page 56)

Bitter Belgian endive, believed to be good for respiratory problems and allergies, equalizes the effects of nature's Wind element (the wet weather) and Water element (the time of day). If you don't like the idea of killing the lobster, ask someone at your fish market to do it. Just be sure to cook it as soon as you get home.

BELGIAN ENDIVE AND GRILLED LOBSTER OR SHRIMP SALAD

HEAT the grill to high.

IF using lobster, drape the lobster tail with a heavy dish towel to flatten it on a cutting board. With the blade of a 10-inch chef's knife facing the head of the lobster, press the knife into the head and cut all the way through, slicing across between the eyes to the end of the head. This will kill the lobster quickly and painlessly. Cut through the center of the lobster tail, crack the claws with a mallet, and put on the grill. Grill until the shell turns red and slightly charred and the meat is firm and white, about 20 minutes. Let cool completely, then extract the meat from the tail and claws. Cut into bite-size pieces.

IF using shrimp, rinse and dry thoroughly. Spray lightly with vegetable oil spray before putting on a fine-mesh rack set over the grill rack. Turn frequently to ensure even cooking. When they are firm, pink, and slightly charred, remove from the grill and let cool completely. Slice each lengthwise.

PUT the lobster or shrimp and endive in a large bowl. Add the dressing and toss. Transfer to a serving platter, garnish with the fried shallots and lime zest, and serve.

MAKES 4 SERVINGS

One-3 pound lobster or 1 pound large shrimp, peeled and deveined

Vegetable oil spray

5 to 6 Belgian endive, thinly sliced lengthwise to make 3 cups

¼ cup or more Apple-Tamarind Dressing (page 56)

2 tablespoons fried shallots (page 100)

1 teaspoon grated lime zest

ot soup on a rainy night blankets an Earth element person's sensitive joints and muscles against the wet and chilled air.

SPINACH, TOFU, AND GLASS NOODLE SOUP

BRING the broth to a boil. Add the salt and soy sauce. (If using canned broth, taste it first, then adjust the seasonings accordingly.) Stir, then add the mushrooms and tofu. Reduce the heat to medium and cook for 5 minutes. Add the spinach and cook for another 5 minutes. Add the noodles. When they turn translucent and soft, add the ginger slivers. Ladle into individual bowls, garnish with the fried garlic, and serve.

MAKES 4 SERVINGS

6 cups homemade (page 26) or canned low-sodium, low-fat chicken broth

1 teaspoon salt

1 tablespoon soy sauce

1 cup oyster mushrooms, sliced into bite-size pieces

One 19-ounce package silken tofu, cubed

2 cups tightly packed spinach with the stems removed

1 cup softened glass noodles (page 86), cut into manageable lengths

1 tablespoon peeled and slivered fresh ginger

1 teaspoon fried garlic (page 100)

This seasoning paste is a perfect balance of opposite elements: Earth and Wind. Warming herbs and spices, the tastes and flavors of the Wind element, are natural protectors of the respiratory and digestive systems.

JUNGLE SOUP Gaeng Paa

IN a mortar, pound ½ teaspoon of the salt and the garlic into a paste. Add the dried chiles, ground pepper, and 6 slices of the galangal and pound until incorporated and reduced to a paste. Add the minced shallot and pound to incorporate. (This will keep, refrigerated, in an airtight container for 2 weeks.)

BRING the water to a boil. Add the chile paste, the remaining galangal, the slightly pounded shallots, lemongrass, krachai, if using, lime leaves, and fresh chiles. When the broth returns to a boil, add the remaining 1 teaspoon salt and the fish sauce. Cover, reduce the heat to low, and let the broth simmer for 7 minutes. Add the eggplants, cover, increase the heat to medium-low, and cook for another 7 minutes. Add the mushrooms, cover, and cook for another 7 minutes, then add the fish. As soon as the fish is cooked through, about 5 minutes, add the parsley and basil. Serve with hot white, brown, or red rice.

MAKES 4 SERVINGS

1½ teaspoons salt

4 cloves garlic, minced

6 to 10 dried de arbol chiles or chiles Japones, softened in warm water, dried thoroughly, and minced

1 teaspoon white peppercorns, dry-roasted and ground (page 70)

12 thin slices galangal or fresh ginger, slightly pounded

4 shallots, peeled, 1 minced, 3 slightly pounded

6 cups water

2 stalks lemongrass, tough outer layers removed, tender inner stalk cut into 3-inch lengths and slightly pounded

3 *krachai* (Chinese keys or lesser galangal; optional), slivered

12 kaffir lime leaves, torn, or zest of 1 lime, cut into slivers

10 fresh Thai or 5 fresh serrano chiles, slightly pounded

3 tablespoons fish sauce

6 Thai eggplants, quartered, or 1 Japanese eggplant, cut into ½-inch-thick slices

2 cups oyster mushrooms

½ pound red snapper, catfish, or halibut fillets, cut into bite-size pieces

10 to 12 sprigs fresh Italian parsley, chopped

½ cup fresh holy or Thai basil or peppermint leaves

$\mathcal{E}$laine, the chef for my brother-in-law Mike and sister-in-law Diane, made a soup similar to this on a wet, rainy June day. She didn't know that the soup was perfect for us all. It was especially soothing for Mike, who had a bad cold, and uplifting for Diane, who was tired. The magic is in the fresh, sweet, cool/refreshing combination of early summer peas, lettuce, and watercress. The healing elements are the warming French tarragon, nutmeg, and white pepper, with spicy leeks protecting and healing the respiratory system.

WATERCRESS AND FRESH PEA SOUP

MELT the butter with the oil in a large saucepan over medium-high heat. Add the leeks and cook, stirring, until softened. Add the peas, broth, tarragon, salt, and sugar and bring to a boil. Reduce the heat to medium-low and cook until the peas are half cooked, about 10 minutes if using fresh, 6 to 7 minutes if using frozen. Add the lettuce and watercress, stir to mix, and cook until the vegetables are very tender, about 20 minutes.

CAREFULLY transfer to a food processor and puree, or use a handheld blender to puree. Transfer to the saucepan and add the almond milk, nutmeg, and white pepper. Mix to combine and cook over medium-low heat until it begins to boil. Ladle into bowls and top with a dollop of the yogurt–sour cream mixture.

MAKES 4 SERVINGS

1 tablespoon unsalted butter

1 tablespoon olive oil

2 leeks (white part only), washed thoroughly to remove grit and minced

3 cups shelled fresh or frozen peas

4 cups homemade (page 27) or store-bought low-sodium vegetable broth

¼ cup chopped fresh tarragon

1 teaspoon salt

1 teaspoon sugar

2 cups chopped butter lettuce

2 cups chopped watercress stems and leaves

1 cup Almond Milk (page 21)

¼ teaspoon freshly grated nutmeg

¼ teaspoon white pepper

½ cup low-fat plain yogurt and sour cream combined

Finish your meal with a dessert spiked with a touch of ginger to warm your respiratory system and ease digestion. Ice cream is a delicious choice, especially when topped with these wonderful bananas.

ICE CREAM TOPPED WITH BANANAS WITH GINGER SAUCE

COMBINE the sugar, water, liqueur, and ginger in a medium skillet over medium heat. Stir to mix. When the mixture begins to bubble and boil, reduce the heat to low and add the bananas. Stir to mix; let the sauce simmer until the bananas begin to soften. Remove from the heat and let cool slightly.

SCOOP the ice cream into individual serving bowls and top it with the warm bananas with sauce.

MAKES 3 CUPS; 3 TO 4 SERVINGS

1 cup palm sugar, firmly packed light brown sugar, or maple sugar

3 tablespoons water

1 tablespoon amaretto or Chambord liqueur

1 tablespoon peeled and minced fresh ginger

2 large ripe bananas, peeled and thinly sliced

1 pint vanilla light, rice, or soy milk ice cream

This is the time for you to indulge in rich desserts made with cream and nuts. Just think of those sensitive joints and tendons—buttery and sweet tastes will lubricate them during damp, rainy weather. This custard is a tasty example.

COCONUT CUSTARD WITH FRESH SEASONAL FRUIT

PREHEAT the oven to 375°F. Fill a roasting pan halfway full with water and place it in the oven.

IN a large bowl, beat the eggs with a fork until the whites and yolks are blended. Do not overbeat. Add the extract, sugar, and salt and beat to combine. Add the coconut cream and mix well to combine.

LADLE the mixture into six 8-ounce ramekins or custard cups and carefully place them in the heated water. Bake until the custard is set, about 45 minutes. Serve warm with sliced seasonal fruits.

MAKES 6 SERVINGS

6 extra-large eggs

2 drops jasmine or almond extract

1 cup palm sugar, firmly packed light brown sugar, or maple sugar

A couple of pinches of salt

3 cups Coconut Cream (page 22)

Peeled, pitted, and sliced peaches, plums, and/or mangos and hulled and sliced strawberries

COLD WEATHER RECIPES

When the weather is cold, who doesn't love to bundle up, hibernate, stay warm, and eat comforting food? The wise Thai traditional healers support your instincts. They have observed how Mother Nature herself seems to like to lie dormant during the winter. Harvests gathered before the cold season (dominated by the Earth element) such as peanuts, lima beans, potatoes and sweet potatoes, taro, winter squashes, and pumpkins, with their buttery, rich, and sweet flavors, are not only nature's comfort foods, but also provide protection from illnesses that can arise when the weather turns chilly. No wonder, with the double force of Earth element (your home element and the weather), that your desire for your "comfort foods" (rich, buttery, sweet, and salty tastes) is especially strong. Just be careful to eat them in moderation to avoid loss of energy and weight gain. Spice up Earth element's favorite vegetables and fruits by adding warm healing herbs and spices such as ginger, cinnamon, nutmeg, anise, and chiles.

BREAKFAST

Cold mornings, dominated by the Earth and Water elements, stimulate our appetite for a warm, comforting breakfast. Eggs, waffles, and pancakes never taste as good as they do when it's cold and snowy outside. For Asians, the perfect way to shake off the morning chill is with a bowl of velvety, piping hot porridge (page 97). Oatmeal and cream of wheat will also satisfy that urge. Add some raisins, dried apricots, or blueberries as well as walnuts for extra fortification.

Citrus juice meets the challenge of nature's Water element dominating chilly morning hours, protecting us against possible colds. Astringent and slightly sour cranberry juice, which is packed with nutrients, will do the same. Prune juice, sweet and loaded with fiber, or apple juice might be needed by Earth element people prone to constipation.

LUNCH

Earth element people can shake off winter's chill with a lunch prepared with the perfect balance in taste, flavor, and aroma to pacify the double influence of Earth element. Remember to pair these dishes with bitter, bland, and cool/refreshing fruits and vegetables, such as bean sprouts, broccoli, bitter salad mixture, and Belgian endive to temper nature's Fire element, which rules the lunch hour.

Cool weather is the time to treat yourself to a rich, hearty curry. Try Green Curry on page 78, preparing it with sliced chicken and 1 cup Thai or Japanese eggplant and 2 cups sliced green beans. Serve it with refreshing Cucumber Relish (page 54). Or make a salad using bitter greens to equalize nature's Fire element. Bitterness, a flavor of Fire element, is believed to clean and purify the blood, while keeping colds and fevers at bay. Or look for the Earth element variations for each of the salad dressing recipes on pages 55 to 62. For added insurance, take a brisk walk after lunch to help your digestion and to stimulate the circulatory system.

For a beverage, a warm cup of cinnamon-orange-honey tea is comforting and settling, as is a glass of pear or apple juice with a sprig of fresh mint. For a midday snack, enjoy an apple or banana, dried fruit, rice cakes with honey, or a glass of hot spiced apple cider.

DINNER

Hearty dishes prepared with winter vegetables are exactly the right winter choices for Earth element people to balance the double rules of Earth element (your home element and the weather). Many tubers and squashes contain important amounts of fiber, helping to ease digestion. Season dishes with aromatic, warm, and healing spices such as star anise, cinnamon, and nutmeg. Spicy flavor promotes appetite and eases digestion, while at the same time, its healing warmth penetrates the tendons, joints, and bones. On cold, wintry evenings, add a touch of spiciness to your dishes as a healing seasoning. To keep nature's Water element, which dominates evening hours and when winter days are cool and dry, in balance with your home element, include some sour taste and bitter and bland flavors. A perfect way to combine these is in salads, stir-fries, soups, and curries. Try Red Curry on page 76, preparing it with 2 cups each sliced chicken and pumpkin chunks.

have lived for decades in California, where winter is considered mild. Nevertheless, it is still not the tropics. I wear layers of sweaters to keep warm while longing for the sun-drenched beaches of Thailand, where food vendors line the sidewalks. Some set up charcoal grills to cook whatever comes in from the sea that day. Squid turn white and firm when cooked on the grill, and here they are chopped and tossed with handfuls of herbs, fiery hot chiles, fish sauce, and squeezes of lime. ∼ As you prepare this salad, the briny aroma of the squid and the pungency of the herbs will warm you against harsh, cold winter.

GRILLED SQUID SALAD

HEAT the grill to medium.

PREPARE the squid. Insert a paring knife into the sac and cut it open. Lay it flat on the chopping board with the inside facing up. Score lightly in a crisscross pattern. Repeat with the remaining squid. Mix with the salt and oil in a medium bowl.

HEAT a fine-mesh rack over the grill. Wait for 3 to 4 minutes before putting the squid on it. Turn the squid pieces frequently until they are slightly charred, white all the way through, firm, and curled, 4 to 5 minutes. Remove from the grill and cool. Slice into bite-size pieces and put in a large bowl. Add the Belgian endive, shallots, lemongrass, and ginger. Toss to combine. Add the dressing and toss again. Add the mint, toss, transfer to a serving plate, and serve immediately.

MAKES 4 SERVINGS

1 pound cleaned squid, bodies only

¼ teaspoon salt

1 teaspoon canola or soybean oil

2 Belgian endive, sliced across

¼ cup thinly sliced shallots

1 stalk lemongrass, tough outer layers removed, tender inner stalk minced

1 teaspoon peeled and minced fresh ginger

¼ cup Roasted Chile Oil Dressing (page 57)

¼ cup tightly packed fresh mint leaves, torn

I call this salad Cambodian coleslaw with chicken. Winter cabbage, slightly sweet but mostly bland and crunchy, pairs well with sweet carrot and spicy sweet onion. The citrus dressing satisfies nature's Water element, which rules dinner hours.

CAMBODIAN SALAD WITH CHICKEN

BRING a medium saucepan of water to a boil. Soak the bean threads in cold water to cover. When softened, about 10 minutes, transfer to the boiling water. Boil until the noodles turn translucent, 10 to 12 seconds. Drain and rinse with cold water. Squeeze out all excess water and cut into manageable lengths. Put them in a large bowl. Add the remaining ingredients, except for the peanuts. Mix well and transfer to individual plates. Garnish with the peanuts and serve.

MAKES 4 SERVINGS

1 cup bean threads (page 86)

1½ cups shredded cabbage

1 cup shredded carrot

¼ cup thinly sliced sweet onion

1½ cups shredded cooked chicken

¼ cup chopped fresh cilantro

¼ cup chopped fresh mint

½ cup Citrus Dressing (page 58)

2 tablespoons crushed peanuts or pine nuts or slivered almonds

Stir-frying helps retain the potato's crunchy texture. Spicy garlic, ginger, and cayenne pepper balance the body's Wind element, warming us on a cool winter night.

STIR-FRIED SHOESTRING POTATOES

PEEL the potatoes and shred in a food processor or on the largest holes of a box grater to make 3 cups. Heat a large skillet over high heat for 1 to 2 minutes. Add the oil and heat for 1 minute. Add the garlic and ginger and stir-fry for 1 minute. Add the potatoes, sprinkle with the cayenne, and stir-fry vigorously until the potato strands are translucent, 4 to 5 minutes. Sprinkle with the salt and stir. Add the soy sauce and sesame oil and stir-fry for another minute or two to incorporate. Serve immediately.

MAKES 4 SERVINGS

2 medium Idaho potatoes

2 tablespoons canola or corn oil

2 cloves garlic, minced

1 teaspoon peeled and minced fresh ginger

¼ teaspoon cayenne pepper

¼ teaspoon salt

1 tablespoon soy sauce

½ teaspoon sesame oil

*T*his version of mussaman curry is lighter than the one most commonly found, usually prepared with potatoes. However, the benefits derived from the warming spices are the same, aiding digestion, protecting the respiratory system, and reenergizing your mind and spirit.

MUSSAMAN CURRY WITH CHICKEN AND DRIED APRICOTS

PUT the salt, peppercorns, coriander seeds, and coriander root in a spice grinder and grind into a paste. Add the remaining ingredients except for the shrimp paste, and blend into a coarse paste. Transfer to a mortar and pound into a fine paste. Add the shrimp paste and pound to combine. This will keep, refrigerated, in an airtight container for up to a month.

HEAT the coconut cream and chile paste together in a large saucepan over medium heat. Stir to keep it from sticking and burning. When oil bubbles with the reddish color of the chile paste appear over the surface, 3 to 4 minutes, add the almond milk. Stir to blend. When it boils, add the remaining ingredients, except for the chicken. Cook over medium-low heat for 10 minutes, stirring occasionally. Add the chicken, stir to mix, cover, and cook until the chicken is just cooked through and tender, about another 7 minutes. Serve with hot white, brown, or red rice.

MAKES 4 SERVINGS

MUSSAMAN CHILE PASTE

1 teaspoon salt

1 teaspoon white peppercorns, dry-roasted (page 70)

1 teaspoon coriander seeds, dry-roasted (page 70)

1 tablespoon minced coriander root or stems

5 cloves garlic, broiled until soft and peeled

2 dried New Mexico chiles, soaked in warm water until softened, dried thoroughly, and minced

15 dried de arbol chiles or chiles Japones, soaked in warm water until softened, dried thoroughly, and minced

1 stalk lemongrass, tough outer layers removed, tender inner stalk minced

5 thin slices galangal or fresh ginger

½ teaspoon ground mace

1 teaspoon cardamom seeds

1 teaspoon ground cinnamon

½ teaspoon freshly grated nutmeg

½ teaspoon cumin seeds, dry-roasted and ground (page 70)

2 shallots, broiled until soft and peeled

1 teaspoon fermented shrimp paste or 1 tablespoon red miso

CURRY

1 cup Coconut Cream (page 22)

3 cups Almond Milk (page 21)

6 cloves

2 bay leaves

⅓ cup palm sugar, dark brown sugar, or maple sugar

1 teaspoon salt

2 tablespoons fish sauce

¼ cup Tamarind Puree (page 25)

20 to 25 shallots, broiled until soft and peeled

¼ cup dried apricots, soaked in warm water until softened and thinly sliced

4 cups (almost 2 pounds) boneless chicken sliced across the grain into bite-size pieces

The jujube date harmonizes and strengthens all elements and calms the mind. They can be found in Asian and specialty food markets such as Whole Foods and online. Lotus root and peanuts nourish the muscles and tendons. Together with cinnamon, star anise, chiles, and ginger, they make a healthful and fortifying stew for winter. ~~&~~ Pork short ribs are mostly meat and fat attached to brittle, thin bones, making it easier to chop them into pieces. For convenience, ask the butcher to do this for you.

LOTUS ROOT SOUP WITH PORK SHORT RIBS, PEANUTS, AND JUJUBE DATES

PUT the pork ribs in a large saucepan, cover with water, and bring to a boil. Drain, discarding the water. Clean the saucepan and return the ribs to it. Cover them with fresh water and bring to a boil again, then add all the remaining ingredients. Cover, reduce the heat to medium-low, and simmer until the ribs are tender, about 1 hour. Serve hot. If making ahead, cool and refrigerate in a container with a lid. Reheat before serving. The soup tastes better the next day.

MAKES 4 SERVINGS

3 pounds pork short ribs, chopped into bite-size chunks

2 cups peeled and thinly sliced lotus root

½ cup shelled raw peanuts

¾ cup dried jujube dates, pitted

6 thin slices fresh ginger

3 dried de arbol chiles or chiles Japones

2 star anise

1 cinnamon stick

2 scallions, cut diagonally into 1-inch pieces

1 teaspoon white peppercorns

1 teaspoon salt

¼ cup soy sauce

3 tablespoons dry vermouth

½ teaspoon sesame oil

*W*hen winter arrives and my house feels like an icebox, I dream of this dish. The steaming fragrance of peppercorns, garlic, ginger, and scallion warms my achy bones, and I am a Water element person. Just think what this can do for Earth element people whose stiff joints and muscle aches cry out for relief.

STEAMED CHICKEN WITH SAVORY RICE KHAO Mun Gai

COMBINE 1 tablespoon of the salt and the ground pepper and massage it into the chicken, inside and out. Insert the garlic, ginger, and sliced scallion in the cavity. Place the chicken on a heat-resistant pie plate.

FILL a large wok halfway full with water and bring it to a boil. Put a small heat-resistant bowl in the center of the wok. Put the chicken in the pie plate carefully on top of the bowl. Cover and steam over high heat. Check the water level every 15 to 20 minutes. If it appears low, replace with boiling water to the original level. Steam until the chicken is cooked, about 1 hour. Turn off the heat. Strain the broth inside the pie plate into a large measuring cup. Extract the garlic, ginger, and scallions from the cavity of the chicken. Mash 2 of the garlic cloves and save the rest for use in another dish. Place the chicken back on the pie plate and place it back in the wok, with the lid on, to keep warm. Slice the meat into bite-size pieces and discard the bones just before serving.

PUT the rice in a rice cooker and rinse with water three times. Drain. Add the mashed garlic and mix with the rice. Add enough chicken broth to the measuring cup with the broth from the steamed chicken to total 3 cups. Pour it into the rice cooker with the rice. Add the pinch of salt and stir to mix. Cook according to the manufacturer's instructions, about 15 minutes. If you do not have a rice cooker, follow the instructions on how to cook rice using a saucepan on page 29. When the rice is cooked, fluff and let sit for another 5 minutes before serving.

MEANWHILE, combine the dipping sauce ingredients, except for the cilantro, in a sauce bowl. Mix well and set aside. Garnish with the cilantro when ready to serve.

TO serve, scoop the rice onto individual plates. Top with slices of the chicken. Garnish on the side with the cucumber slices and whole scallions. Serve with the dipping sauce.

MAKES 4 SERVINGS

1 tablespoon plus a pinch of salt

1 teaspoon white peppercorns, dry-roasted and ground (page 70)

One 3- to 4-pound chicken, rinsed and dried thoroughly

6 cloves garlic, slightly mashed

10 thin slices fresh ginger, slightly pounded

1 scallion, thinly sliced on the diagonal

3 cups long-grain jasmine rice

Homemade (page 26) or canned low-sodium, low-fat chicken broth as needed

1 cucumber, peeled, seeded, and thinly sliced

4 scallions, trimmed

DIPPING SAUCE

1 clove garlic, thinly sliced

1 teaspoon peeled and minced fresh ginger

2 teaspoons sugar

1 tablespoon or more minced fresh serrano chiles

¼ teaspoon cayenne pepper

1 teaspoon bean paste

2 tablespoons dark sweet soy sauce

¼ cup regular soy sauce

1 tablespoon white wine

1½ tablespoons distilled white vinegar

½ teaspoon sesame oil

¼ cup chopped fresh cilantro

ound in the refrigerated section of Asian supermarkets, Sichuan pickled turnip is coated with red chile liquid. Slice the amount needed and rinse well. It will keep, tightly wrapped, in the refrigerator for months.

CHICKEN WONTON SOUP WITH MUSTARD GREENS AND SPICY SICHUAN PICKLED TURNIP

IN a medium bowl, thoroughly mix together all the wonton ingredients, except for the wrappers. Set a wrapper in front of you, with one of its corners facing you. Place ½ teaspoon or more of the mixture on the corner. Tuck and roll the wrapper around the filling toward the center of the wrapper. Fold the right and left corners over the center. Wet the bottom flap with a bit of water and pinch the top flap over to secure. As you finish them, place the wontons on a baking sheet lined with wax paper. Repeat with the remaining ingredients. You only need 24 wontons for this recipe, so freeze the rest on the baking sheet. Once they are frozen, transfer them from the sheet to a zip-top plastic bag. They'll keep for up to a month in the freezer. Besides making a hearty addition to soup, when deep-fried, they make delicious finger food.

COMBINE the broth, pickled turnips, salt, and soy sauce in a large saucepan and bring to a boil. (If using canned chicken broth, taste and adjust the seasonings accordingly.) Add the mustard greens and cook until the color brightens, about 3 minutes. Add the wontons and cook until the wrappers turn translucent, about 5 minutes. (Add an extra minute if you're adding frozen wontons.) Ladle the wontons and broth into individual bowls and serve garnished with the scallion and cilantro, with the chiles in vinegar on the side.

MAKES 4 SERVINGS

WONTONS

½ pound ground chicken or turkey

⅛ teaspoon salt

⅛ teaspoon white pepper

1 teaspoon peeled and minced fresh ginger

1 scallion (white part only), minced

1 tablespoon soy sauce

½ teaspoon sesame oil

1 package wonton wrappers (about 40 sheets)

SOUP

6 cups homemade (page 26) or canned low-sodium, low-fat chicken broth

¼ cup Sichuan pickled turnips, rinsed and slivered, or capers, drained and rinsed

1 teaspoon salt

2 tablespoons soy sauce

1½ cups sliced mustard greens

1 scallion, minced

¼ cup chopped fresh cilantro

Fresh Chiles in Vinegar (page 84)

*T*apioca is a comfort food for winter nights. When made with almond milk, it is both wholesome and healthy.

BANANAS WITH TAPIOCA AND ALMOND MILK

COMBINE the tapioca pearls and the almond milk in a medium nonstick saucepan and let stand for 5 to 7 minutes. Cook over high heat and stir constantly.

WHEN the milk begins to get hot, in 3 to 4 minutes, reduce the heat to medium-low. Add the sugar, salt, and extract and continue to stir until the mixture is thick and the tapioca pearls appear, about 3 minutes. Add the banana and stir to mix. Turn off the heat and let the mixture cool for 20 minutes. Serve slightly warm.

MAKES 4 SERVINGS

¼ cup instant tapioca pearls

2½ cups Almond Milk (page 21)

3 tablespoons palm sugar or ¼ cup firmly packed light brown sugar or maple sugar

Pinch of salt

3 drops almond extract

1 ripe banana, peeled and thinly sliced

BLISS

When Uncle Non was forced to move from his home in Nonthaburi, which he built and where he lived for over 50 years, he dismantled it and hauled the wood, piece by piece, across the river, to the site of his new house. With additional wood salvaged from the neighborhood, he built a larger and more contemporary home, but the teak post that served as the old house's foundation was planted in the front near the new kitchen. Uncle Non said that with the post relocated to the new home, the spirit of the house would never abandon him or his family.

Like Uncle Non, who faithfully cared for his home and its spirit, you must respect and care for your "structure" or body, as well as your emotional and spiritual needs. As life's inexorable forces shift and gradually alter your appearance and test your emotional and spiritual outlook, be guided by the mantra "lightness of being." Take good care of your body's structure by providing constant maintenance and proper care. By doing so, you will remain strong and youthful looking.

"Lightness of being" brings forth an acceptance of life's changes. Your emotional and spiritual health, as an Earth element person, depends on achieving a steady, light, playful, and optimistic attitude. Realization of this will bring joy and beauty to your life.

"Realization" is your vision, "lightness of being" is your mantra, and blissful living your reward.

YOUR PHYSICAL BEING

Part of your Earth element physical maintenance is taking good care of your skin and hair. Here are some traditional Thai beauty treatments, made with natural ingredients that will make your skin and hair glow with health and beauty.

This facial mask cleans the skin, as well as neutralizes and rejuvenates the complexion. If your skin feels oily or puffy, use it once a week.

WATERMELON, YOGURT, HONEY, LEMON JUICE, AND CUCUMBER MASK

PUT all the ingredients, except for the cucumber, in a blender and puree. The puree will keep, refrigerated, in an airtight container for up to a week; mix it well before using it.

WHEN ready to use, wash and dry your face, then apply half the puree. Be careful not to get it in your eyes. Relax, close your eyes, put the cucumber slices over your eyes and leave the mask on for 15 to 20 minutes. Wash the mask off with cool water. Dry your face thoroughly. Lie down and place the 3 tablespoons of slightly mashed cucumber slices on your entire face. Empty your mind and rest for another 10 minutes before removing the slices. Rinse your face with cool water. Dry thoroughly and apply facial toner and moisturizer.

MAKES ENOUGH FOR 2 APPLICATIONS

⅓ cup mashed watermelon

2 tablespoons plain yogurt

1 tablespoon honey

1 teaspoon fresh lemon juice

2 thin slices cucumber for each application

3 tablespoons peeled, thinly sliced, and slightly mashed cucumber for each application

This refreshing mask, especially soothing after being in the hot sun, reduces puffiness, soothes sunburn, and rejuvenates your delicate complexion. If needed, repeat every other day for 1 week.

CUCUMBER, PAPAYA, AND CHAMOMILE FACIAL MASK

PLACE the chopped cucumber, papaya, and oil in a blender and puree at high speed. The puree will keep, refrigerated, in an airtight container for several days.

WHEN ready to use, wash and dry your face, then apply half the puree. Avoid getting it in your eyes. Lie down, close your eyes, and place the cucumber slices over your eyes. Relax and let the mask set for 15 minutes. Rinse your face with cool water, dry thoroughly, and apply facial toner and moisturizer.

MAKES 2 APPLICATIONS

3 tablespoons peeled and chopped cucumber

3 tablespoons peeled and diced ripe papaya

10 drops chamomile essential oil

2 thin slices cucumber for each application

146

n o one likes swollen or clammy hands and feet. Sore feet can be a problem particularly for Earth element people. To soothe and relax these tired and overworked limbs, apply this natural formula weekly.

ROSE AND PATCHOULI HAND AND FOOT RUB

COMBINE the almond oil and 2 drops of the rose essential oil and set aside.

FILL a soaking basin with the lukewarm water. Add the remaining rose oil and the patchouli oil. Remove the petals from the roses, crush slightly, and add to the water. Soak your feet and relax until the water is cool. Dry your feet thoroughly and massage them with the reserved almond and rose essential oil. While you're at it, also apply the oil to your hands.

MAKES 1 APPLICATION

1 teaspoon almond oil

7 drops rose otto, rosewood, or rose absolute essential oil

10 cups lukewarm water

5 drops patchouli essential oil

2 to 3 fresh roses

Dandruff can be banished and limp or oily hair transformed into a lustrous, silken mane by using this treatment. After a couple of weekly applications, use once a month to keep the follicles healthy.

BANANA, LEMONGRASS JUICE, AND CEDAR HAIR CONDITIONER

PUT all the ingredients in a blend and puree.

WET your hair before applying. Massage the mixture into the scalp and hair, taking care not to get it in your eyes. Wrap your hair with a warm, wet towel. Sit and relax for 20 minutes, then rinse and shampoo.

MAKES 1 APPLICATION

1 stalk lemongrass, tough outer layers removed, tender inner stalk finely chopped

⅓ cup water

½ ripe banana, peeled and mashed

10 drops cedar essential oil

U se this treatment to rejuvenate lackluster or color-damaged hair.

EGG, HONEY, LIME, AND LEMONGRASS JUICE HAIR CONDITIONER

PUT all the ingredients in a blender and puree.

WET your hair before applying. Massage the mixture into the scalp and hair, taking care not to get it in your eyes. Wrap your hair with a warm, wet towel. Sit and relax for 20 minutes, then rinse and shampoo.

MAKES 1 APPLICATION

1 stalk lemongrass, tough outer layers removed, tender inner stalk finely chopped

⅓ cup water

1 large egg

1 tablespoon honey

Grated zest of 1 lime

1 tablespoon fresh lime juice

mind and spirit

From the depths of thick, black mud arises the perfumed, silken lotus blossom. Like the lotus, set your mind and spirit free from the heavy burden of daily chores and responsibilities. Pamper yourself with aromatherapy and attain the magical "lightness of being." Use essential oils that will rejuvenate your mind and raise your spirit.

Buy soaps, bath oils, body lotions, facial mist, and shampoos with these special scents. Indulge in scented candles or incense that emits these scents to transport your mind and rally a happy spirit.

CEDAR: Bitter and pungent, it calms the nerves and relieves tension.

JASMINE: Sweet, warming, and floral, jasmine is a good anti-inflammatory for joints. It also relieves stress, refreshes the mind, and soothes the heart.

JUNIPER BERRY: Astringent and pungent, an antiseptic and cleansing agent, it also relieves bloating and sluggishness.

PATCHOULI: Sweet, warming, and floral, like jasmine, patchouli works as an antidepressant, anti-inflammatory, antiseptic, and anti-toxin. Soothing and sensual, it also helps relieve colds, headaches, and nausea.

ROSE OTTO, ROSEWOOD, ROSE ABSOLUTE: Sweet and aromatic, and an antiseptic, it's used for dry skin and sensitive complexions, and to smooth out wrinkles. It helps relieve coughs and hay fever as well as depression, stress, nervous tension, and insomnia.

SANDALWOOD: Sweet, slightly woody, and warming, it's a stimulant and is used for chapped skin, oily skin, and sensitive skin, and to minimize scarring. It is believed to help relieve anxiety, nervous tension, stress, and insomnia and to heighten the ability to concentrate and focus. The Chinese use it to treat stomachache, nausea, sore throats, and bronchitis.

YLANG-YLANG: Sweet, warming, and floral, it is used in the tropics as a remedy for skin infection, as well as a sedative, an antidepressant, and a tonic for the nervous system. It calms and rebalances the mind and spirit.

MASSAGE OILS

The healing hands of a trained masseuse can smooth away tired and achy muscles, banish stress, and restore balance and tranquility. Have a massage regularly and, when you do, request or provide your masseuse with the essential oil most suited for your needs. Relax, enjoy, and leave the oil on for at least an hour after the massage before showering. Be sure to drink plenty of water afterward to flush away toxins and prevent soreness from vigorous massage.

FOR MUSCLE ACHES AND PAIN AFTER VIGOROUS EXERCISE: Combine ½ cup mustard oil and 10 drops each cedar and sandalwood essential oils in a bottle. Seal tightly and shake well. Massage into the affected areas or where the body is experiencing stress.

TO REFRESH AND RELIEVE SLUGGISHNESS AND STRESS: Combine ½ cup almond oil with 10 drops each patchouli, ylang-ylang, and rose otto, rosewood, or rose absolute essential oils in a bottle. Seal tightly and shake well. Use it to massage over the entire body, especially the neck, shoulders, hands, and feet. Or, combine ½ cup almond oil with 10 drops each jasmine and rose otto, rosewood, or rose absolute essential oils. Apply to your body, especially your face around your temples and neck.

SACHETS

To rekindle your Earth element spirit, make sachets to perfume drawers, closets, and your work area. To make a fragrant sachet, choose a pretty handkerchief and place 4 to 5 cotton balls in the center. Sprinkle 9 to 10 drops of an essential oil of your choosing on them, then wrap up in the handkerchief and tie with a ribbon. The sachet's scent will last a month in the drawer, less time if exposed to air.

FOR INTIMATE APPAREL: Sprinkle 10 drops each sandalwood (uplifting) or patchouli (sensuality) and rose otto, rosewood, or rose absolute (refreshes the heart) essential oils on the cotton balls and tuck the sachet among your intimate apparel.

FOR CLOTHING: In closets, drawers, or storage containers, sprinkle 10 drops each ylang-ylang (refreshing) and jasmine essential oils (uplifting) on the cotton balls.

TRADITIONAL REMEDIES FOR MINOR AILMENTS

Earth element people are prone to colds and muscle and joint aches, as well as insomnia. Try these natural healing remedies.

FOR COLDS: Combine 2 tablespoons minced fresh ginger; 6 cloves, roasted and ground (page 70); and 10 drops sandalwood essential oil in a small bowl. Heat in the microwave for 25 seconds. Lightly massage your chest and neck with the mixture. Leave on for at least 1 hour before washing off.

FOR COLD HANDS AND FEET: Combine 2 tablespoons fresh ginger, pulverized by pounding in a mortar with a pestle; 1 stalk lemongrass, tough outer layers removed and tender inner stalk pulverized in the same manner as the ginger; and 7 drops each cedar and sandalwood essential oils in a small bowl and microwave for 25 seconds.

Rub and massage on the affected area. Leave on for at least 1 hour before washing off.

FOR INSOMNIA: Combine 3 drops each sandalwood, rose otto or rose absolute, and chamomile essential oils in a small bottle. Shake to combine. Rub and gently massage into your chest, neck, and upper back. Take deep breaths, inhaling and absorbing the scent. Close your eyes, empty your mind, and relax.

FOR MUSCLE AND JOINT ACHES: Combine and place on a thin cotton cloth or several layers of cheesecloth 1 stalk lemongrass, tough outer layers removed and tender inner stalk

pulverized by pounding in a mortar with a pestle; one 2-inch piece fresh ginger, pulverized in the same manner as the lemongrass; 1 cup Asiatic pennywort leaves, pulverized in the same manner as the lemongrass; and 9 drops cedar essential oil. Tie to secure. Heat in the microwave for 30 to 40 seconds. Rub, press, and massage the hot cotton compress in a circular motion around the affected area. Continue until the compress cools. Repeat 3 times a day for 2 days with the same compress. After the second day, discard the old compress. Repeat the treatment weekly with a new compress until healed.

CHAPTER FOUR

Nam is the Thai word for water and, to Thai people, water is life's eternal spring. For centuries, Thais have chosen to live by the water's edge, next to rivers, lakes, and oceans. Water has nourished our lives, transformed our culture, and purified our spirituality. Our dependence on water binds us to its source, the rivers, and their paths have guided us as we searched for peaceful, fertile land to settle and build our cities.

Whenever I return to Thailand, I never feel that I have truly arrived home until I have seen and traveled on the splendid Chao Phraya River. On this river, two of Thailand's capitals, Thonburi and Bangkok, were founded. Majestic royal palaces, ornate temples, and grand government buildings stood by its banks, testament to the river's importance in the history of the people. Today, much around the river, with its constantly churning chocolate brown water, has changed, yet it remains heavily trafficked by commercial interests, ordinary folks, and tourists alike. Rivers, including the Chao Phraya with its endless tributaries, are our life source. Thais honor all rivers by calling every river *mae nam,* or the "mother of waters."

Like nature's benevolent *mae nam,* Thai traditional healers honor people whose home element is *nam,* or the Water element, as sources of love and compassion. If Water is your home element, you are generous and faithful to your friends and family. Some of you are gifted with an excellent memory. You are admired at work for your precision, dedication, and reliability.

According to Thai folk medicine, your kindred spirits are the Earth and Wind elements, which means that you share some of those traits. Read the chapters on Earth and Wind for additional insight into who you are. As for your own unique characteristics, you resemble sparkling, cool water, always looking youthful for your age. Many marvel at your elegance and self-assuredness. Yet hidden behind this outwardly confident appearance is a delicate, sensuous, and sensitive person.

WATER

Like life, the river flows along its course; It sometimes ebbs, and at times is blocked, requiring strong currents to push through debris and obstacles. Preoccupation and self-absorption, in particular, can dam up the flow of a Water person's giving spirit, making it seem as if you are oblivious to and without concern for others.

I have several family members and friends who are Water element people. When they are out of sorts, it's almost always because they did not get enough sleep. To stay centered, get a long night's sleep and indulge in the urge to nap. A regular midday nap to the Water element person is like giving water to a wilting plant, instantly reviving and replenishing its spent energy.

Another distinct characteristic of the Water element person is the constant need to replenish fluids. Their chief complaint is a parched, dry throat, which leads them to drink water all day long. According to traditional Thai medicine, the health of Water element people depends on the quality and quantity of the fluid they take in, which nourishes the respiratory, digestive, urinary, and reproductive systems. An imbalance in any of these areas will plague you with recurring colds, bronchitis, allergies, water retention, or indigestion.

FOOD FOR HEALTH

"Everything in its place and every task performed to perfection" is the motto for Water element people. Your sense of well-being and peace depends on a disciplined and orderly lifestyle, including your diet. My daughter, Angela, for example, is a Water element person. For years, her favorite indulgence was a greasy breakfast with heaps of bacon strips, fried eggs, and home fries smothered in a sea of ketchup. She paid dearly for her excessive tastes.

When she met her boyfriend, who is a vegetarian, she decided to follow suit. While her friends teased her, she stuck to this rather difficult new eating regimen. Her occasional bursts of acne began to disappear, and her troublesome digestive tract ceased giving her problems. She has learned that a Water element person should eat fatty, rich, and sweet foods in moderation. Angela feels much better now that she eats light meals prepared with locally grown seasonal vegetables flavored with warming herbs and spices.

According to traditional Thai healing beliefs, bitter and sour tastes in combination with bland flavors in fruits and vegetables contain the necessary rebalancing remedies for Water element people. Bitter-flavor vegetables such as Chinese broccoli (also known as Chinese kale) and collard greens are also thought to strengthen and heal the respiratory, digestive, and immune systems.

Water element people love sour-tasting fruits such as cranberries, oranges, limes, lemons, cherries, and tomatoes, which are ideal for their sensitive respiratory and digestive systems. Thai healers believe that sour tastes eliminate excessive phlegm, aid in fighting upper respiratory congestion, quench the thirst, purify the blood, and cleanse the digestive tract, especially the lower intestine. No wonder Thais reach for glasses of orange juice when they have a cold or cold lemonade on a rainy day.

Bland vegetables might sound uninspiring, but they can be as uplifting as the quiet whisper of wind on a calm day. Imagine dishes prepared with bean sprouts, Chinese or regular okra, both dried and fresh mushrooms (especially enoki, portobello, shiitake, straw, and wood ear mushrooms), as well as rice and winter melon. These flavors nurture the respiratory system and act as a diuretic, which benefits the urinary tract.

Water element people should drink coffee and tea in moderation, especially during hot weather, because both are diuretics and believed to be warming agents.

HOT WEATHER RECIPES

While others wilt in the heat, Water element people reach out to the sun and dance in its glistening, warm rays. To keep this healthy glow in balance, whet your appetite and appease nature's Fire element, which influences the hot weather, with small, light meals. Prepare dishes made with cool, refreshing fruits and vegetables such as summer melons, cucumbers, and salad greens. Sour tastes, considered one of the healing and nurturing food groups for Water element people, should be eaten sparingly during hot weather, as they elevate the internal body temperature already naturally induced by the climate. Eat fewer tangy-sour as well as sweet fruits, which also increase body temperature, and instead double up on bland- and bitter-flavor vegetables such as Chinese and regular mustard greens, broccoli, Asiatic pennywort, chayote, and summer squash, which will balance nature's Fire element.

BREAKFAST

As a Water element person myself, I start the day with a cool, refreshing smoothie. Traditional Thai doctors taught me both the reason for and the value in my cravings for them. Thai medical practice identifies the early hours of the day as being under the influence of nature's Water element. As a Water element person, you have sensitive respiratory, digestive, and immune systems. During the morning hours, nature's Water element is present. For everyone, regardless of their home element, nature's Water element can be taxing on their respiratory, digestive, and immune systems. For a Water element person, in particular, when these double forces of Water element are present, extra precautions must be taken to avoid catching a cold or suffering from indigestion. To that end, Thai folk healers have advised me to start the day with a light, nourishing breakfast that balances sour and sweet summer fruits with Fire element's cool/refreshing flavor. Berries with a tart/sweet taste such as blueberries, strawberries, and blackberries are a delicious choice. Enjoy them in combination with a rice cereal, as rice, with its bland, nurturing flavor, will balance nature's Fire element, which rules the weather. You can also enjoy jams or preserves made with these berries on toast. Corn is another great choice, in the form of a corn-based cereal, or the corn cakes on page 33.

Start the morning with a glass of cranberry-apple or tomato-celery juice. Sun-ripened pineapple, with its sweet and tart flavor, energizes the Water element as you race through the day with personal demands for perfection in everything you do. Make personalized juices by blending together sweet summer melons, cucumber, orange, pineapple, tomato, kiwi, celery, and/or carrot.

LUNCH

When the weather becomes unbearably hot, a traditional Thai saying, *Kom pben ya* or "bitterness is medicine," is often repeated, because of the belief that bitter-flavor vegetables and greens have the ability to cool and reduce fever. To keep the Fire element, which dominates the hot weather and the noon hour, in balance, a wholesome lunch of bitter greens will keep you refreshed. Add a bit of pungent and plenty of cool/refreshing herbs and spices to your luncheon dishes and they, in turn, will perk up your appetite.

Summer soups prepared with bland-flavor vegetables such as chayote, cucumber, or summer melons and squashes come alive when you add warm, herbal spices such as coriander and peppercorn. The combination calms the heat radiated by nature's Fire element, while at the same time clears your delicate circulatory and respiratory systems.

Your home element taste for sourness will dominate your desire when it comes to picking the ingredients for a salad. Having Water as your home element, you need and can withstand a bit of sourness in your food, even when the weather is hot. However, it is very important to balance that with the addition of crispy, bland-, and cool/refreshing-flavor vegetables to lessen the heat induced by the sour taste and that of nature's Fire element. Try Northeastern Thai Salad on page 53, preparing it with ¾ cup peeled and shredded green papaya and ⅓ cup each shredded fresh pineapple and thinly sliced strawberries.

For beverages, refreshing Chrysanthemum Tea (page 46), laced with honey ice-cold Lemongrass Tea (page 46) with a sprig of fresh mint, and Asiatic Pennywort Drink (page 43) would be cooling and satisfying.

Most Water element people aren't prone to eating between meals, but if you do get the urge, have a small handful of roasted almonds, sunflower or pumpkin seeds, or a slice or two of fresh fruit. Better yet, a tall, cool glass of Watermelon Juice (page 45) will refresh and satisfy you.

DINNER

Warm, summery evenings are a time for rejoicing. These fleeting moments of easy living are made for the pleasures of light dishes with a touch of exotica. Fresh seasonal fruits such as watermelons, peaches, Pluots, mangos, papayas, and apricots, cool/refreshing vegetables, and bitter greens are good combinations for Water element summer salads. Dress them with a light citrus-based dressing, as the sour taste will balance the double influence of Water element (your home element and the dinner hour). Adding bland-flavor ingredients will steady your home element and moderate nature's Fire element (the weather). Mixing in cool/refreshing- and bitter-flavor vegetables adds surprising contrast to the salad, as it balances the heat of the domineering Fire element.

One way to satisfy your cravings for the clean, crisp taste of bitter- or bland-flavor vegetables is to cook them together in stir-fry dishes. Season them with ginger and garlic to keep your respiratory system healthy and to ease digestion.

Both the Chinese and Thai people believe that ice, rather than being cooling, increases inner heat. Hot tea, believed to ease digestion, is the best drink to accompany the evening meal during hot weather. Hot Chrysanthemum Tea (page 46) is especially cooling and calming.

TASTE	VEGETABLES	FRUITS	HERBS/SPICES	GRAINS	
BITTER	Belgian endive, broccoli raab, Brussels sprouts, collard greens, dandelion greens, escarole, mustard greens, kale, radicchio	Olives	Kaffir lime leaves; rosemary; star anise; lemon, lime, and orange zests		
BITTER/ASTRINGENT	Tea				
BITTER/BUTTERY					
BITTER/COOL/ REFRESHING	Bitter melon, bitter salad mix, frisée		Aloe vera, Asiatic pennywort		
BITTER/SPICY	Arugula				
BLAND		Bottle gourd, chayote, fuzzy melon			
BLAND/ASTRINGENT	Artichoke, cauliflower, Swiss chard, green beans, yard-long beans, wing beans	Unripe guava			
BLAND/BITTER	Broccoli, Chinese broccoli, eggplant				
BLAND/BUTTERY	Mushrooms, potato, taro	Unripe papaya			
BLAND/COOL/ REFRESHING	Bamboo shoots; bean sprouts; bok choy; Boston, butter, green-leaf, iceberg, red-leaf, and romaine lettuces; Chinese okra (luffa); okra; cucumber; Napa cabbage; summer squashes; tatsoi; watermelon rind; water spinach; winter melon				
BLAND/SWEET	Hearts of palm, kholrabi, rutabaga				
SOUR	Sorrel, purslane, tomatillo	Lemon, unripe mango, unripe tamarind	Rose hip		
SOUR/ASTRINGENT	Rhubarb	Cranberry			
SOUR/BITTER		Blood orange, grapefruit, kaffir lime, kumquat, lime			
SOUR/SWEET	Tomato	Apricot Cheery orange, passion fruit, pineapple, Pluot, pommelo, star fruit, tangerine, tangelo, tamarind			
BUTTERY				Oat, wheat	
BUTTERY/ASTRINGENT				Quinoa	
BUTTERY/SWEET					
BUTTERY/COOL/ REFRESHING				Rice	
AROMA					
WARM/SPICY					
SWEET/WARMING					
SWEET/FLORAL/ WARMING					
SWEET/FLORAL/COOL/ REFRESHING					
SWEET/FLORAL/WARM/ SPICY					

SEEDS/NUTS	BEANS/LEGUMES	COOKING OILS	ESSENTIAL OILS	SEASONINGS
	Fava beans			
				Vinegar
Pumpkin, sunflower	Black beans, black-eye peas, mung beans, red beans, soybeans	Canola, corn, olive, sunflower		
Almond				
			Sage	
			Benzoin, coriander	
			Geranium	
			Honeysuckle, ylang-ylang	
			Lavender	

Shrimp dressed with aromatic, spicy ginger and garlic sit prettily on delicate strands of rice noodle adorning a bed of cool, sweet, and crunchy lettuce and carrot and smoky, peppery chiles, which add unexpected texture to the slithery noodles. To top it all, a sauce of sweet-sour-spicy flavors and crunchy peanuts balances the influences of Water and Fire elements, while at the same time making you swoon with its delicious mouth-watering taste. Ground fresh chile paste can be purchased at Asian supermarkets. Canned whole fire-roasted Anaheim chiles are available in most supermarkets.

COOL RICE VERMICELLI WITH GRILLED SHRIMP, FIRE-ROASTED ANAHEIM CHILE, AND SWEET-SOUR SAUCE

IN a small saucepan, combine the sugar and water, and heat over medium heat. When the sugar is dissolved, set aside to cool. Add the remaining sauce ingredients and stir to combine. If making ahead, refrigerate and taste before serving, as the lime juice may lose its sourness. Add more to balance the flavor.

BRING a pot of water to a boil. Soak the rice vermicelli in cool water to cover for 10 minutes. Drain, then add to the boiling water and cook until the strands are softened and cooked, 3 to 4 minutes. Rinse immediately under cool water. Drain, pat dry thoroughly, cut into manageable lengths, and set aside.

HEAT the grill to high. Put a fine-mesh rack on top of the grill rack.

COMBINE the shrimp with the salt, garlic, ginger, white pepper, and lime zest in a large bowl. Mix well. Spray the shrimp generously with vegetable oil spray before placing on top of the mesh. Grill until the shrimp turn pink and are slightly charred and firm, 5 to 7 minutes, turning them frequently. Remove from the grill. (This can be done the day before, when you've got the grill going for dinner. Refrigerate until ready to use.)

DIVIDE the shredded lettuce between four serving bowls and top with equal amounts of vermicelli. Add equal amounts of the Anaheim chiles, carrots, and shrimp. Garnish with the cilantro, mint, and peanuts. Ladle equal amounts of the sweet-sour sauce over the noodles and serve.

NOTE: If making ahead for the next day's lunch, store the sauce separately and add right before serving. Warm the noodles to room temperature in the microwave for about 20 seconds.

MAKES 4 SERVINGS

SWEET-SOUR SAUCE
3 tablespoons sugar

⅓ cup water

2 tablespoons ground fresh chile paste

¼ cup fish sauce

⅓ cup fresh lime juice

TO FINISH THE DISH
6 ounces rice vermicelli (page 86)

⅔ pound medium shrimp, peeled and deveined

½ teaspoon salt

1 teaspoon minced garlic

1 teaspoon peeled and minced fresh ginger

¼ teaspoon white pepper

Grated zest of 1 lime

Vegetable oil spray

1 cup shredded iceberg lettuce

3 canned fire-roasted Anaheim chiles, thinly sliced

1 cup shredded carrot

¼ cup chopped fresh cilantro

3 tablespoons minced fresh mint

¼ cup crushed dry-roasted unsalted peanuts

For Water element people who can't resist fresh summer fruits, this is the salad for you. It's paired with bitter-spicy Asiatic pennywort, guaranteed to keep you cool and calm no matter how hot the weather. Since this healing herb is sometimes unavailable, watercress is a good substitute.

FRUIT SALAD WITH GRILLED SCALLOPS AND CITRUS DRESSING

HEAT the grill to medium.

MIX the scallops with the salt and lime zest in a small bowl. Spray them generously with vegetable oil spray and put them in a single layer on a fine-mesh rack set over the fire. Turn frequently to prevent burning. Grill until the outer surface is slightly charred and the scallops are firm to the touch, 5 to 6 minutes. Remove to a plate to cool. Slice each in half.

COMBINE the fruit, pennywort, and slivered lime leaves in a large bowl and toss lightly. Add the scallops and dressing. Toss again. Transfer to a serving platter, garnish with the fried shallots, and serve.

MAKES 4 SERVINGS

½ pound large scallops (about 1 cup)

¼ teaspoon salt

1 teaspoon grated lime zest

Vegetable oil spray

2 cups cubed peeled mango

2 cups cubed sweet melon such as Crenshaw, Persian, or cantaloupe

2 cups cubed peeled kiwi

2 cups cubed peeled pineapple

1 cup tightly packed Asiatic pennywort or watercress, slivered

1 tablespoon slivered kaffir lime leaves or grated lime zest

¼ cup or more Citrus Dressing (page 58)

1 tablespoon fried shallots (page 100)

This is an adaptation of an ancient Thai recipe that used tomatoes grown in Thailand that were smaller and tarter. It's for that reason that I call for an underripe tomato. Seasoning of fish sauce, lime juice, chile, and cilantro not only complements but also highlights the sweet-tangy taste of tomato, creating a balance to satisfy the requirements for all elements.

GRILLED SHRIMP AND TOMATO SALAD

HEAT the grill to high.

COMBINE the fish sauce and lime juice in a small bowl and set aside. Combine the shrimp with the salt and lime zest in another bowl; mix well and set aside.

PLACE a fine-mesh rack over the grill rack and wait a minute or two for it to get hot. Lightly coat the shallots and Anaheim chiles with vegetable oil spray and place on the grill. Cook until both are slightly charred on the outside and soft and tender to the touch, turning them often. Remove from the grill. Put the chiles in a paper bag and seal. Rub the bag against the chiles to remove the charred skins. Remove them from the bag, rinse, seed, and slice into strands. Put on a platter.

WHEN the shallots are cool to the touch, remove the skins, slice each in half, and place on the platter with the chiles.

LIGHTLY coat the shrimp with the vegetable oil spray and place on the grill. Cook until pink and firm, about 7 minutes, turning frequently to prevent burning. Transfer to the platter. Top with the tomato, cilantro, and minced Thai chiles. Pour the reserved dressing over the top and mix to combine. Serve with hot white, brown, or red rice.

MAKES 4 SERVINGS

2 tablespoons fish sauce

3 tablespoons fresh lime juice

1 pound medium shrimp, peeled and deveined

½ teaspoon salt

Grated zest of 1 lime

15 shallots

3 fresh Anaheim chiles

Vegetable oil spray

1 cup thinly sliced underripe tomato

¼ cup chopped fresh cilantro

1 to 2 fresh Thai or 1 fresh serrano chile(s), minced

S tir-fried okra is crunchy and not slimy, as its bland flavor succumbs to the pungency of garlic, ginger, and chiles, creating a delectable integration among Water, Wind, and Fire elements.

STIR-FRIED OKRA

HEAT a wok or large skillet over high heat for 1 minute. Add the oil and let heat for another minute. Add the garlic and ginger and stir-fry until the garlic turns golden, 10 to 15 seconds. Add your choice of protein and stir-fry until partially cooked or heated through. Season with the salt and soy sauce, then add the okra and chile and stir-fry until the okra turns slightly limp. Transfer to a serving platter and serve with hot white, brown, or red rice.

MAKES 4 SERVINGS

1 tablespoon rice bran, canola, or corn oil

1 tablespoon minced garlic

1 tablespoon peeled and minced fresh ginger

About 6 ounces chicken breast or pork tenderloin, thinly sliced; 10 ounces small shrimp, peeled; or 8 ounces firm tofu, cubed

¼ teaspoon salt

1 tablespoon soy sauce or fish sauce

3 cups okra thinly sliced on the diagonal

1 fresh serrano chile, minced

This was my favorite dish while growing up. Whenever I felt out of sorts, our housekeeper, Ah Sum, would make it to cheer me up. It always worked. Having Water as my home element, I love the crisp, clean taste of watermelon rind. Nowadays, as new varieties of watermelon with thin rinds are grown and sold, it might be hard to make this dish. Substitute peeled and seeded cucumber.

STIR-FRIED CHICKEN OR PORK WITH WATERMELON RIND

HEAT a wok or large skillet over high heat for 1 minute. Add the oil and heat for another minute. Add the seasoning and stir-fry for 1 minute. Add the chicken and stir-fry until partially cooked. Season with the soy sauce and stir to mix. Add the watermelon rind and chiles and stir-fry until the chicken is cooked and the watermelon rind turns translucent. If the skillet appears dry, add a tablespoon of water. Transfer to a serving platter, garnish with the cilantro, and serve with hot white, brown, or red rice.

MAKES 4 SERVINGS

1 tablespoon rice bran, canola, or corn oil

1 tablespoon Bean Paste Stir-Fry Seasoning (page 66)

6 to 8 ounces chicken breast or pork tenderloin, thinly sliced to make 1 cup

1 tablespoon soy sauce

3 cups peeled watermelon rind cut into small cubes or peeled and seeded cucumber

1 to 2 fresh Thai or 1 fresh serrano chile(s), minced

1/3 cup coarsely chopped fresh cilantro

O n many warm summer evenings, I have made this succulent dish for my husband, Bob (who also has Water as his home element), and myself and served it with hot rice on the side. Whiffs of orange zest, ginger, and sesame put us in a relaxed mood. Bob, who is very picky about his vegetables, loves bok choy. I suppose its bland flavor and unassuming character appeal to his Water element needs.

STIR-FRIED FISH WITH BABY BOK CHOY

IN a medium bowl, combine the orange zest, 1 tablespoon of the ginger, ½ teaspoon of the salt, ½ teaspoon of the pepper, 2 tablespoons of the soy sauce, and the sesame oil. Mix well, then add the fish and turn to coat all the pieces. Let stand for 10 minutes.

LINE a plate with paper towels and place next to the stove. Heat a large skillet over high heat. Put the cornstarch in a paper or plastic bag and add the fish. Add the canola oil to the heated skillet. Close and shake the bag to coat the fish with the cornstarch. Tap off any excess and gently lay the fish in the oil. Cook just until it is beginning to look opaque. Remove to the paper towels.

REMOVE all but 1 tablespoon of the oil from the pan and place back over high heat. Add the remaining 1 tablespoon ginger and stir-fry for a couple of seconds. Add the bok choy, vermouth, broth, and the remaining ½ teaspoon each salt and pepper and 1 tablespoon soy sauce. (If using canned broth, taste and adjust the seasonings accordingly.) Stir-fry for 10 to 12 seconds, then add the fish and mix in gently. Cover and cook for a minute. Uncover and let cook for another minute, until the broth thickens. Transfer to a serving platter and serve with hot white, brown, or red rice.

MAKES 4 SERVINGS

Grated zest of 1 orange

2 tablespoons peeled and minced fresh ginger

1 teaspoon sea salt

1 teaspoon white pepper

3 tablespoons soy sauce

½ teaspoon sesame oil

1 pound sea bass or red snapper fillets, cut into bite-size pieces

⅓ cup cornstarch

¼ cup canola or corn oil

4 cups baby bok choy (only the inner clusters), blanched in boiling water with ½ teaspoon salt added for less than 1 minute, drained, and dried thoroughly

2 tablespoons dry vermouth

½ cup homemade (page 26) or canned low-sodium, low-fat chicken broth

This Asian-style panna cotta is light and slightly sweet, with a nutty texture, and is the kind of dessert Water element people love. Fresh, sweet-tart berries also meet Water element's requirement.

ALMOND FLOAT WITH FRESH BERRIES

COMB!NE the gelatin and water in a small saucepan over medium heat. Stir to mix until the gelatin is dissolved. Let cool.

IN a medium saucepan, combine the almond milk and sugar over medium heat. Stir to mix until the sugar is dissolved. Remove from the heat and add the gelatin mixture and extract. Mix to combine. Pour into an 11 x 7 x 1½-inch glass baking dish. Refrigerate until firm, 2 to 3 hours. Slice into tiny squares and serve with the fresh fruit.

MAKES 4 SERVINGS

3 envelopes Knox unflavored gelatin

1 cup water

2 cups Almond Milk (page 21)

⅔ cup sugar

2 to 3 drops almond extract

2 cups mixed fresh berries, sliced peaches, and/or melons

Fresh fruits such as sweet summer melons mixed with tart berries or fruit sorbets are a lovely ending to a meal, equalizing the presence of nature's Water element (time of day) and Fire element (climate) with that of your own home element.

RICE CREPES WITH RASPBERRIES

PUT the milk, water, rice flour, cooked rice, sugar, salt, and oil in a blender and blend until smooth. Add the eggs and blend for another minute. Transfer to a container, cover, and refrigerate for at least 2 hours or overnight.

WHEN ready to cook, whisk the batter well. Heat a medium nonstick pan over medium heat for 1 to 2 minutes. Coat the pan generously with the vegetable oil spray. Add ⅓ cup of the batter. Tilt and rotate the pan to coat the surface with the batter. Put the pan back on the stove and cook until the top is dried and the bottom lightly brown, about 1 minute. Use a thin spatula to loosen the edges. Lift the crepe up lightly from the pan with the spatula and insert a thin, long spatula underneath. Flip the crepe over. Cook until the other side is lightly brown. Use the spatula to transfer the crepe to a plate lined with wax paper. Cover to keep warm. Mix the batter well and repeat the process with the remaining batter. Place each crepe on top of the wax paper, adding another sheet of paper.

SPREAD each crepe with a tablespoon or two of strawberry jelly. Top with 6 to 7 raspberries. Gently roll each crepe up over the filling. Serve warm.

MAKES ABOUT 12 CREPES; 4 SERVINGS

1 cup milk

⅓ cup water

½ cup fine rice flour

½ cup cooked long-grain white rice, at room temperature

1 tablespoon sugar

¼ teaspoon salt

2 tablespoons rice bran, canola, or corn oil

3 large eggs

Vegetable oil spray

One 10-ounce jar strawberry jelly

2 cups fresh raspberries

RAINY WEATHER RECIPES

As the rain begins to fall, you might be tempted to frolic in the wet outdoors without your hat or umbrella. Even in the warm tropical rain, the wise Thai traditional healers caution against going outside without a raincoat and hat. They would tell you that wet air can aggravate the sensitive respiratory system of Water element people. To keep your system in balance as nature's Wind element dominates the rainy and damp weather, stay dry and warm. Include healing herbs and spices such as warming ginger, garlic, onion, peppercorns, and star anise in your food. Use them as seasonings with fruits and vegetables that have bitter and bland flavors as well as sour taste. Bitter-flavor vegetables such as escarole, kale, and radicchio are nurturing to the muscles and bones. Eggplant, bamboo shoots, bok choy, broccoli, and cauliflower are all good choices for bland-flavor vegetables. They keep the cardiovascular, respiratory, and digestive systems in balance. Eat sour-tasting citrus fruit when it rains to add warmth to your system. Pick among an abundance of choices, including grapefruit, lemon, lime, kumquat, orange, pomelo, and tangerine. The taste of cherry, grape, and pomegranate will also make those endless rainy days sparkle like diamonds.

Together, bland, bitter, and sour tastes regulate the inner heat, steady the circulatory system, and protect Water element types against damp air.

BREAKFAST

Turn rain-soaked mornings into cozy, warm beginnings with a comforting breakfast. Protect yourself against the wet, damp mornings dominated by Water (the hour) and Wind (the weather) elements by including sour and tangy tastes in your breakfast. You can accomplish this by reaching for a glass of orange, tangerine, or grapefruit juice, or try Tamarind Juice with Cloves (page 44) or Banana and Papaya Smoothie with Kumquat, Honey, and Ginger Preserves (page 41). A fresh fruit salad with an abundance of citrus will also do the trick. Hot cereals garnished with a sprinkling of cinnamon or nutmeg lighten dark and stormy mornings. Or warm yourself with oatmeal topped with dried cranberries, slices of banana, and a dollop of honey to fortify yourself against nature's Wind element. Chinese-style rice porridges add stamina to the Water element person's delicate constitution. Pancakes (page 31) topped with fruits packed with your home element's tastes and flavors make you hum with delight.

LUNCH

Wet heat (dominated by nature's Wind and Fire elements) is the way Thais describe a rainy midday. To keep your chest and throat warm, some of you will need a protective cloak.

Pick among the best produce of the season and combine sweet- and sour-flavor fruits with bland or bitter vegetables to nourish your home element. Take extra care because of the rain brought on by nature's mighty Wind element. To keep your body in balance and healthy, add a touch of spicy and cool/refreshing flavors.

A wonderful way to combine these spicy and cool/refreshing flavors is in salads:

- Combine grapes, cut in half, with shredded cooked chicken, torn arugula leaves, torn fresh mint leaves, and 1 minced stalk lemongrass, then toss with Kumquat, Ginger, and Clove Preserve Dressing (page 59).

- Combine broccoli florets you've blanched in boiling water for 30 seconds with slivers of tart mango, and shredded cooked chicken, cooked medium shrimp, or thinly sliced baked tofu. Toss together with toasted almond slivers and Kumquat, Ginger, and Clove Preserve Dressing (page 59). Garnish with fried shallots (page 100).

If you crave warm soups, try one of those offered on pages 89 to 96. In particular, Noodle Soup (page 82), prepared with an extra dose of slivered ginger and chopped cilantro, will keep nature's Wind element in its place.

For beverages, treat yourself with a cup of hot or cold Lemongrass Tea (page 46), rose hip tea, or mint tea with honey. Any of them will soothe you.

For a snack in the middle of the afternoon, when Wind element dominates, a hot cup of Red Zinger or ginger tea, or spiced apple cider served with a cookie made with dried cherries or cranberries will warm and comfort you. A bowl of freshly made popcorn without butter will satisfy hunger cravings until dinner.

DINNER

Cool, wet evenings call for extra protective measures to balance nature's dominant Wind and Water elements. Hot soups or stews with a tangy punch or a spicy kick from added herbs and spices perk up a dreary night and nurture your immune system. While most people grill food only in the summer, I love it best when the weather is wet or cold. I inherited this habit from my mother, who, during the monsoon season, would hold an umbrella in one hand to shield her from the pouring rain as she cooked in our outdoor kitchen. Rain, Mother said, was "extra seasoning." I don't ever remember Mother suffering a day of cold or flu.

Tangy fruits such as oranges, tangerines, pomelos, apricots, and pomegranates make wonderful additions to salads. Contrast them with some bitter- and astringent-tasting vegetables, then toss everything together with a fruity-sour dressing. Add the spicy flavors of chiles, ginger, garlic, and shallots. This bountiful assortment will protect you against the drenching rains of the harsh Wind element. For a beverage, comforting Almond Milk (page 21) with honey or hot Chrysanthemum Tea (page 46) will soothe the digestion while warming the spirit.

During one of those weeks when the rain seems to come down nonstop, put up a pot of soup when you have a moment. Add everything called for in the recipe except the bean threads and garnishes. While it is cooking, the smell of ginger and sesame oil will warm your chest and calm you down. After the soup is done, let it cool and put in the refrigerator. As the Wind element keeps the rain coming, heat the soup, add the bean threads, and ladle it into serving bowls for you and your guests for lunch. You'll be sorry to see the rain go.

TOMATO, CUCUMBER, AND TOFU SOUP

BRING the broth to a boil in a large saucepan, then reduce the heat to medium. Add the ginger, salt, soy sauce, and sesame oil. (If using canned broth, taste and adjust the seasonings.) Stir to mix, then add the chicken, tomato, cucumber, and tofu. When it comes back to a boil, reduce the heat to medium-low. Cover and cook for another 8 minutes. Uncover and add the bean threads. Stir and cook until they turn translucent, about 1 minute. Ladle into individual serving bowls, garnish with the white pepper and cilantro, and serve hot.

MAKES 4 SERVINGS

6 cups homemade (page 26) or canned low-sodium, low-fat chicken broth

6 thin slices fresh ginger

1 teaspoon salt

1 tablespoon soy sauce

½ teaspoon sesame oil

6 to 8 ounces boneless chicken breast, thinly sliced

1 large or 2 medium tomatoes, peeled, seeded, and quartered

1 cucumber, peeled, seeded, and thinly sliced to make 1 cup

8 ounces silken tofu, cut into chunks

1 cup tightly packed softened bean threads (page 86)

Pinch or two of white pepper

⅓ cup coarsely chopped fresh cilantro

Wash away concerns about deluges of rain brought on by nature's Wind element with your home element's tastes and flavors. Sweet and tangy orange protects your respiratory system. Pomegranate, bursting with antioxidants, cleanses the cells of impurities.

GRILLED CHICKEN, ORANGE, AND POMEGRANATE SALAD

PREHEAT the oven to 375°F.

COMBINE the chicken breasts with the orange zest and salt in a large baking dish. Coat generously with vegetable oil spray and bake until the chicken is just cooked through, 10 to 15 minutes. Let cool, then slice into thin strips.

COMBINE the orange segments, watercress, and pomegranate seeds in a large bowl. Toss gently, then add the chicken and dressing. Toss again, transfer to a serving platter, and serve.

MAKES 4 SERVINGS

2 boneless chicken breasts

1 tablespoon grated orange zest

¼ teaspoon salt

Vegetable oil spray

2 oranges, peeled and separated into segments

2 cups watercress, torn into bite-size pieces

½ cup pomegranate seeds

¼ cup or more Citrus Dressing (page 58)

*T*he pomelo resembles a giant grapefruit, but is firmer. The fruit has a sweet-tangy juice, and the sections are easier to separate than those of a grapefruit. These giant green- or yellow-peeled grapefruits are in season during the fall and winter, piled high in the produce section of most major supermarkets.

POMELO AND GRILLED SHRIMP SALAD

SLICE about ½ inch off the top of the pomelo on the stem end. Score the rind into quarters. Peel away the thick rind until you reach the membrane. Separate the fruit into sections. Slice across the very top of each section and push the fruit out of the membrane. Gently separate the sacs, trying not to bruise them. Use 1½ cups and save the rest for snacking. Put them in a large bowl. Top with the arugula and set aside. If using oranges, use a knife to peel them. Section the orange to remove the pith and use a total of 1½ cups.

HEAT the grill to medium-high.

PLACE a fine-mesh rack over the grill rack. Put the shrimp in a medium bowl and toss with the orange zest, ginger, salt, and white pepper. Coat them generously with vegetable oil spray before placing on the grill. Turn frequently to prevent burning. Cook until the shrimp are firm, pink, and slightly charred, about 7 minutes, turning them frequently. Let cool slightly, then add them to the bowl containing the pomelo and arugula. Sprinkle with the lemongrass, mint, coconut flakes, and shallots. Add the dressing, mix gently, and transfer to a serving platter. Serve immediately.

MAKES 4 SERVINGS

1 large pomelo or 4 to 6 oranges

1 cup arugula, torn into pieces

½ pound medium shrimp, peeled and deveined

Grated zest of 1 orange

1 teaspoon peeled and minced fresh ginger

¼ teaspoon salt

¼ teaspoon white pepper

Vegetable oil spray

1 stalk lemongrass, tough outer layers removed, tender inner stalk minced

9 fresh mint leaves, torn into pieces

2 tablespoons Dry-Roasted Coconut Flakes (page 101)

2 tablespoons fried shallots (page 100)

¼ cup or more Apple-Tamarind Dressing (page 56)

ere is a quick and healthy way to energize you at the end of the day. Garlic and ginger cloak your respiratory system against the wet Wind element, while bland-flavor broccoli boosts enzymes to ward against cell damage, and tangy-sweet tomato enriched with vitamins, minerals, and, in particular, lycopene acts as a preventative against colon and prostate cancer. Imagine that, all in one delicious dish!

STIR-FRIED RICE NOODLES WITH BROCCOLI AND TOFU OR CHICKEN

HEAT a large nonstick skillet over high heat for 1 minute. Add the oil and heat for 1 minute. Add the garlic and ginger and stir-fry for 10 to 15 seconds. Add the tofu or chicken and stir-fry until partially heated through or cooked, 1 to 2 minutes. Season with the bean paste, soy sauce, tomato paste, and fish sauce and stir to mix. Add the broccoli and tomato and stir-fry until the tomato softens, 1 to 2 minutes. Add the noodles and stir to mix. If the contents of the pan seem dry, add a tablespoon or two of water. Continue to stir-fry until the noodles soften, 2 to 3 minutes. Transfer to a serving plate, garnish with the white pepper, and serve with additional fish sauce and fresh chilies in vinegar on the side.

MAKES 1 SERVING

1 tablespoon canola, corn, rice bran, or olive oil

1 teaspoon minced garlic

1 teaspoon peeled and minced fresh ginger

½ cup thinly sliced baked tofu or chicken

1 teaspoon bean paste

1 teaspoon dark soy sauce

1 teaspoon tomato paste

1 tablespoon fish sauce (for vegetarians, substitute light soy sauce)

¾ cup broccoli florets, thinly sliced, or Chinese broccoli, blanched in boiling salted water for less than a minute and drained

¼ cup sliced ripe tomato

1½ cups fresh wide rice noodles (page 86), loosened and separated into strands, or dried pad thai rice noodles, softened in warm water until pliable and dried thoroughly

A couple pinches of white pepper

Fresh Chiles in Vinegar (page 84)

*n*eed a light, simple vegetarian soup after a day of dodging the rain? Here's one with a variety of mushrooms, sprouting with healing remedies, easing digestion, and increasing stamina. Cool/refreshing celery and warming ginger, shallot, and scallion mingled with aromatic cilantro meet nature's Wind element's rules, keeping your home element in harmony with its presence.

MUSHROOM AND TOFU SOUP

BRING the broth to a boil in a large saucepan, then reduce the heat to medium. Add the ginger, shallots, salt, soy sauce, and sesame oil. (If using canned broth, taste and adjust the salt accordingly.) Add the mushrooms, celery, and tofu. Bring to a boil, then reduce the heat to medium-low, cover, and cook until the mushrooms are soft, 5 to 7 minutes. Uncover, add the bean threads, and cook until they turn translucent, about 1 minute. Transfer to a soup tureen, garnish with scallion, cilantro, and white pepper, and ladle into individual bowls.

MAKES 4 SERVINGS

6 cups homemade (page 27) or canned low-sodium vegetable broth

3 to 4 thin slices fresh ginger

3 to 4 shallots, peeled

1 teaspoon salt

2 tablespoons soy sauce

1 teaspoon sesame oil

3 cups tightly packed thinly sliced mixture of shiitake, white, and oyster mushrooms

¼ cup thinly sliced Chinese or regular celery

One 12-ounce carton silken tofu, drained and cut into bite-size chunks

1 cup tightly packed softened bean threads (page 86), cut into manageable lengths

1 scallion, minced

⅓ cup coarsely chopped fresh cilantro

¼ teaspoon freshly ground white pepper

It is believed that this soup was invented by Thai cooks for Jews who had a settlement in Thailand at the beginning of the nineteenth century. Eating meat was a rarity among Thais, who are Buddhist. In addition, potato was seldom used in Thai cooking. Thai cooks seasoned the soup with aromatic star anise to mask what they perceived to be the unpleasant smell of cooked meat. It also aids indigestion and eases a stomachache. Chiles are added to stir the appetite. *Kraphrao,* a basil with a hot, spicy kick, settles indigestion. Since this variety of basil is rare, I have substituted it with peppermint. Then there is tamarind, with its fruity, tangy flavor, added to balance the salty-spicy taste of the soup.

THAI JEWISH SOUP Geang Tom Jew

PUT the beef bones, star anise, and ginger in a large pot. Cover with water and bring to a boil. Reduce the heat to medium-low, cover, and let it cook slowly for 1 hour. Strain the broth and discard the bones. Rinse out the pot, pour the broth back into it, and bring to a boil. Reduce the heat to medium-low and add the beef. Cover and let simmer for 30 minutes, or until the meat is tender. Add the potato, tamarind puree, salt, fish sauce, onion, and chiles. Cover and cook until the potato is cooked, 15 to 20 minutes. Add the peppermint; stir to mix until the leaves turn limp. Serve hot.

MAKES 4 SERVINGS

6 beef bones

2 star anise

3 to 4 thin slices fresh ginger

½ pound cubed beef tenderloin

1 large russet potato, peeled and diced

2 tablespoons Tamarind Puree (page 25)

½ teaspoon salt

2 tablespoons fish sauce

1 medium onion, diced

2 to 3 fresh Thai or 1 to 2 fresh serrano chiles, slightly pounded

1 cup fresh peppermint leaves, torn and slightly crushed

This was a favorite dish of my former mother-in-law, who was born in Nebraska. Although Thai food was totally foreign to her when I married her son, Ruthy was careful not to offend me. To her surprised delight, she loved my Asian cooking and became one of my biggest fans. ⌇ Ruthy was also a Water element person. Cauliflower, with its bland taste, meets one of Water element's taste requirements. The stir-fry is seasoned with Madras curry powder made from a combination of healing spices, all of which are under Wind element's category of taste. In this recipe, the powder coats the cauliflower and chicken during the stir-fry process as it would cloak a Water element person against Wind element's rain.

STIR-FRIED CAULIFLOWER AND CHICKEN WITH MADRAS CURRY

HEAT a wok or large nonstick skillet over high heat for 1 to 2 minutes. Add the oil and heat for 1 minute. Add the garlic and ginger and stir-fry for 10 to 15 seconds. Add the chicken and stir-fry until partially cooked. Add the salt, soy sauce, curry powder, cayenne, vermouth, and sugar and stir to mix. Add the cauliflower and scallion and stir-fry until the cauliflower turns translucent and is still slightly crunchy, 3 to 4 minutes. If the skillet seems dry, add a tablespoon or two of water. Serve with hot white, brown, or red rice.

MAKES 4 SERVINGS

1 tablespoon canola, corn, rice bran, or olive oil

1 tablespoon minced garlic

1 tablespoon peeled and minced fresh ginger

1 cup thinly sliced chicken

½ teaspoon salt

1 tablespoon soy sauce

1 teaspoon Madras curry powder

½ teaspoon cayenne pepper

2 tablespoons dry vermouth

½ teaspoon sugar

2 cups thinly sliced cauliflower florets

1 scallion, cut into 1-inch lengths

u nlike your typical sweet and sour sauce, which tends to be thick and gooey, this version is fruity and aromatic, with just the right bit of clingy texture. And blending Wind element's spicy ginger, cloves, and star anise with your home element's sour citrus, plum, and raspberry makes it both healthful and delicious. Double or triple the sauce recipe and keep it stored in the refrigerator for last-minute dinner guests. It keeps for at least a month.

CRISPY SHRIMP WITH SWEET AND SOUR SAUCE

COMBINE the sauce ingredients in a small saucepan and bring to a boil. Reduce the heat to medium and cook until the sauce thickens and clings to the back of the spoon, about 5 minutes. (If making ahead, let cool completely before storing in an airtight container in the refrigerator. Reheat before using, adding more orange juice to dilute if necessary.)

PUT the salt, pepper, flour, and cornmeal in a small paper bag. Seal and shake to mix. Set aside. Put the lime zest, ginger, paprika, and egg white in a medium bowl. Add the shrimp and mix well to coat them with the mixture. Set aside.

LINE a colander with several layers of paper towels and place near the stove. Heat the oil in a large skillet over high heat until hot, 6 to 7 minutes. Test for readiness by sprinkling a bit of flour into it. If it sizzles, it's ready. Put the shrimp in the bag with the flour mixture and toss to coat. Transfer to a strainer to discard any excess flour. Gently add a handful of the shrimp to the oil. Try not to overcrowd the skillet. Turn the shrimp frequently and cook until lightly golden and firm to the touch. Using a slotted spoon, transfer the cooked shrimp to the colander lined with paper towels. Repeat with the remaining shrimp.

SPOON several spoonfuls of the sweet and sour sauce onto a platter. Scatter the shrimp on top. Drizzle several more spoonfuls of the sauce over the shrimp. Serve immediately.

MAKES 4 SERVINGS

SWEET AND SOUR SAUCE

1 teaspoon peeled and minced fresh ginger

¼ cup orange juice

2 tablespoons chopped plum

2 tablespoons raspberries

1 tablespoon minced Kumquat, Ginger, and Clove Preserves (page 100)

½ teaspoon salt

¼ cup sugar

2 tablespoons red wine vinegar

1 teaspoon balsamic vinegar

2 cloves

1 star anise

TO FINISH THE DISH

½ teaspoon salt

½ teaspoon white pepper

½ cup all-purpose flour

2 tablespoons fine cornmeal

Grated zest of 1 lime

1 teaspoon peeled and minced fresh ginger

½ teaspoon paprika

1 large egg white, slightly beaten

1 pound medium shrimp, peeled, deveined, and patted dry

3 cups canola or corn oil

One of my favorite childhood Thai desserts was a bright neon pink sponge cake sold by vendors throughout Bangkok. First introduced by the Portuguese in the eighteenth century, the Thais took regular sponge cake and added iridescent pink food color to the batter. How could any child resist such a dessert? In this version, I have added warming and aromatic cinnamon, instead of pink food dye, to shield and warm us against the Wind element. I also added pureed kumquats, which turn the cake a pretty orange-yellow hue instead of pink.

SPONGE CAKE WITH CINNAMON AND KUMQUATS

PREHEAT the oven to 350°F.

COMBINE the kumquats and water in a blender and puree. Remove and set aside.

USING an electric mixer, beat the egg whites with the cream of tartar in a large bowl until foamy. Add ½ cup of the sugar, a couple of tablespoons at a time. Beat until the sugar is dissolved and the whites turn glassy and stand in soft peaks.

CLEAN and dry the beaters, then beat the egg yolks in a medium bowl until thick and lemony in color, 3 to 5 minutes. Gradually add the remaining sugar, the salt, and pureed kumquat.

COMBINE the flour with the cinnamon in a small bowl and mix with a fork. Pour it through a sieve over the beaten egg whites. Add the beaten egg yolks and fold gently and thoroughly. Do not overwork the batter, otherwise the cake will be chewy. Pour into an ungreased 9-inch tube pan. Gently cut through the batter with a knife to get the air bubbles out. Spread the batter evenly.

BAKE until the top springs back when lightly touched with finger and the edges begin to pull away slightly from the pan, 35 to 40 minutes. Remove from the oven and invert the cake pan over a long-necked glass bottle. Let cool completely, remove from the bottle, and use a narrow spatula to loosen the cake from the pan. Place a plate over it and turn it upside down to remove the cake from the pan.

SERVE with sliced seasonal fruits such as peaches, cherries, or berries.

SERVES 6 TO 8

5 kumquats, seeded and minced

2 tablespoons water

5 large eggs, separated, at room temperature

¾ teaspoon cream of tartar

1 cup sugar

½ teaspoon salt

1 cup sifted all-purpose flour

1 teaspoon ground cinnamon

COLD WEATHER RECIPES

Winter days, dominated by nature's Earth element when cold and damp, and Water when cool and dry, can be a potential health problem for Water element people. Your extra-sensitive respiratory and circulatory systems are even more vulnerable when a cold day turns wet and gray. You are prone to catching colds, and your joints, muscles, or bones might feel achy and become stiff. Dress warmly, wear a hat and scarf to protect the head, throat, and chest areas, and pay special attention to what you eat.

Water element people who take extra precautions and nutritional remedies can enjoy cold, wintry days. Start by staying fit and limber with exercise such as walking and stretching. Get regular massages to ease the aches and pains that attack muscles and joints. Remember to drink plenty of fluids, especially vitamin-packed citrus juices and warming herbal teas. Cold days bring the blessings of seasonal sweet-tangy citrus, bitter greens, and freshly harvested grains, perfect for shielding Water element people from the effects of wet weather. The right protective remedies will keep you in good health during cold days.

BREAKFAST

Our bodies hunger for warm, comforting food such as oatmeal or cream of wheat on dark, cold mornings; add dried cranberries or tart cherries to provide the sour taste you crave. Pancakes (page 32) smothered with a fruit compote (page 34) and maple syrup make for a glorious breakfast. A Rice Porridge with Brown or White Rice (page 97) or fluffy omelet made with vegetables befitting your home element (page 37) will also light the fires within Water element people. For once, you can even indulge in rich, buttery foods such as hot chocolate or sweet muffins and cakes without feeling any guilt about extra calories. After all, your joints and muscles need that extra lubrication to balance nature's strong Earth element, which rules the season.

If you have a juice-making machine, put in an array of cold-season fruits and vegetables, such as celery, orange, grapefruit, carrot, apple, and pear, and ginger with shakes of cinnamon, nutmeg, or cloves for a heavenly drink. Or enjoy your citrus straight up—orange, grapefruit, or tangerine. For something warm, try a cup of Hot Cocoa with Almond Milk (page 47).

LUNCH

What a welcoming feeling when the sun warms up a wintry day! You are thankful to nature's Fire element for the warmth it brings during the lunch hours. Bask in it and let it fuel your appetite. To nurture your home element and to stay in balance with nature's Fire element, eat bland-flavor foods and sour-tasting fruits. Shake the chills from your circulatory system during winter days with bitter-flavor vegetables and pungent herbs and spices like garlic and peppercorns. Seasonal mushrooms and greens, needed to balance your body elements, will bloom with sprinkles of salty taste. And warm your body with curative herbs such as ginger and chiles. Try the Fried Rice on page 69, making it with crabmeat and adding 2 tablespoons of coarsely pickled garlic (available in Asian supermarkets) for a nice flavor punch.

Cold weather vegetables with buttery, astringent flavors make ideal salads for Water element people, especially when paired with your home element's love for sour tastes. Together they strengthen and lubricate the joints, bones, and tendons. Spicy chile will stimulate your appetite.

Hot soups made with healing chicken or vegetable broth will keep your Water element flowing in a steady current, strengthening both the circulatory and respiratory systems. To balance nature's Fire element, add bland- or bitter-flavor vegetables to the broth. Or indulge with a creamy and rich curry. Pick one of the recipes on pages 72 to 81. A good choice would be *Gaeng Liang* (page 94), prepared with 1 cup each bite-size chunks of pumpkin, sliced zucchini, baby corn, and quartered white or brown mushrooms. Or make chicken rice soup, adding 2 slices fresh ginger; 1 stalk lemongrass, tough outer layers removed and tender inner stalk thinly sliced and pounded; ¼ cup each diced onion, celery, and carrot; ¼ cup sliced cabbage; and 1 cup shredded cooked chicken to 4 cups boiling homemade (page 26) or canned low-sodium, low-fat chicken broth. Season with ½ teaspoon salt and 1 tablespoon fish sauce. Cover and simmer for 10 minutes, then add ½ cup cooked rice and cook over low heat for 10 to 15 minutes. Garnish with ¼ cup chopped fresh cilantro and serve with lime or lemon slices.

For a beverage, cozy up to a cup of hot rose hip, ginger, lemon balm, or lime tea with a tad of honey. Chai tea with pinches of cinnamon and nutmeg and cool pomegranate juice with a twist of orange rind are other choices.

For a midday break, stretch to stay limber before enjoying some applesauce, gingersnaps, and a cup of hot mandarin orange or mint tea.

DINNER

As the night turns colder, a hearty dinner to balance Earth element's cold, wintry weather should include piping hot soups or dishes seasoned with ginger, lemongrass, garlic, and shallots. They will warm the body and brighten the spirit. Furthermore, you need to nurture the multiplied demands from the Water element (your home element, the element of the dinner hour, and also nature's dominant element when winter days are cool and dry), which means dishes prepared with bland or bitter flavors and sour tastes. Try a spicy, rich soup or stew like *Gaeng Som* (page 92), prepared with 1 cup each tightly packed sliced zucchini, sliced beet greens, and oyster mushrooms. Fresh lime wedges are a good accompaniment; a squeeze to any dish adds zest, as well as soothing and protecting the throat and chest against the chilled air. And instead of salads made with lettuce, cold evenings call for winter vegetables packed with buttery-rich flavors or winter greens combined with pungent chiles and garlic and dressed with a sweet, fruity, creamy dressing.

Fruit pies, tarts, or warm, sweet cakes made with banana, pumpkin, sweet potato, tart cranberries, or apples are your kind of comforting desserts. Give extra sustenance to your bones, joints, and tendons with red and black beans cooked in date sugar. For Thais, creamy coconut tops the list as dessert comfort food during cold weather.

For a beverage, warm your chest with hot mint tea, or hot rice milk with a spoonful of Kumquat, Ginger, and Clove Preserves (page 100) mixed into it. Stir a glass of apple-cranberry juice with a cinnamon stick to uplift your mind and spirit.

Uncooked Thai eggplant's slightly astringent flavor matches the call from winter's Earth element. Raw baby artichoke hearts can be used as a substitute. To prevent both from browning, squeeze a bit of lemon juice on them. Both vegetables bloom with this simple Thai dressing combining tastes and flavors from the opposing elements Earth and Wind. Sour taste from your home element adds a balanced note to it all.

SHRIMP AND THAI EGGPLANT SALAD

COMBINE the salt, sugar, and fish sauce in a small saucepan over low heat. Cook until the salt and sugar are dissolved. Let cool completely, then stir in the lime juice and chiles. Set aside.

PREHEAT the broiler. In a medium bowl, combine the shrimp with the salt and pepper. Spray a baking sheet with vegetable oil spray and lay the shrimp on top in a single layer. Lightly coat the shrimp with the spray. Broil until the shrimp turn pink and are slightly charred, 5 to 6 minutes. Remove, drain away any liquid, and set aside to cool.

IN a large bowl, combine the eggplants with the lemon juice. Add the turmeric, garlic, and ginger and toss. Add the shrimp and mix well. Add the dressing and mix again. Let sit for 5 minutes, then add the cilantro. Mix and transfer to a serving platter. Serve with hot white, brown, or red rice.

DRESSING

½ teaspoon salt

1½ tablespoons sugar

3 tablespoons fish sauce

¼ cup fresh lime juice

8 fresh Thai or 3 fresh serrano chiles, minced

SALAD

1 pound medium shrimp, peeled and deveined

1 teaspoon salt

½ teaspoon white pepper

Vegetable oil spray

6 to 8 Thai eggplants, sliced paper thin, or 12 fresh artichoke hearts, sliced paper thin

1 teaspoon fresh lemon juice

1 fresh turmeric root, peeled and slivered, about 2 inches or ⅓ cup mixed carrots and peeled fresh ginger cut into matchsticks

1 clove garlic, slivered

1 tablespoon peeled and slivered fresh ginger

7 to 8 fresh cilantro sprigs, torn into pieces

Khmer means "Cambodian," and this is a traditional Cambodian salad.

KHMER SALAD Yum Khmer

PUT the sugar and fish sauce in a small saucepan over low heat. When the sugar is dissolved, add the garlic and simmer for 1 to 2 minutes. Let cool completely, then add the remaining dressing ingredients and mix well.

COMBINE the lemongrass, galangal, salt, and garlic in a small bowl. Divide the mixture in half. Rub one portion on the pork, and the other on the scallops.

PREHEAT the broiler. Spray a baking sheet with vegetable oil spray and put the pork and scallops on it. Spray with more vegetable oil spray. Broil until the scallops are firm and opaque, about 5 minutes. Remove the scallops from the sheet. Turn the broiler off, turn the oven to 375°F, return the pork to the oven, and roast until it is cooked and slightly charred, about 45 minutes. Let cool, then cut into thin slices.

BRING the almond milk to a boil in a medium saucepan, then add the endive and simmer until slightly cooked, about 1 minute. Remove the endive from the milk with a strainer to a plate.

ADD the beans to the almond milk and simmer until they are tender-crisp, about 2 minutes. Using a strainer, remove them to a medium bowl. Repeat the process with the bean sprouts, cooking them about for 1 minute and then transferring them to the bowl. Simmer the almond milk until it is reduced to a thick, creamy sauce. Add to the reserved salad dressing and mix well.

ADD the pork and scallops to the bowl with the vegetables. Toss gently. Add the arugula and jalapeño and toss again. Add the dressing, mix well, and serve.

MAKES 4 SERVINGS

DRESSING

3 tablespoons palm sugar, dark brown sugar, or maple sugar

3 tablespoons fish sauce

1 tablespoon minced garlic

2 fresh serrano chiles, minced

¼ cup fresh lime juice

SALAD

1 stalk lemongrass, tough outer layers removed, tender inner stalk minced

5 to 6 thin slices galangal or fresh ginger, minced

1 teaspoon salt

1 tablespoon minced garlic

½ pound pork tenderloin

1 pound large scallops or medium shrimp, peeled and deveined

Vegetable oil spray

2 Belgian endive, thinly sliced lengthwise

1½ cups Almond Milk (page 21) or Coconut Cream (page 22)

1 cup green beans or yard-long beans cut into matchsticks

2 cups bean sprouts

1 cup arugula, torn into pieces

1 fresh red jalapeño, slivered

Daikon turns slightly sweet when cooked and yet, at the same time, retains its nice crunchy texture. Asians love daikon for its ability to absorb and take on the flavor of other ingredients. It is also valued for its healthful benefits, including fighting inflammation and easing indigestion.

SHRIMP AND DAIKON SALAD

PUT the salt, sugar, and fish sauce in a small saucepan over low heat and heat until the salt and sugar dissolve. Let cool, then mix in the lime juice and chile. Set aside.

BRING a pot of water to a boil, salt it, and blanch the daikon for 1 to 2 minutes. Rinse with cool water, dry thoroughly, and set aside. Heat a large skillet over high heat for 1 minute. Add the oil and heat for another minute. Add the mushrooms and stir-fry until tender, 2 to 3 minutes. Add the shrimp and stir-fry until pink and firm, 2 to 3 minutes. Transfer to a bowl and let cool. Add the daikon, onion, celery, and cashews and mix well. Just before serving, mix in the salad dressing. Toss in the mint and serve.

MAKES 4 SERVINGS

DRESSING

½ teaspoon salt

1½ tablespoons sugar

2 tablespoons fish sauce

¼ cup fresh lime juice

1 to 2 tablespoons minced fresh serrano chile

SALAD

½ cup peeled and thinly sliced daikon

1 tablespoon canola, rice bran, or corn oil

1 cup oyster mushrooms cut in half lengthwise

½ pound medium shrimp, peeled and deveined

½ cup sweet onion thinly sliced into half-moons

½ cup minced Chinese or regular celery

1 cup dry-roasted unsalted cashews

½ cup torn fresh mint leaves

*I*f you love a hearty stew on a cold winter night and want to try something new, perhaps, with an Asian flavor, this particular recipe is worth making. Sour mustard greens can be bought in Asian markets or online. Because of the pickling process, after being securely sealed in plastic wrap, they keep for at least a month without refrigeration. Bean threads, made with mung beans, are sold in most major supermarkets and specialty food stores. They add a delightful texture to the stew. Warming herbs and spices used for seasoning will keep your home element in proper balance with nature's Earth element. For convenience, ask the butcher to chop the pork ribs into bite-size pieces for you.

PORK RIBS WITH SOUR MUSTARD GREENS

PUT the pork, star anise, ginger, garlic, and scallions in a large saucepan. Fill it with water to cover and bring to a boil. Reduce the heat to medium and add the remaining ingredients, except for the bean threads and sriracha. Cover and reduce the heat to medium-low. Check occasionally; if the broth has evaporated, add ½ cup water. Cook until the meat is tender, about 1 hour.

ADD the bean threads, stir to incorporate, and when the noodles are soft and transparent, 1 to 2 minutes, turn off the heat. Serve with hot white, brown, or red rice and sriracha sauce, if using. (If not serving immediately, do not add the bean threads. Turn off the heat and let cool. Refrigerate until ready to serve. It will keep overnight. Reheat over high heat. When the stew comes to a boil, lower the heat to medium and add the bean threads.)

MAKES 4 TO 6 SERVINGS

2 pounds country-style pork ribs, cut into bite-size pieces

2 to 3 star anise

5 to 6 thin slices fresh ginger

1 clove garlic

3 scallions, cut into 1-inch pieces

1 teaspoon sugar

1 teaspoon salt

1 teaspoon white peppercorns

1 tablespoon dark soy sauce

3 tablespoons regular soy sauce

One 10.5-ounce package pickled Chinese mustard greens, rinsed, dried thoroughly, and cut into bite-size pieces

½ teaspoon sesame oil

1 cup softened bean threads (page 86), cut into manageable lengths

Sriracha sauce (optional)

ealing spices such as cinnamon, nutmeg, and Sichuan peppercorns act like a blanket, shielding your chest against the cold. Garlic, chiles, and lime will do the same. Cook them with easily digested vegetables and ingredients such as tofu, potatoes, pumpkin, and/or mushrooms to help you sleep through the night.

STIR-FRIED TOFU

ADD the oil to a heated skillet over high heat. After 10 to 20 seconds, add the bean paste seasoning and stir for 10 to 20 seconds. Add the tofu and stir-fry until heated through, about 1 minute. Add the remaining ingredients, except for the scallion and cilantro, and stir until well combined, 1 to 2 minutes. Add the scallion and cilantro, mix in gently, and serve with hot white, brown, or red rice.

MAKES 4 SERVINGS

1 tablespoon canola, corn, olive, or sunflower oil

1 tablespoon Bean Paste Stir-Fry Seasoning (page 66)

One 19-ounce carton silken tofu, drained and cut into bite-size pieces

1 teaspoon Sichuan peppercorns, dry-roasted and ground (page 70)

1 tablespoon peeled and minced fresh ginger

1 teaspoon soy sauce

½ teaspoon sesame oil

1 scallion, minced

2 tablespoons chopped fresh cilantro

This is best prepared with a tender fine-flaked fish, but a firmer fish such red snapper, rock cod, or black cod can also be used.

STEAMED FISH WITH LIME, CHILES, AND GARLIC

PLACE the fish skin down in a heat-resistant pie plate.

COMBINE the broth, chiles, lime juice, and soy sauce in a small bowl, and pour over the fish. (If using canned broth, taste and adjust the seasonings accordingly.) Arrange the garlic and lime slices over the fish.

FILL a large wok at least halfway with water and bring to a boil. Put a heat-resistant rice bowl upside-down in the center. Carefully put the fish in the pie plate on top of the bowl. Cover and steam until the fish turn white and firm, about 10 minutes. Serve with hot white, brown, or red rice.

MAKES 4 SERVINGS

Two ½-pound boned trout, patted dry

¼ cup homemade (page 26) or canned low-sodium, low-fat chicken broth

2 to 4 fresh Thai or 1 to 2 fresh serrano chiles, minced

2 tablespoons fresh lime juice

2 tablespoons soy sauce

3 to 4 cloves garlic, thinly sliced

1 lime, thinly sliced

*L*ight up a bleak winter night with this grand finale of a salad. It will thaw out the deepest winter chill. Feast on a bouquet of bland-flavor mushrooms and tart-tasting orange and salad greens accentuated with spicy radish spread before succulent grilled ahi steaks, dressed with streams of aromatic Citrus Dressing (page 58).

GRILLED AHI WITH ENOKI MUSHROOMS, ORANGES, SALAD GREENS, AND RADISHES

IN a small bowl, mix together all the marinade ingredients.

PLACE the ahi in a shallow pan and pour the marinade over them. Coat well and let marinate at room temperature for 20 minutes. Meanwhile, peel the oranges with a knife over a bowl and section them to remove the pith. Save the sections along with the juice.

HEAT a grill. Generously spray the ahi with vegetable oil spray and place on the hot grill. Brush the tops with the marinade and spray again with the vegetable oil spray. After 2 minutes, flip the ahi over. Spoon the marinade over the top again and spray again with vegetable oil spray. After 2 minutes, flip the ahi over again and coat with the marinade and spray. Repeat the process after a minute or two. For rare ahi, cook for 6 minutes total, for medium rare, 7 to 8 minutes. Remove from the grill.

COMBINE the mushrooms, salad greens, radishes, and mint in a medium bowl. Toss with about ¼ cup of the citrus dressing; divide between four salad plates. Arrange the orange slices on top of the salad. Slice the ahi into ½-inch pieces and place them over the orange slices. Drizzle the remaining 2 tablespoons salad dressing over the ahi and serve.

MAKES 4 SERVINGS

MARINADE

1 kumquat, minced, or 1 tablespoon grated orange zest

1 tablespoon light miso

1 tablespoon peeled and minced fresh ginger

2 tablespoons soy sauce

½ teaspoon sesame oil

¼ cup fresh lemon juice

2 tablespoons minced fresh cilantro

SALAD

1 pound ahi steaks

3 navel oranges

Vegetable oil spray

1 cup enoki mushrooms or thinly sliced white mushrooms

2 cups salad greens

1 cup thinly sliced radishes

¼ cup fresh mint leaves, torn into pieces

6 tablespoons Citrus Dressing (page 58)

*T*his is my friend Patty Clark's recipe. She is the only other Asian person I know who shared my experience of growing up in a small Kentucky town. She has been making this pudding for more than four decades from the original recipe (which is written on an old envelope) and using the same pan. There is something about persimmons that Asians go wild over. Aside from its brilliant and jewel-like color, persimmon's sweet and gelatin-like texture is packed with fiber and vitamins. Lemon sauce is the perfect taste for Water element people, especially on a cool evening. This recipe works best if you have a traditional pudding pan about 6 inches wide at the base, 7 inches wide at the top rim, and 2 inches deep, with a lid. For a substitute, use any ovenproof round pan with the same depth as the pudding pan, preferably with a lid. If you don't have a lid, you can use heavy-duty aluminum foil to cover the pan.

STEAMED PERSIMMON PUDDING WITH WARM LEMON SAUCE

PREHEAT the oven to 375°F. Fill a roasting pan big enough to hold the pudding pan halfway full with hot water and set in the oven. Grease the pudding pan and dust it lightly with flour.

SIFT the dry ingredients together in a small bowl. Beat the egg and sugar together with an electric mixer at high speed in a large bowl until smooth and lemony in color. With the mixer running, add the vanilla and milk. Add the persimmon pulp and continue to beat. Fold in the dry ingredients ⅓ cup at a time. Continue to beat until the ingredients are well incorporated. Add the melted butter, prunes, and raisins and continue to beat until the mixture is smooth and a bit more liquidy than cake batter. Pour into the prepared pudding pan. Cover with the lid or seal well with heavy-duty aluminum foil. Carefully set it in the pan of hot water in the oven. Bake until a toothpick in the center comes out clean, about 1 hour and 20 minutes. Remove the pudding from the stove and from the pan of water. Cover the top with wax paper and a plate to keep warm. When ready to serve, remove the wax paper and invert the pudding onto the plate.

IF making ahead, invert the pudding while it's still lukewarm onto a plate lined with wax paper. Wrap it with wax paper. Wrap once again in aluminum foil, place in a plastic bag, and refrigerate for up to several weeks.

MAKES 4 TO 6 SERVINGS

PUDDING

1 cup all-purpose flour, plus more for dusting the pan

½ teaspoon salt

1 teaspoon baking soda

1 teaspoon baking powder

1 teaspoon ground cinnamon

½ teaspoon ground ginger

½ teaspoon freshly grated nutmeg

1 large egg, slightly beaten

1 cup sugar

1 teaspoon vanilla extract

½ cup 2% or nonfat milk

1 cup Hachiya persimmon pulp (from about 2 ripe persimmons)

TO make the sauce, beat the egg and water together in a medium bowl and set aside. Fill the bottom of a double boiler halfway with water and bring to a boil. Put the sugar and butter in the upper pan of the double boiler and set over the boiling water. Reduce the heat to medium and stir to mix until the butter melts. Add the lemon zest and juice and mix well. Reduce the heat to low and add the egg mixture. Mix and stir to incorporate. Make certain that the heat is low enough that the egg doesn't curdle. Continue to whisk until the mixture thickens slightly, about 20 minutes.

REMOVE the sauce from the heat and serve warm over slices of the pudding. (If making ahead, refrigerate. It will keep for a couple of weeks. To reheat, warm in the top of the double boiler or spoon a couple of spoonfuls directly onto individual slices of pudding, microwave for 30 seconds, and serve warm.)

2 tablespoons unsalted butter, melted

1 cup chopped pitted prunes

1 cup dark or golden raisins

LEMON SAUCE

1 large egg

¼ cup water

1 cup sugar

½ pound (2 sticks) unsalted butter

Grated zest and juice of 1 lemon

BLISS

It is the custom among some older Thais to have their fortune told at the beginning of the new year. Once, a friend took me to have my future read by an elderly monk who lived in a remote Buddhist temple in the province of Petchburi. I had experienced a sad, difficult year, and my friend thought a prediction of bright future prospects might cheer me up, even though I was fearful and nervous about the outcome. The old monk sat on the shiny wooden floor in front of an immense altar crowded with several golden statues of Buddha. Framed by stacks of books and pictures of him and his flock, he smiled through thick reading glasses as my friend told him of my misgivings. He asked only for my birth date and to study the palms of my hands. After flipping through a couple of well-worn books and scribbling on a notebook, he looked up at me and spoke gently, "To travel through the labyrinth of the innumerable courses of the river, a person can forget the way and become lost. Such could also be said of our journey through life. Visualize the river that flows past the debris, channeling through obstruction. You, too, can learn to live with the flow of life. You can channel past the 'context,' which colors your thoughts and feelings. Live in the moment and believe in your generous loving spirit. You shall understand the reason for this moment of sadness and despair."

Like the flowing stream of the river, being in the moment is the life path for Water element people. Love is your vision, which you feel and give generously. Love also shines through your work and your steadfast commitment to high performance. To attain bliss, live by your mantra, "being in the moment." Make quiet time for reflection. Pamper yourself to rejuvenate body, mind, and spirit.

YOUR PHYSICAL SELF

Keep your delicate and beautiful body in shape all year round by exercising regularly and pampering yourself with skin, hair, and nail treatments. You will retain your youthful physique and be an envy of your friends.

The skin of Water element people, especially the face, is susceptible to harsh weather changes. A weekly facial mask helps keep the skin moist. After washing, apply the toner and lotion as a nightly ritual. It will keep your skin supple and youthful. ⁓⦵ Fresh almond puree, the solid residue from the extraction of Almond Milk (page 21), is the best treatment for chapped or dry skin. This mask will do more than cleanse the skin; as you relax, the scents of geranium and lemongrass will soothe and calm the mind.

ALMOND PUREE, GERANIUM, LEMONGRASS, AND HONEY FACE MASK

COMBINE all the ingredients in a small bowl. Stir vigorously to mix well. Wash and dry your face before applying the mask. Be careful to avoid contact with your eyes. Lie down, relax, and leave the mask on for 15 to 20 minutes. Rinse it off and gently dry your face. Use the Lemongrass Skin Toner before applying a moisturizer of your choice.

MAKES 1 APPLICATION

2 tablespoons Lemongrass Skin Toner (recipe follows)

2 tablespoons almond puree (page 21)

7 drops geranium essential oil

1 tablespoon honey

*T*his marvelous toner is best made from freshly picked lemongrass. I recommend you grow your own, as it grows easily, even in pots. To use, cut a stalk or two just above the dirt. New sprouts will appear in a week or two. Lemongrass toner opens facial pores, allowing for a deep cleansing, while at the same time disinfecting the skin. Refreshing, invigorating, and soothing, it leaves the skin with a cleansed afterglow. I have used it every day for years. I make a fresh batch every 3 weeks. Instead of discarding any of the old batch that is left, I use it as a hair rinse, massaging it into my scalp and hair after shampooing. I leave it on while showering before rinsing. It will leave your hair fresh smelling and shiny.

LEMONGRASS SKIN TONER

PUT the lemongrass and water in a blender, cover, and blend at high speed for 1 to 2 minutes. Pause for a minute and repeat. Do this twice more, or until the lemongrass turns to pulp. Transfer the contents to a 12 inch square of cheesecloth draped over a small storage container. Cover and refrigerate for 30 minutes. Squeeze to extract the liquid. Store the liquid in a bottle with a secure cap and refrigerate. Keep the pulp to use in a compress to relieve aching muscles. (Add to the pulp ½ cup bruised fresh peppermint leaves and 5 drops each of benzion, sage, and coriander essential oils. Wrap cheesecloth around this mixture and microwave for 30 seconds. Knead in a circular motion around the affected areas for 10 minutes. Repeat every 3 to 4 hours two to three more times, putting the compress in a container in the refrigerator between treatments, then discard.)

WASH and dry your face. Shake the bottle well before applying the toner with a cotton pad. Rub in a circular motion, especially around the eyes, temples, and the creases around the nose and lips, moving downward toward the neck. Apply facial moisturizer.

THIS toner can also be combined with other herbs and essential oils to make other treatments. For example, for deep facial cleansing, combine 2 tablespoons lemongrass toner with 1 tablespoon fine rice flour, 1 tablespoon mashed avocado, and 2 drops each of geranium and ylang-ylang essential oils. Mix well and apply to the face and neck area. Be careful not to get it into your eyes. Lie down, close your eyes, and empty your mind of worry and concern for 10 minutes. Wash your face with cool water, pat it dry, and apply the moisturizer of your choice.

MAKES ABOUT ½ CUP

2 stalks lemongrass, tough outer layers removed, tender inner stalk finely chopped (about 1 cup)

½ cup distilled water

The delicate, soft skin of Water element people can become parched and dry. Scrub away the dead skin with a loofah or a brush, then apply this for a vigorous body scrub. ∽⧗ Sit on a chair or a stool in your shower or bathtub. Apply this heavenly paste all over your body, and breathe in the soothing lavender fragrance. Let the paste work its magic on your skin while its lavender scent calms and relaxes you.

ALMOND AND LAVENDER BODY SCRUB

REMOVE the lavender flowers and leaves from the stems, put them in a mortar, and pound them into a paste. Transfer to a bowl; mix in the almond puree and milk and lavender essential oil.

THE paste is dry, so it will flake easily. Gather up the loose paste and work it into your skin. Rub in a circular motion all over your body, face, and hair. Sit back, close your eyes, and breathe in the heavenly fragrance. Leave the paste on for at least 10 minutes before rinsing and showering.

MAKES 1 APPLICATION

5 to 6 sprigs fresh lavender

¼ cup almond puree (page 21)

¼ cup Almond Milk (page 21)

8 drops lavender essential oil

I created this cool, refreshing mask for my daughter, Angela, who needed it after long days of surfing in the hot sun. After showering, Angela applied the mask to her face and neck, then covered her eyes with cucumber slices. The mask replenished her skin with moisture lost from being in the sun. She glowed with radiance. Aloe vera juice can be bought in health food stores.

CUCUMBER, ALOE VERA, AND CARROT FACE MASK

PLACE all the ingredients in a blender and puree at high speed until smooth. Wash and dry your face before applying the mask, taking care not to get it in your eyes. Lie down, close your eyes, and place two cucumber slices over your eyes. Relax; empty your mind of worry and anxiety. Leave the mask on for 15 to 20 minutes. Wash and dry your face before applying Lemongrass Skin Toner (page 196). Rejuvenate the skin with the moisturizer of your choosing.

STORE the remaining mask mixture in an airtight container in the refrigerator. Apply it again in a couple of days. Better yet, share the remaining mask mixture with friends who have a Water or Wind home element.

MAKES 4 APPLICATIONS

½ cup peeled and chopped cucumber

2 tablespoons aloe vera juice or 1 tablespoon chopped fresh aloe vera

1 tablespoon fine rice flour

2 tablespoons finely chopped carrot

2 tablespoons plain yogurt

10 drops rose otto, rosewood, or rose absolute essential oil

10 drops sweet orange essential oil (for daytime use) or wild chamomile essential oil (for evening use)

*T*ired feet and hands will spring to life after a soak in this perfumed water.

LEMONGRASS, KAFFIR LIME, LAVENDER SPRIG, AND ROSE PETAL SOAK

FILL 2 small basins with warm water. Divide the ingredients, except for the lime, into two equal portions; scatter them into the basins. Squeeze the lime halves to extract the juice, adding the juice of one half to each basin. Use one of the basins to soak your feet and the other to soak your hands. Scrub and massage your hands and feet with the ingredients. Close your eyes, breathe in the wonderful perfume, and relax. When the water is cool, dry your hands and feet. Massage them with Almond Oil Infusion with Sage or Lavender Essential Oil (see page 200).

MAKES 1 APPLICATION

2 to 3 stalks lemongrass, tough outer layers removed, tender inner stalk thinly sliced and slightly pounded

12 kaffir lime leaves, slightly bruised, or grated zest of 2 to 3 limes

12 fresh lavender sprigs, slightly bruised

Petals from 3 fresh roses, bruised

1 kaffir or regular lime, cut in half

Almond oil softens skin while the sweet, warming scents of sage and lavender ease tense muscles, banishing stress.

ALMOND OIL INFUSION WITH SAGE OR LAVENDER ESSENTIAL OIL

MIX the ingredients together in a glass bottle. Tighten the lid and shake well to combine. Massage the oil into hands and feet. Leave it on for at least 1 hour or longer.

MAKES ¼ CUP

¼ cup almond oil

12 drops sage or lavender essential oil

This is an old Thai remedy used by housewives and farmers to treat calloused areas.

LIME AND BROWN SUGAR CALLUS TREATMENT FOR FEET

DIP one half of a lime into a bowl of the sugar, then rub in a circular motion around the calloused area for 5 to 7 minutes, dipping the lime back in the sugar as needed and using up the other lime halves as they lose their juice. Rinse and dry. Massage the area with Almond Oil Infusion with Sage or Lavender Essential Oil (see above).

MAKES 1 APPLICATION

1 to 2 limes, cut in half

¼ cup firmly packed brown sugar or palm sugar

$\mathcal{H}$air can become dry and brittle with age or from the use of coloring chemicals. Regular care keeps it shiny and healthy. Thai women combine kaffir lime and honey to maintain the luster in their hair. Although Water element people are usually blessed with beautiful hair, it is important to care for it. Treat yourself to this rich hair-care treatment once a month. Your hair will be the envy of your friends and hairdresser.

ALMOND, LEMONGRASS, KAFFIR LIME, ORANGE RIND, AND HONEY HAIR TREATMENT

PUT all the ingredients in a blender and puree at high speed until smooth. Wet, then towel dry your hair. Apply the paste generously to the hair, and massage it into your scalp. Wrap a warm, wet towel around your hair; leave it on for at least 10 minutes before rinsing. Shampoo and dry your hair.

STORE any remaining treatment in an airtight container and refrigerate. Repeat after 2 to 3 days.

MAKES 1 TO 2 APPLICATIONS

3 tablespoons almond puree (page 21)

¼ cup Almond Milk (page 21)

1 stalk lemongrass, tough outer layers removed, tender inner stalk minced and pounded

Zest of 1 kaffir or regular lime, minced

Zest of 1 orange, minced

1 tablespoon honey

mind and spirit

"The highest goodness is like water. Water is beneficent to all things but does not contend. It stays in places others despise. Therefore it is near Tao (the way)." This writing of Lao Tze, a Chinese sage, in the book *Tao Te Ching*, describes the mind and spirit of the Water element person.

To flow with the path of life, one remembers that the well of goodness and love is bountiful. Love begins with loving yourself. Begin the day with quiet time in a space where you find serenity. Surround the space with treasured objects. Perfume the room with one or two of these scents. Use them as your guide when you buy soaps, bath oil, face toner, or body lotions, which will usher in *suk-sabai,* or happiness.

BENZOIN: Sweet, warm, and soothing, it eases tired muscles.

CORIANDER: This is a sweet, warm, and spicy stimulant to combat fatigue and lethargy.

GERANIUM: A warming stimulant, it helps reduce inflammation. It's especially good to lessen the blues during menstruation.

HONEYSUCKLE: It restores hope and is a preventative against sadness and longing for the past.

LAVENDER: It has a restorative, calming effect and the ability to lessen stress or sluggishness. Lavender eases one into a restful sleep; try it in a sachet tucked into your pillowcase.

SAGE: Warm and spicy, sage relieves work-related stress and also relieves the sluggishness one can feel during menstruation and the restlessness and unsettledness one can feel during menopause. It also aids in healing colds and congestion.

YLANG-YLANG: Earthy and warm, it is especially good for hair and skin, soothing insect bites, easing insomnia, and stimulating the circulatory system.

MASSAGE

I give myself the gift of a regular massage every few weeks to lessen those aches and pains that have become more frequent as I get older. A professional, therapeutic massage relaxes and rejuvenates me, since like many Water element people I have a tendency to overwork.

Try getting a massage and relaxing afterward. Let the massage oil penetrate your skin for at least an hour before showering. Remember to drink plenty of fluid afterward to detoxify your system and prevent soreness from vigorous massage.

FOR MINOR MUSCLE ACHES AND PAINS: Combine ½ cup flaxseed oil or mustard oil with 8 drops benzoin essential oil and 8 drops sage essential oil. Seal tightly and shake well; it will keep for at least a month. Massage into the affected areas or where the body is experiencing stress.

TO CALM AND RELIEVE STRESS: Combine ½ cup almond oil with 10 drops each coriander and lavender essential oils. Or, combine ½ cup almond oil with 5 drops each lavender, rose, jasmine, and ylang-ylang essential oils. Seal tightly and shake well. Apply to your body, especially your face around your temples and neck.

SACHETS

Create lovely sachet pouches with perfumed cotton balls wrapped in handkerchiefs and tied with ribbons and lace. Hang them in closets or place them in dresser drawers. Wrap dried sprigs of lavender or perfumed blossoms in silk gauze to freshen and scent your intimate apparel.

FOR DRAWERS: Sprigs of lavender blossoms and leaves (sweet, warming, and uplifting)

FOR CLOTHING CLOSETS: 10 drops each lavender (uplifting), honeysuckle (restorative), or ylang-ylang (soothing) essential oils

FOR PILLOWS AND BED: Lavender mist (refreshing and calming) by combining 6 drops lavender essential oil with 2 oz. drinking water

FOR WORK AREAS: 10 drops each coriander (stimulating), geranium (rejuvenating), or sage (stress relieving) essential oils

TRADITIONAL REMEDIES FOR MINOR AILMENTS

These remedies are prescribed for the Water element people in Thai folk medicine, to help speed recovery. Combine them with prescribed medications.

FOR MINOR BRUISES: Combine 3 cups Asiatic pennywort leaves; 3 stalks lemongrass, tough outer layers removed, tender inner stalk minced; and 1 cup water in a blender and puree. Line a strainer with several layers of cheesecloth and strain the mixture. Save the liquid to drink. Tie up the cheesecloth to secure the mixture inside. Heat it in the microwave for 40 seconds. Massage the area in circular motions with the hot compress until the compress cools. Repeat several times a day for 3 to 4 days. Between treatments, store the compress in a container with a lid and refrigerate. Discard the compress after 3 to 4 treatments.

FOR COLDS: Process a 2-inch chunk of fresh ginger and 6 star anise together in a food processor until reduced to paste. Transfer the paste to the center of a square of cheesecloth and add 8 drops sage essential oil. Tie up the cheesecloth to secure the mixture inside. Heat in the microwave for 40 seconds. Rub the hot cloth in circular motions around the chest and throat area until the cloth cools. Repeat 2 to 3 times a day for a couple of days. If the symptoms persist, start another compress. Use for a week.

CHAPTER FIVE

Lom, or wind, is revered by Thai people as the breath of nature, its energy and force. Wind is also the symbol for our own breath. For those with Wind as your home element, your health rides on the even, flowing stream of your breath. According to Thai healers, on most days, you are lighthearted and free-spirited, like the gentle trade winds. In Thailand and other tropical countries, this breezy air relieves the sticky humidity that weighs us down and challenges our spirit. We are grateful for the wind's quiet and reassuring presence, even if it teases us with occasional stirrings that bring only a brief relief. But when the month of June approaches, however, the wind changes its course and arrives as a mighty force, ushering in the monsoon season. During the rainy season, the wind becomes fickle and powerful. Clouds spread like wet, heavy blankets over the sky. Then the stagnant air, pregnant with moisture, begins to change. The light breeze gathers its strength and, picking up more energy, sends crescendos of thunder exploding into fiery flashes of lighting. For a split second, there's silence. Then it starts. A droplet here, one there. The wind begins to howl, throwing around sheets of heavy, elephant-size raindrops, drumming its deafening, artillery-like musical chorus on the roofs and streets below.

Like the monsoon wind, your usually carefree nature as a creative, artistic, passionate, and perceptive person can change without warning. All of a sudden, you can become forgetful, restless, anxious, or melancholy. "The reason," Thai folk doctors as my mentor and friend, Dr. Pennapa, explained, "is because fear is Wind people's worst enemy. It can grab you unexpectedly, affecting your most vulnerable areas: the heart, central nervous and circulatory systems. When this occurs, you suffer an emotional and spiritual storm, as well as severe stress to your digestive system."

Learn to breathe deeply and evenly when you feel turbulent stirrings of emotions. Channel the gathering storm into creative and artistic endeavors. Another alternative is to seek a quiet haven where you can calm the fear and rein in the storm. You can also lessen your "monsoon gale" before its onset by expending excess energy through regular exercise. Dancing and aerobics, accompanied by music, or water ballet are not just good workouts, they are also ways for you to release tension and revel in your artistic nature.

Since some of you are light sleepers, a bedtime ritual will help you get a long, uninterrupted night's sleep. Invest in a comfortable bed with luxurious sheets and blankets. Take a hot bath infused with calming and relaxing herbal oil, read a book, or find your own routine that will help soothe you to sleep. Since you are sensitive to noise, situate your bedroom in a quiet place, where you are less likely to be disturbed. A Wind element friend of mine wears earplugs to bed every night.

WIND

FOOD FOR HEALTH

To better control and balance the forces of your home element, take heart and adopt some of the Water element's ways. According to the Thai healers, Wind and Water home elements are closely linked and have similar characteristics because the months in which they are born follow sequentially.

Many Wind element people think of eating as a necessary chore. An artist friend is such a person. If not for friends who love food, he would be happy eating alone, snacking on whatever is left over in the refrigerator. Often distracted or preoccupied, he eats while painting, talking on the telephone, or watching television.

If you have eating habits like my friend's and were to consult a Thai folk doctor, he would gently suggest that you change your ways. This is because when, how, and what you eat can help settle and calm your windy disposition. He would advise that you schedule regular mealtimes as well as enjoy healthy snacks between breakfast and lunch and again between lunch and dinner, since such snacking is better suited to your disposition. Eat less red meat, and avoid hard-to-digest foods such as clams, oysters, and mussels. Instead, eat foods that lessen gastric irritability or bloating such as melons, seedless cucumbers, jicama, bamboo shoots, fresh peas, and lettuce. Stay clear of gas-producing vegetables such as cabbage, Brussels sprouts, and cauliflower, or minimize their effects by cooking them with herbs and spices such as caraway, cardamom, cumin, mint, or ginger. Root vegetables, including potatoes and sweet potatoes, are easier on your digestive tract, as are carrots, though you're better off enjoying them cooked rather than raw. Wheat, rice, and oats are among the nourishing grains your body needs. While beans aren't a good food source for you, with the exception of mung beans, if you do choose to eat them, soaking them overnight before cooking them will eliminate their gas-producing tendencies. Almonds, walnuts, pecans, pine nuts, and sesame seeds are good choices for their monounsaturated and polyunsaturated fats and

omega 3 oil, all of which are good for the heart. Sesame, almond, rice bran, soybean, and olive oils are better for your sensitive digestive system. Yogurt and warm soy milk can be soothing and settling, while coffee's astringent flavor might not agree with your digestive and nervous systems.

When it comes to selecting fruits, herbs, spices, and vegetables, Thai healers recommend spicy and cool/refreshing flavors for Wind element people. Aside from being the perfect match for you, they're perhaps the most important ingredients in Thai regional cooking, because they balance our bodies against the abrupt climate changes, such as unpredictable shifts in the wind, that affect circulatory, nervous, and digestive systems.

Spicy flavors, especially in herbs and spices, soothe the body's gastric juices, lessening bloating and indigestion while heightening appetite. Spicy is also good for joints and bones, another sensitive area of Wind element people, and chiles in particular are good for the circulatory system. Cool/refreshing flavors, on the other hand, nurture Wind element people's tender hearts, calming sensitive emotions and easing tension and feelings of exhaustion. Rice, the most important Thai food source, is classified as cool and refreshing and is the perfect food for Wind people.

HOT WEATHER RECIPES

Warm, sunny days lure Wind element people into the open air, like bees drawn to nectar. You feel relaxed, energized with the urge to live, work, eat, and sleep outdoors.

When it comes to eating, remember that in hot weather nature's Fire element dominates. To steady your Wind element against its fiery force, combine Fire element's bland, bitter, and cool/refreshing (also your flavor) fruits and vegetables with your home element's spicy flavor. Some of you would be perfectly happy living on simple, no-fuss foods such as cool summer melons and fruits, salads, or yogurts. You should add a bit of pizzazz to help you to fare better

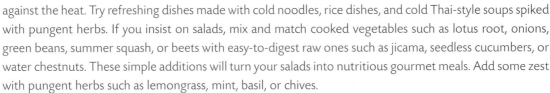

against the heat. Try refreshing dishes made with cold noodles, rice dishes, and cold Thai-style soups spiked with pungent herbs. If you insist on salads, mix and match cooked vegetables such as lotus root, onions, green beans, summer squash, or beets with easy-to-digest raw ones such as jicama, seedless cucumbers, or water chestnuts. These simple additions will turn your salads into nutritious gourmet meals. Add some zest with pungent herbs such as lemongrass, mint, basil, or chives.

Go light on dishes that use large quantities of chiles. Eat sour fruits and sweet, rich desserts in moderation, unless you plan to spend the rest of the day on the sofa. Sour- and sweet-tasting foods will exacerbate fluctuations in your body temperature, something to which Wind element people are already predisposed.

Drink plenty of slightly sweet, refreshing juices such as apple, carrot, or pear. Plain water with mint sprigs and slices of peeled seedless cucumber, or with a tablespoon of orange blossom syrup, will refresh your heart and uplift your spirits. A cup of lemongrass or mint tea will feel like a fresh breeze, keeping you well hydrated and cool.

BREAKFAST

Wind element people are blessed with an abundance of imagination and creativity, which can cause them to jump right into the day, without thought of breakfast. This is a mistake. Give fuel to your passions and enjoy a summer melon smoothie such as Mumbo Jumbo Melon and Banana Smoothie (page 39) or a scrambled egg with finely chopped basil. Other choices might be a breakfast cereal topped with fresh berries or banana, applesauce mixed with yogurt and garnished with a tad of honey and fresh fruit, or sourdough or whole-wheat toast spread with apple or pear butter.

Go easy on sour-tasting fruits such as grapefruit or orange; for breakfast drinks, enjoy apple, pear, or a blend of carrot, apple, and celery juice with a sprig of mint instead. Although you need a touch of sourness to balance nature's Water element, which governs the breakfast hours, too much might spike your body's temperature. Eat cooked sweet and cool/refreshing summer fruits such as peaches, plums, and nectarines—perfumed with orange zest, they will energize you, despite the sweltering heat. Any of these breakfast choices can also be eaten as a midday snack before lunch.

LUNCH

Have you noticed that on some hot summer days, as the sun glides steadily to the top of the sky, the wind seems to slowly disappear? As a Wind person, it behooves you to act like the wind, making a hasty retreat when the sun peaks. Nature's Fire element rules this time of day, so stay and work in cool, shaded areas.

When lunchtime arrives, eat a light, restorative meal to ease your digestion and steady your heart and mind. Shapes and colors, even in food, are important considerations for artistic-minded Wind element types. Think about lunching on cool, calming colored fruits and vegetables combined with bland- and clean/refreshing-tasting ones, like cucumbers, radishes, artichokes, peas, lettuce, grapes, watermelon, and summer melons. Spice your selections with white pepper, mint, basil, ginger, or lemongrass. Try Fried Rice (page 69) prepared with baby shrimp; omit the cubed vegetables and substitute fresh mint for the cilantro. Enjoy small portions of refreshing soups made with cucumbers or summer squashes and salads with tangy dressings, like Northeastern Thai Salad (page 53), made with carrots, tart green apple, and seedless cucumber, or a salad of diced grilled chicken, diced grilled beets, and arugula tossed with Citrus Dressing (page 58) and garnished with toasted pine nuts.

For beverages, flavor ice water with slices of peeled seedless cucumber and sprigs of mint. Carrot and sweet melon juices are tasty and refreshing. On hot days, warm Lemongrass Tea (page 46), Chrysanthemum Tea (page 46), or rose hip, jasmine, or orange tea provides comforting relief for your easily overtaxed digestion.

A midday snack is an important fueling stop for Wind element people. It keeps you operating at normal speed without running out of gas. Given your tendency to spend life in the fast lane, take a breather with a calming Popsicle or some yogurt and cut-up fresh fruit. To keep your motor running, try the tasty Thai snack *Mieng Khum* (page 48) or top chilled chunks of watermelon with Grated Fresh Coconut (page 101), toasted and coarsely ground sesame seeds, a little sugar, and a pinch of salt.

DINNER

You love gathering with friends and family on summer nights when the sky is blanketed with stars. Play sweet melodic music, place lit candles everywhere, and adorn the dinner table with fresh flowers. If there is a chilling breeze, cloak yourself with a mixture of sweet-, sour-, and bland-flavor seasonal fruits and vegetables—they will stave off a possible cold caused by the evening's dominant Water element. Oranges, pineapples, peaches, plums, grapes, and berries along with sorrel, watercress, green beans, carrots, mushrooms, and peas are the best choices.

Further temper the seasonal heat with your home element's spicy-flavor herbs such as mint or basil. A salad embellished with tastes of cool and pungent herbs will whet your appetite, balance your body's elements, and bring *sabai* (happiness) to your spirit.

The night also calls for a richly flavored soup or curry, seasoned with aromatic herbs and spices to arouse your appetite. As you relish each bite, with its alluring combination of pungent spices blended with cool/refreshing-tasting ones, your home element will be blissfully buoyed, even in the midst of the domineering Water and Fire elements. Try *Gaeng Koa* (page 72), increasing the palm sugar in the curry broth to 1 tablespoon and adding for main ingredients 2 cups fresh pineapple chunks and 2 cups peeled and deveined medium shrimp.

For a beverage, a blend of cherry and pear juice with orange slices, a half portion of ice tea mixed with a half portion of orange juice, or hot green or hibiscus tea will comfort the body and the mind.

TASTE	VEGETABLES	FRUITS	HERBS/SPICES	GRAINS	
SPICY	Green onion, onion, horseradish, leek, nasturtium, shallot, turnip		Chile, galangal, garlic, ginger, paprika, peppercorn		
SPICY/AROMATIC			Cardamom, cinnamon, cumin, fennel, nutmeg, mace, sage, Sichuan peppercorn		
SPICY/ASTRINGENT			Marjoram, turmeric		
COOL/REFRESHING			Borage, pandanus		
COOL/REFRESHING/AROMATIC			Lemon balm, lemongrass, lemon verbena		
COOL/REFRESHING/ ASTRINGENT	Lotus root, pea shoot				
COOL/REFRESHING/BITTER	Bitter melon, bitter salad mix, frisée		Asiatic pennywort, aloe vera		
COOL/REFRESHING/BLAND	Bamboo shoot, bean sprout, bok choy, Boston bibb lettuce, butter lettuce, Chinese okra, cucumber, green leaf lettuce, iceberg lettuce, okra, Napa cabbage, red leaf lettuce, romaine lettuce, summer squashes, tatsoi, watermelon rind, water spinach, winter melon				
COOL/REFRESHING/SPICY	Daikon, mache, radish, watercress				
COOL/REFRESHING/SPICY/ AROMATIC	Chinese chive, chive		Italian basil, Thai basil, cilantro, culantro, dill, peppermint, spearmint, parsley, tarragon, thyme		
COOL/REFRESHING/SWEET	Fennel bulb	Jicama, canary melon, cantaloupe, Crenshaw, honeydew, loquat, sugarcane, water chestnut, watermelon			
BUTTERY				Oat, wheat	
BUTTERY/ASTRINGENT					
BUTTERY/BITTER					
BUTTERY/COOL/REFRESHING				Rice	
BUTTERY/SWEET					
AROMA					
SPICY/AROMATIC					
SPICY/AROMATIC/WARMING					
WARMING					
SWEET/AROMATIC					
AROMATIC/ASTRINGENT					
SWEET					

SEEDS/NUTS	BEANS/LEGUMES	COOKING OILS	ESSENTIAL OILS	SEASONINGS
Mustard				
Pecan, pine	Mung, soy	Almond, olive, sesame, soy		
Walnut				
Black sesame, white sesame				
Almond				
			Basil, lemongrass, peppermint, spearmint	
			Caraway	
			Mustard, tea tree, turmeric	
			Bergamot, Melissa, absolute, rose otto, rosewood, rose absolute	
			Lemon, lime, sweet orange	
			Mandarin	

*C*ool, refreshing cucumber blended with anise, fragrant fennel, a blush of oniony taste from the leek, and the bold, peppery flavor of mint restores Wind element to a state of peace and contentment. This soup actually tastes better the next day.

MINTY CUCUMBER SOUP

HEAT a medium skillet over high heat for 1 minute, then add the oil. Add the sliced cucumbers, leek, and fennel; reduce the heat to medium-high and cook, stirring, until translucent. Add all but 3 to 4 mint leaves, the salt, and sugar. Stir and cook until the mint leaves turn limp, then add the flour and stir to incorporate. Slowly add the broth; continue to stir and mix well. (If using canned broth, taste and adjust the seasonings accordingly.) Cover and simmer over medium heat for 20 minutes.

CAREFULLY transfer the hot soup to a food processor and puree. While the machine is running, add the pepper, almond milk, and 2 tablespoons of the lemon juice through the feed tube. Transfer to a medium bowl and add the grated cucumber. Cover and chill in the refrigerator for at least 4 hours.

IN a small bowl, combine the honey, yogurt, and the remaining 1 tablespoon lemon juice. Mince the remaining mint leaves and fold into the mixture. When ready to serve, spoon the chilled soup into chilled serving bowls. Garnish with the yogurt mixture and serve.

MAKES 4 SERVINGS

1 tablespoon olive or rice bran oil

3 large cucumbers, peeled, seeded, and thinly sliced

1 leek (white part only), washed thoroughly to remove grit and chopped

¼ cup chopped fennel bulb

½ cup fresh mint leaves

2 teaspoons salt

1 teaspoon sugar

1 tablespoon all-purpose flour

2 cups homemade (page 26) or canned low-sodium, low-fat chicken broth

¼ teaspoon white pepper

1 cup Almond Milk (page 21)

3 tablespoons fresh lemon juice

1 large cucumber, peeled, seeded, and grated on the largest holes of a box grater

1 tablespoon honey

¼ cup low-fat plain yogurt

Grilling fruits coaxes out their natural sweetness with a brush of smoky aroma, drawing the Wind element people to the dinner table.

GRILLED PEACH AND PINEAPPLE SALAD

HEAT the grill to medium.

TOAST the almond slivers in a small skillet over medium heat, shaking the pan, until lightly brown. Let cool.

BRING a pot of water to a boil. Drop the peaches into the boiling water for 1 to 2 minutes, transfer to ice water to cool, then slip off the skins. Slice each in half to remove the stone. Put the peach halves and pineapple rings on a fine-mesh rack set on the grill rack and grill until the outer surface is slightly charred, turning them once, 7 to 10 minutes total. Transfer to a plate to cool before slicing the peaches into thin half-moons and the pineapples into cubes.

COMBINE the fruits in large bowl. Add the lemongrass and watercress and toss lightly. Add the dressing and toss again. Transfer to a serving platter, garnish with the goat cheese and almond slivers, and serve.

MAKES 4 SERVINGS

2 tablespoons slivered almonds

1 to 2 ripe peaches

5 pineapple rings

1 stalk lemongrass, tough outer layers removed, tender inner stalk minced

3 cups loosely packed watercress, torn into pieces

¼ cup or more Citrus Dressing (page 58)

⅓ cup crumbled goat cheese

CHINESE SAUSAGE SALAD

Don't feel much like cooking when the weather is too hot to bear? All you need is this salad with some crackers or bread on the side. It has all the taste, flavor, and aroma you need to satisfy your home element and balance nature's Fire element and Water element.

MIX the dressing ingredients together in a small bowl and set aside. (This will keep, refrigerated, in an airtight container for a day or two. Taste before using. The lime juice might lose its sourness. Add more to balance.)

IF using Chinese sausage, soak them in lukewarm water to cover for 10 minutes. Dry thoroughly with paper towels. Line a toaster oven pan with aluminum foil. Puncture the sausages with a fork. Put them on the pan and broil until slightly charred, about 5 minutes. Remove from the toaster oven, turn the uncooked side upward, and broil until slightly charred, another 5 minutes. If using chicken-and-apple sausage, grill on a stovetop grill pan or an outdoor grill. Let cool enough to touch. Slice into thin diagonal pieces and set aside.

WHEN ready to eat, put the cucumber, tomatoes, onion, and kaffir lime threads in a medium bowl. Toss gently before adding the dressing. Toss again, then add the sausage, mint, and cilantro. Toss to combine, then transfer to a platter. Garnish with the pine nuts and serve.

MAKES 4 SERVINGS

DRESSING

1 teaspoon minced garlic

1 teaspoon salt

1 tablespoon fish sauce

3 tablespoons sugar

2 tablespoons distilled white vinegar

1 tablespoon fresh lime juice

1 tablespoon crushed red pepper

SALAD

4 links dried sweet Chinese-style pork or chicken sausage or chicken-and-apple sausage

1 seedless cucumber, peeled and thinly sliced on the diagonal

12 cherry tomatoes, cut in half

½ cup sweet onion thinly sliced into half-moons

1 tablespoon slivered kaffir lime leaf or grated orange zest

½ cup fresh mint leaves, coarsely chopped

½ cup fresh cilantro leaves, coarsely chopped

2 tablespoons pine nuts, toasted in a small skillet over medium heat until lightly brown

Bitter endive and peppery watercress put out the heat brought on by nature's Fire element. Tangy and sweet fresh mango balances the Water element ruling the dinner hours.

ENDIVE, MANGO, AND WATERCRESS SALAD

HEAT the grill to medium-high.

PUT the mango slices on a fine-mesh rack set over the grill rack and grill, turning frequently, until they are slightly charred, about 7 minutes. Remove to a plate to cool before slicing into chunks.

SPRAY the shrimp with vegetable oil spray and set on the mesh rack. Grill, turning frequently, until they are firm, pink, and slightly charred, about 5 minutes. Transfer to a plate to cool.

COMBINE the mango, shrimp, endive, watercress, basil, cilantro, and candied ginger in a bowl. Toss with the dressing and serve.

MAKES 4 SERVINGS

1 large ripe mango, peeled and sliced in half off the seed

½ pound medium shrimp, peeled and deveined

Vegetable oil spray

1 Belgian endive, thinly sliced lengthwise

1 cup loosely packed watercress, torn into pieces

1 cup fresh Thai or regular basil leaves, torn into pieces

½ cup fresh cilantro leaves, torn into pieces

1 tablespoon minced candied ginger

½ cup or more Citrus Dressing (page 58)

*i*f you need reviving from the heat, these spices will do just that.

SPICY CHINESE BROCCOLI AND HALIBUT SOUP

PUT all the chile paste ingredients, except for the miso, in a blender. Blend at high speed until reduced to a coarse paste. Remove and pound in a mortar into a fine paste. Stir in the miso. This will keep, refrigerated, in an airtight container for several weeks.

PEEL the tough outer layer from the broccoli stems. Separate the florets from the stems. Slice the stems thinly on the diagonal (about 3 cups sliced).

BRING the broth to a boil in a large saucepan, then stir in the chile paste, bean paste, sugar, and fish sauce. (If using canned broth, taste and adjust the seasonings accordingly.) Taste for a pleasing balance of spicy and salty. Add the sliced broccoli stems. When their color brightens, add the florets. When their color brightens, add the halibut and stir to mix. Cook until the fish is firm and white, 5 to 6 minutes. Ladle into individual serving bowls, garnish with the slivered chile, and serve with hot white, brown, or red rice.

MAKES 4 SERVINGS

CHILE PASTE

½ teaspoon salt

3 cloves garlic, minced

1 tablespoon Sichuan peppercorns, dry-roasted and ground (page 70)

6 fresh Thai or 2 to 3 fresh serrano chiles, minced

1 teaspoon peeled and minced fresh ginger

1 stalk lemongrass, tough outer layers removed, tender inner stalk minced

1 shallot, minced

1 teaspoon red miso

SOUP

6 to 7 stalks Chinese or regular broccoli

4 cups homemade (page 26) or canned low-sodium, low-fat chicken broth

1 tablespoon bean paste

1 teaspoon sugar

2 tablespoons fish sauce

1 pound halibut, ling cod, or sea bass fillet

1 fresh red Thai or serrano chile, seeded and slivered

*T*he blending of your home element's spicy and cool/refreshing tastes together with Fire element's bitter, bland, and cool/refreshing tastes and Water's element's sour taste make this a glorious Wind element dish that everyone can enjoy.

COOL RICE VERMICELLI WITH GRILLED VEGETABLES

COMBINE the dressing ingredients in an airtight container and shake vigorously until well combined. This will keep, refrigerated, for several days. Mix well before using. If it is too thick, dilute it with another 1 to 2 tablespoons apple juice.

HEAT the grill to high.

PUT a fine-mesh rack over the grill rack.

COMBINE the oil, soy sauce, salt, wine, and mint in a large bowl. When your grill is hot, place the green beans in the bowl and coat generously with the mixture. Use tongs to transfer them to a large tray and spray them with vegetable oil spray. Repeat with the remaining vegetables. Transfer them to the grill and cook, turning frequently to prevent them from charring. Brush with the remaining sauce as you turn them. As they finish cooking (they should all be tender but still slightly firm, between 4 to 8 minutes), remove them from the grill to a plate. When cool enough to touch, slice the corn from the cob and add to the bowl. Slice the remaining vegetables into thin diagonal pieces and place in the bowl. Mix lightly to combine.

COMBINE the rice vermicelli with the apple in a medium bowl. Mix lightly. Divide among four individual serving bowls. Top with equal portions of the vegetables and dressing. Toss to combine. Serve immediately.

MAKES 4 SERVINGS

DRESSING

⅓ cup tahini

2 teaspoons salt

3 tablespoons sugar

¼ cup distilled white vinegar

3 tablespoons soy sauce

1 teaspoon paprika

1 teaspoon cayenne pepper

1 tablespoon peeled and minced fresh ginger

1 stalk lemongrass, tough outer layers removed, tender inner stalk minced

3 tablespoons apple juice

TO FINISH THE DISH

1 tablespoon olive, soybean, or rice bran oil

2 tablespoons soy sauce

1 teaspoon salt

¼ cup white wine

½ cup fresh mint leaves, minced

1 cup green beans

Vegetable oil spray

1 ear corn, husked

2 cups shiitake mushrooms, stems removed

1 carrot, cut in half across

2 zucchini, each cut into 8 lengthwise slices

1 small head radicchio, quartered

2 leeks (white part only), cut in half and rinsed well to remove any grit

6 ounces rice vermicelli (page 86), soaked in cool water, cooked in boiling water until soft (2 minutes), rinsed under cool running water, and patted dry

½ cup shredded tart green apple, with peel left on

*L*aab refers to a spicy minced meat salad from northeastern Thailand and Laos. Tofu takes the place of meat here; remember to press the tofu either in the morning or the night before.

LETTUCE WRAP WITH TOFU Laab

PLACE the tofu in a pie plate. Top with a dinner plate and put several heavy cans on top. Refrigerate for 2 to 3 hours, until the water is extracted from the tofu. Discard the water, mince the tofu, and put it in a large bowl. Cover and microwave for 1 to 2 minutes to warm.

PUT the rice in a small skillet and dry-roast over medium-high heat until golden. Let cool before grinding in a spice grinder, small food processor, or coffee grinder. Set aside.

ADD the garlic to the tofu. Mince the shallots and add to the tofu. Add the ginger, chili powder, salt, sugar, and soy sauce. Mix well, then add the juice of 1 lime. Taste for balance, adding more lime juice if necessary. Add the rice powder, lemongrass, lime leaves, scallion, parsley, cilantro, and mint. Mix well and let sit for 10 to 15 minutes before serving. Scoop a good portion into each of the lettuce leaves and enjoy.

MAKES 4 SERVINGS

One 19-ounce carton extra-firm tofu

1 tablespoon Thai long-grain jasmine rice

5 cloves garlic, roasted in a 450°F oven until soft (10 minutes) and peeled

4 shallots, roasted in a 450°F oven until soft (15 minutes) and peeled

1 tablespoon peeled and minced fresh ginger

1 tablespoon or more chili powder or cayenne pepper

1 teaspoon salt

1 teaspoon sugar

1½ tablespoons soy sauce

Juice of 1 to 2 limes

1 stalk lemongrass, tough outer layers removed, tender inner stalk minced

6 kaffir lime leaves, slivered, or grated zest of 1 lime

1 scallion, minced

10 sprigs fresh Italian parsley, minced

12 sprigs fresh cilantro, chopped

½ cup fresh mint leaves, minced

10 to 12 iceberg lettuce leaves

how off your artistic flare by wrapping fried rice in banana pouches. Some Whole Foods markets carry fresh banana leaves. Asian supermarkets sell frozen banana leaves. If you cannot find any, line aluminum foil with fresh grape leaves or corn husks or soaked dried corn husks to form a pouch.

GRILLED CURRY FRIED RICE IN BANANA POUCHES

COMBINE the almond milk and chile paste in a large skillet over medium-high heat. Stir to mix. When the mixture begins to bubble, add the mushrooms, peas, green beans, and eggplant. Stir to mix until the vegetables are cooked but still firm, about 5 minutes. If the mixture is dry, add a couple tablespoons of water. Add the salt, fish sauce, lime leaves, and basil. Stir to mix, then add the rice. Stir to mix well. Remove from the heat.

CAREFULLY unwrap the banana leaves and clean them with dishwashing soap. Rinse and dry thoroughly. Cut out the spine. Cut the leaves along the grain into twelve 10-inch-wide squares. Turn a stovetop burner to low and brush the leaf lightly over the heat to soften. Put one on top of another to make 6 sets. Divide the rice mixture evenly among the banana leaves, placing it in the center of each leaf. Divide the crumbled trout evenly, placing it on top of the rice mixture. Fold one side of each of the banana leaves along the grain over the filling. Fold the opposite side over. Fold both ends to overlap into a pouch. Secure with a toothpick. (If making ahead, put the banana pouches in a zip-top plastic bag. Seal and refrigerate. They will keep for a day.)

HEAT the grill to hot, or preheat the oven to 375°F.

Grill the pouches over high heat until aromatic, 6 to 8 minutes. Spray lightly with water to prevent the leaves from burning. Or, bake for 10 minutes. When ready to serve, open the banana pouches and serve. (If making ahead, after grilling, cool the banana pouches before refrigerating. They will keep for a day or two. When ready to eat, microwave at high heat for 1 to 2 minutes.)

MAKES 6 POUCHES; ABOUT 4 SERVINGS

½ cup **Almond Milk (page 21)**

1 tablespoon **Red Curry Chile Paste (page 76)**

1 cup **thinly sliced mushrooms**

¼ cup **fresh peas**

1 cup **thinly sliced green beans**

1 cup **Japanese eggplant thinly sliced across into rounds, salted for 5 to 7 minutes, rinsed, and patted dry**

½ teaspoon **salt**

1 tablespoon **fish sauce**

3 **kaffir lime leaves, slivered, or grated zest of 1 lime**

½ cup **fresh Thai basil or peppermint leaves**

2 cups **cooked Thai jasmine, brown, or red rice**

1 package **banana leaves**

1 **boneless smoked trout fillet, skin removed and shredded**

6 **toothpicks, soaked in water for 2 to 3 minutes and dried thoroughly**

Young coconut, with its sweet-fruity juice and tender, gelatin-like meat, makes a wonderful and refreshing-tasting gelatin dessert. Serving it inside the coconut makes it fun to eat as well.

COCONUT JELL-O

LAY each coconut on its side and use a cleaver and mallet or electric knife to hack off or saw halfway through the top of the coconut. Be careful not to spill the sweet juice inside. Transfer the juice to a medium saucepan and finish hacking off or sawing off the tops. Scrape out the tender flesh inside the coconuts and slice it into thin ribbons. Put it in a large bowl and set aside.

ADD the gelatin to the coconut juice and mix well. Bring to a boil over medium heat and stir until the gelatin is dissolved, 3 to 4 minutes. Remove from the heat.

PUT the coconut ribbons back into the coconuts. Pour the liquid over the ribbons until it reaches the brim. Cover and refrigerate overnight, until the gelatin sets.

SERVE directly out of the coconut, using a spoon to scoop out the gelatin.

MAKES 4 SERVINGS

4 young tender coconuts

3 envelopes Knox unflavored gelatin

This pretty dessert showcases Wind element's artistic flair.

MANGO, MELONS, AND BERRIES WITH COCONUT SYRUP

COMBINE the coconut cream, sugar, and salt in a small saucepan over medium-low heat. Stir until both the sugar and salt are dissolved. Don't let the cream boil, or it will curdle. Let cool completely. If making ahead, refrigerate until ready to use.

TO serve, divide the mangos, melon balls, and berries equally in four individual serving bowls. Garnish with crushed ice and drizzle the coconut cream syrup over the ice. Sprinkle with the sesame seeds and enjoy.

MAKES 4 SERVINGS

½ cup Coconut Cream (page 22)

2 tablespoons sugar

Pinch of salt

2 ripe mangos, peeled and cubed

2 cups mixture of melon balls such as watermelon, Crenshaw, and cantaloupe

1 cup mixed berries such as strawberries, raspberries, and blueberries

Crushed ice

1 tablespoon sesame seeds, toasted in a small skillet over medium heat until lightly golden

RAINY WEATHER RECIPES

My friend Pim jokes that she can always predict the weather by how she feels. As the rainy season approaches, she gets the sniffles and her bones start to ache. It was not until after meditating one day at a Buddhist temple, where we visited afterward with an elderly monk who is also a traditional healer, that she finally became convinced of the connection between the weather and her ailments. According to the monk, my Wind element friend's problem is the double influence of the Wind element: her home element and rainy-damp weather. She becomes more vulnerable during these periods, which often results in stiff joints and aching muscles. Rainy days also wreak havoc on her respiratory system, resulting in colds and fevers, and make her feel bloated and lethargic.

If you have similar problems when the weather is damp and rainy, protect yourself by eating right. You can strengthen your home element by cooking seasonal vegetables and fruits mixed with pungent-flavor herbs and spices such as cilantro, ginger, galangal, garlic, shallots, lemongrass, and white peppercorns. Select buttery-flavor and salty-tasting fruits and vegetables, which will add extra nourishment to protect your body's sensitive Earth element. Add sour- or sour/sweet-tasting berries, pineapple, plums, lime, or lemon and bland-flavor foods such as chayote, okra, mushrooms, or summer squashes to your grocery list, which will help nurture and maintain balance when the Water element is ruling your vulnerable respiratory and digestive systems.

BREAKFAST

Wake up to breakfast treats prepared from ingredients that balance and neutralize the terrible twosome of Wind elements (your home element and rainy weather). Cravings for rich, sweet-tasting muffins, pancakes (pages 31–32), or bread on cold wintry mornings are your inner voice, urging you to bathe and lubricate bones, muscles, and joints with your Earth element's buttery, salty, and sweet tastes. Try blueberry muffins with 1 to 2 tablespoons minced candied ginger added to the batter, or blend the ginger into some butter before spreading it on top. Banana-walnut bread would be an excellent choice, with extra shakes of warming cinnamon and nutmeg added to the batter, served with a mixture of cream cheese and orange zest. A light snack before lunch is also suggested.

Tangy fruits will balance nature's Water element in the damp morning air. Citrus juices such as orange, tangerine, or grapefruit are like putting on an extra raincoat, guarding you against chilly weather that can affect your respiratory system, as is hot apple cider with a cinnamon stick. Hot ginger tea will warm and soothe the throat and chest. Fortify your Earth element body parts with a smoothie made from sweet bananas or papayas. Lessen the impact of Water element mornings by mixing in tart fruits such as blueberries, strawberries, or raspberries. The Berry and Papaya Smoothie (page 40) is perfect.

LUNCH

When the weather turns wet, damp, and humid from rain, shield your chest and circulatory system by seasoning your cooking with pungent ginger, garlic, onions, and shallots. They are believed to prevent colds and reduce fevers while adding zest to bitter-flavor greens like kale, escarole, radicchio, and Belgian

endive and bland-flavor vegetables such as summer squash, cucumbers, and mushrooms that will quiet the dominant midday Fire element. To nurture bones and muscles, it is time to indulge in rich and creamy soups such as Thai Coconut Cream Soup (page 91), making it with thinly sliced chicken or ½-inch cubes of firm tofu and thinly sliced oyster mushrooms instead of straw mushrooms, or Thai Hot and Sour Soup with Roasted Chile Oil (page 89), with thinly sliced pork tenderloin or chicken, 1 sliced Japanese eggplant, and 2 cups sliced green beans added as the main ingredients. Wouldn't it be nice if all medicines tasted as good as these healing foods do?

For a beverage, drink hot Lemongrass Tea (page 46) or Ginger Tea (page 47) to protect your chest and throat against the damp air. Stirring pomegranate juice with a cinnamon stick will do the same thing. A cup of fragrant orange-flavored tea, on the other hand, is uplifting for a melancholy mood.

For a midday break, take a moment, sit by a window, and listen to the sound of the rain. Relish a hot cup of mint, cinnamon, or orange tea. Enjoy the weather and indulge in cookies baked with dried apricots or cranberries. Fig Newtons or applesauce with yogurt laced with fresh mint threads will also take the gloom out of rainy days.

DINNER

Thais like me cannot understand how some Wind people in America will settle for a boring bowl of cold cereal for dinner. Instead, engage your creative and artistic talents by turning dinnertime into a playful, beautiful, or dramatic event. Imagine the sounds of the rain as music and the darkening night as the backdrop. Light up your home with candles and decorate the dinner table with the warm colors of summer.

Make nature's Water element, which rules the dinner hour, sing in harmony with bland- and bitter-flavor vegetables such as green beans, peas, and Belgian endive, together with the double Wind element's spicy taste and cool/refreshing flavor. Remember, you want to get your circulatory system flowing as steadily as the rain. Pungent garlic and spicy aromatic ginger, lemongrass, mint, and basil pair beautifully with tangy lemon or lime. Jazz the meal up even more with peppercorns or chiles. For the grand finale, create a dessert with tangy-tasting berries, apples, and other seasonal fruits to cheer your spirits and cloak the respiratory system. Black Sticky Rice Pudding with Mangos or Peaches (page 236) is guaranteed to earn you a standing ovation.

For a beverage, a cup of hot herbal tea, like orange, mint, or ginger, will wrap you in its warm, comforting embrace.

many supermarkets call dried rice noodles "pad thai noodles." To prepare them for use, refer to page 85. Each package generally makes 2 to 3 servings. ⁓᥎ Instead of the slightly sweet pad thai served in Thai restaurants in foreign countries, this ancient recipe displays the true culinary genius of ancient Thai cooks, who turned ordinary and bland noodles into an extraordinary dish.

STIR-FRIED RICE NOODLES, ANCIENT THAI STYLE
Phad Thai Boran

IN a mortar, combine the salt, garlic, chiles, galangal, and shallot and pound into a paste. Set aside. In a small bowl, combine the sugar, fish sauce, and tamarind puree; set aside.

HEAT a large nonstick skillet over high heat for 1 to 2 minutes. Add the coconut milk and the garlic mixture. Stir-fry for a minute or two, until the mixture begins to bubble and thicken. Add the chicken and stir-fry until it is partially cooked. Add the noodles and tamarind mixture. Continue to stir. If the pan appears dry and the noodle strands are still hard, sprinkle with a tablespoonful of water. Add more water if needed and stir-fry until the strands are limp and soft. Add the bean sprouts and chives. Continue to stir-fry for another minute. Add the pine nuts and stir to mix. Serve garnished with the mango slivers.

MAKES 1 SERVING

¼ teaspoon salt

2 cloves garlic, minced

3 dried de arbol chiles or Japones chiles, softened in warm water, dried thoroughly, and minced

3 thin slices galangal or fresh ginger, minced

1 shallot, minced

2 teaspoons palm sugar, dark brown sugar, or maple sugar

1 tablespoon fish sauce

2 tablespoons Tamarind Puree (page 25)

About ¼ cup Coconut Milk (page 22) or Almond Milk (page 21)

⅓ cup thinly sliced chicken, small shrimp, or bay scallops

1½ cups softened thin rice noodles (page 86)

¼ cup bean sprouts

2 stalks Chinese chives or 1 scallion, thinly sliced on the diagonal

1 tablespoon pine nuts, toasted in a small skillet over medium heat until lightly golden

2 tablespoons slivered peeled green mango or unpeeled tart green apple

Wind element people bring a sense of flair to anything they do. This salad gives you a chance to do just that. Stir-frying the ingredients for this salad leaves the crispy vegetables slightly crunchy, the moist ones turn a tad buttery, the carrot and zucchini get a bit sweeter, and the green beans, mushrooms, and asparagus become a bit nuttier. And the intense heat brightens the color of everything.

STIR-FRIED VEGETABLE SALAD WITH BLACK SESAME DRESSING

HEAT a large nonstick skillet over high heat for 1 minute. Add the oil and wait another minute, then add the shallot and stir-fry until translucent. Add the vegetables one at a time, adding the next one only after the color of each brightens, 1 to 2 minutes each. Season with the salt, mix to combine, and transfer to a serving bowl. Add the dressing, basil, and mint and toss gently to combine. Let rest for 5 minutes before serving.

MAKES 4 SERVINGS

1 tablespoon olive, soybean, or rice bran oil

1 shallot, minced

1 cup green beans thinly sliced on the diagonal

1 large carrot, thinly sliced on the diagonal

2 large zucchini, thinly sliced into rounds

6 to 8 white or brown mushrooms, thinly sliced

1 red or green bell pepper, seeded and cut into thin strips

6 to 7 stalks asparagus, peeled and thinly sliced

½ teaspoon salt

⅓ cup Black Sesame Dressing (page 55)

¼ cup firmly packed fresh Thai basil, torn

¼ cup firmly packed fresh peppermint leaves, torn

W hile most fried rice recipes should be made one serving at a time, there is always an exception. Here is one. ~~~ Historically, Persian cooking has had a strong influence on the development of Thai dishes, particularly on the use of dried spices in combination with dried sweet fruits to create a savory dish. Wind element people benefit from these warming spices, which are a restorative to the mind and spirit, as well as an aid to digestion.

PERSIAN-THAI FRIED RICE

IN a small bowl, combine the cinnamon, nutmeg, cloves, mace, turmeric, cayenne, and ginger. Set aside.

HEAT a large skillet or wok over high heat for 1 minute, then add the oil and wait another minute. Add the shallot and stir-fry until golden, then add the spice mix, star anise, and chicken and stir-fry until the chicken is cooked through. Add the rice and stir to mix, breaking up any clumps. Add the salt and both soy sauces and stir to mix well. Add the raisins and stir to mix well. Transfer to a serving platter, garnish with the cilantro, and serve hot with the lime slices.

MAKES 4 SERVINGS

⅛ teaspoon ground cinnamon

⅛ teaspoon freshly grated nutmeg

⅛ teaspoon ground cloves

⅛ teaspoon ground mace

½ teaspoon ground turmeric

1 teaspoon cayenne pepper

½ teaspoon ground ginger

1 tablespoon olive, rice bran, or soybean oil

1 shallot, thinly sliced

1 star anise

1 cup thinly sliced chicken
or cubed baked tofu

3 cups cooked white, brown, or red rice

½ teaspoon salt

1 tablespoon light soy sauce

1 teaspoon dark soy sauce

¼ cup golden raisins, softened in warm water for 2 to 3 minutes, drained, and patted dry

¼ cup chopped fresh cilantro

1 lime, thinly sliced

Working with rice paper is like doing a magic trick. These brittle, paper-thin, translucent sheets turn soft and pliable after being bathed in warm water (page 282). Salad rolls are fun to make, especially for children. Other fresh vegetable and/or fruit combinations can be used with your choice of meat, poultry, seafood, or firm tofu. For a Wind element person, this is your opportunity to display your artistic imagination.

SALAD ROLLS WITH CHICKEN, MANGO, AND GRILLED ASPARAGUS

FILL a large bowl with very warm water. Bathe a rice paper in it, then shake off the excess water and place on a work surface. Repeat with 5 more. As the rice paper begins to soften, line the upper half of the center of the rice paper with half a lettuce leaf. Top with 2 chives and a piece each of cucumber, mango, avocado, and asparagus. Spread a generous tablespoon of the chicken on top together with 1 mint leaf and 1 cilantro sprig. Fold the bottom edge of the rice paper to slightly cover the filling. From left to right, fold in the edges, and roll the rice paper over the filling into a cylinder. Repeat with the remaining ingredients, moistening the remaining 6 rice papers when needed. Keep the finished rolls moist by covering them with a wet paper towel. (If making ahead, cover the rolls tightly with plastic wrap. You can put these together early in the day and refrigerate, but the rice papers may dry out. Refresh them by patting lightly with water and letting them sit for 10 minutes before eating.)

COMBINE the sauce ingredients, except for the mint, in a small bowl. Garnish with the mint just before serving. Serve the rolls with the sauce for dipping.

MAKES 12 ROLLS

ROLLS

Twelve 6-inch rice papers

6 red leaf lettuce leaves, hard stems removed and torn in half lengthwise

24 fresh chives

1 large cucumber, peeled, cut in half lengthwise, seeds scooped out, and each half cut into 6 long slices (12 total)

1 ripe mango or peach, peeled, cut off the seed, and each half cut into 6 long slices (12 total)

1 ripe avocado, cut in half lengthwise, peeled, each half cut into 6 long slices (12 total), and lightly mashed

12 stalks asparagus, grilled or broiled until lightly charred

1 cup shredded cooked chicken, roast duck, or smoked fish

12 fresh mint leaves

12 sprigs fresh cilantro

HONEY PEPPER SAUCE

¼ teaspoon salt

½ teaspoon cayenne pepper

2 tablespoons honey

1 tablespoon distilled white vinegar

1 tablespoon fresh lime juice

1 teaspoon minced fresh mint

I altered this ancient recipe by substituting coconut cream with almond milk, as Wind element people fare better with less saturated fat. It is still delicious, with a profusion of herbs that will nurture your Wind element.

CEVICHE, THAI STYLE Plah Pla

PUT the chile paste ingredients in a spice grinder or blender and puree. Remove to a mortar and pound into a paste.

COMBINE the chile paste, salt, fish sauce, and sugar in a saucepan. Heat over low heat until the sugar is dissolved. Let cool completely, then stir in the lime juice. Put the salmon in a single layer in a glass baking dish and pour the mixture over it. Cover and refrigerate for at least 1 hour and up to 2 hours, until the salmon turns pale pink and firm.

BEFORE serving, add the almond milk and stir lightly to coat the fish. Toss gently with the chiles, mango, mint, and cilantro. Serve with hot white, brown, or red rice.

CHILE PASTE

½ teaspoon salt

4 cloves garlic, minced

1 stalk lemongrass, tough outer layers removed, tender inner stalk minced

Grated zest of 1 kaffir or regular lime

6 to 7 fresh Thai or 3 fresh serrano chiles, minced

2 shallots, minced

CEVICHE

1 teaspoon salt

¼ cup fish sauce

1 tablespoon sugar

½ cup fresh lime juice

One 1-pound salmon fillet, bones removed and sliced paper thin

1 cup Almond Milk (page 21)

3 fresh Thai or 1 to 2 fresh serrano chiles, slivered

1 cup shredded peeled green mango or unpeeled tart green apple

½ cup fresh mint leaves, torn

½ cup fresh cilantro leaves, torn

*L*emongrass is one of the most commonly used ingredients in Thai cooking. It is an equalizer for all home elements while giving an extra boost to the circulatory system. Rain or shine, lemongrass steadies the Wind element toward its proper course.

SHRIMP AND LEMONGRASS SALAD WITH TAMARIND DRESSING

COMBINE the dressing ingredients in a small saucepan over medium-low heat and stir until the sugar is dissolved. Set aside to cool.

PEEL the oranges with a knife. Section the orange segments from the pith and place in a large serving bowl. Add the remaining ingredients, except for the fried lemongrass, and mix gently. Add the dressing. Toss lightly. Add the fried lemongrass and toss again. Serve with hot jasmine, brown, or red rice on the side.

MAKES 4 SERVINGS

TAMARIND DRESSING

½ teaspoon salt

1 tablespoon palm sugar, dark brown sugar, or maple sugar

1 tablespoon fish sauce

1 teaspoon crushed red pepper

2 tablespoons Tamarind Puree (page 25)

SALAD

4 navel oranges

2 cups cooked medium shrimp

6 thin slices young ginger, slivered (if using older ginger, peel, then soak it in a couple tablespoons of water with ⅛ teaspoon salt for 5 to 6 minutes, rinse, dry, and mince)

½ cup pine nuts, toasted in a small skillet over medium heat until lightly golden

½ cup fresh mint leaves, torn

1 cup nasturtium blossoms or other edible flower or peppery green, like watercress

¼ cup fried lemongrass (page 100)

The Karen people are an ethnic tribe living in the north and northwest of Thailand, many of whom are refugees from Myanmar. They are known to eat superhot food, which seems to stir up their appetite when the food might not be all that palatable. ⚬ With the double force of the Wind element at play, chile in combination with lemongrass, galangal or ginger, mint, basil, and peppercorns helps center the inner force of Wind and leaves you feeling nice and warm for the rest of the evening.

KAREN JUNGLE SOUP Gaeng Pa Galieng

PUT the chile paste ingredients in a spice grinder and puree. Transfer to a mortar and pound into a paste. Set aside.

HEAT a saucepan over high heat for 1 minute. Add the oil, wait another minute, and add the chile paste. Stir until fragrant, 10 to 15 seconds. Add the water and bring to a boil. Add the eggplants, bamboo shoots, corn, mushrooms, salt, fish sauce, ginger, and peppercorns. Taste for balance. Cover and cook over medium-low heat for 15 to 20 minutes. Uncover, increase the heat to medium, and add the trout. When it is firm and cooked through, about 5 minutes, add the basil. Stir to mix. Serve with hot white, brown, or red rice.

MAKES 4 SERVINGS

CHILE PASTE

½ teaspoon salt

6 cloves garlic, minced

10 or more fresh Thai or 5 to 6 fresh serrano chiles, minced

1 stalk lemongrass, tough outer layers removed, tender inner stalk minced

5 to 6 thin slices of galangal or fresh ginger, minced

Grated zest of 1 kaffir or regular lime

1 shallot, minced

SOUP

1 tablespoon olive, rice bran, or soybean oil

4 cups water

6 to 7 Thai eggplants, quartered, or 1 Japanese eggplant, cut across into 1-inch-thick slices

½ cup sliced bamboo shoots

Kernels cut from 1 ear corn

1 cup sliced oyster mushrooms, sliced

1 teaspoon salt

2 tablespoons fish sauce

1 tablespoon peeled and slivered fresh ginger

1 tablespoon green peppercorns, dry-roasted (page 70)

1 pound skinless trout or catfish fillets, cut into bite-size pieces

1 cup fresh Thai basil or peppermint leaves

my granddaughter Claire has Wind as her home element. She doesn't care much for sweets except for a couple of simple cakes. One is a pound cake with cinnamon and sugar dusted over it, and another is a pineapple upside-down cake. I have combined her favorite ingredients to make this cake. Cinnamon will keep Claire calm and happy while the slightly sweet and tart tastes of the pineapple will balance nature's Water element, protecting her chest from the cool evening air.

CLAIRE'S PINEAPPLE UPSIDE-DOWN CAKE

POSITION a rack in the center of the oven and preheat to 350°F.

SIFT together the flour, baking powder, baking soda, and salt in a medium bowl. Grease the bottom and side of a round 9 x 2-inch nonstick cake pan with 4 tablespoons of the butter. Combine the brown sugar and cinnamon in a measuring cup and sprinkle evenly over the bottom and slightly up the side of the pan. Arrange the pineapple over the bottom of the pan, starting in the center and working around in a circle, with some slices slightly overlapped.

BEAT the remaining 6 tablespoons butter with the granulated sugar and vanilla with an electric mixer at high speed in a large bowl until light and fluffy, about 2 minutes. Add the eggs one at a time, beating each one well into the mixture. Reduce the speed to low and add the flour mixture in increments, alternating it with the milk, and continue beating until the batter is smooth.

SPOON and spread the batter evenly over the pineapple. Bake until a toothpick inserted in the center of the cake comes out clean, 40 to 45 minutes. Let cool in the pan on top of a wire rack for 15 minutes. Loosen the edge with a knife, then invert the cake onto a plate and let cool to room temperature. Slice into and serve, if you wish, with whipped cream.

SERVES 8

1⅔ cups all-purpose flour

1½ teaspoons baking powder

¼ teaspoon baking soda

½ teaspoon salt

10 tablespoons (1¼ sticks) unsalted butter, softened

⅔ cup firmly packed light brown sugar

1 teaspoon ground cinnamon

½ large pineapple, peeled, cut into ¼-inch-thick rings, each ring quartered and core cut out

⅔ cup granulated sugar

1 teaspoon vanilla extract

2 large eggs

⅔ cup whole milk

Whipped cream (optional)

Black sticky rice can be purchased in Asian supermarkets, specialty food markets, and online. The grain is long, unlike the short white or brown Japanese rice used for making sushi rice. This dessert is a rare treat not only because it tastes marvelous, but also because the black coating on the rice is the bran, which is very nutritious.

BLACK STICKY RICE PUDDING WITH MANGOS OR PEACHES

SOAK the black and white sticky rice together in cool water to cover overnight. Drain. Transfer the rice to a steamer basket lined with softened dried or fresh corn husks or a double thickness of cheesecloth. Fill the steamer pot halfway full with water. Bring to a boil. Insert the steamer basket with the rice, cover, and steam over high heat until tender, 30 to 45 minutes. Check the water level at regular intervals and replenish with boiling water as needed. Keep warm.

IN the meantime, heat the coconut cream and milk, ⅔ cup of the sugar, ¼ teaspoon of the salt, and the nutmeg in a medium saucepan over medium-low heat. When the mixture begins to boil, remove from the heat.

TRANSFER the cooked rice to a large bowl. Stir vigorously with a wooden paddle to release the steam, about 1 minute. Pour the coconut cream mixture over the rice and mix well. The mixture will be soupy. Cover tightly with plastic wrap and let sit until the liquid has been absorbed into the rice, about 20 minutes. Add the grated coconut and mix well. (If making ahead, divide the rice into individual serving portions and wrap in plastic wrap. Refrigerated, it will keep for a week. When ready to serve, microwave for 1 minute.)

TO make the coconut syrup, combine the coconut cream with the remaining ⅓ cup sugar, ¼ teaspoon salt, and the rice flour in a small saucepan. Stir to mix well and cook over medium-low heat, stirring constantly, until the mixture thickens, about 5 minutes. Do not boil, or the coconut cream will curdle. Set aside to cool. (If making ahead, cool completely, then refrigerate for up to a week. When ready to serve, microwave for 10 to 20 seconds to warm.)

TO assemble, pour a ladle of warm coconut syrup over each portion. Serve with the fruit slices on the side.

MAKES 4 SERVINGS

½ cup black long-grain sticky rice

1½ cups white long-grain sticky rice

3 cups Coconut Cream and Milk combined (page 22)

1 cup sugar

½ teaspoon salt

½ teaspoon freshly grated nutmeg

½ cup Grated Fresh Coconut (page 101)

1 cup Coconut Cream (page 22)

1 teaspoon rice flour

2 ripe mangos or 4 peaches, peeled, pitted, and sliced

*T*hai people love bananas and consider them to be the best food for the very young and old because they are so easily digestible. For a sensitive digestive system, this is a nice dessert for Wind element people.

BANANAS IN MAPLE SYRUP AND ALMOND MILK SAUCE

COMBINE the almond milk, sugar, and salt in a small saucepan and heat over medium-low heat. When the sugar and salt are dissolved, add the almond extract and stir to mix. Remove from the heat.

COMBINE the maple syrup and amaretto in a medium saucepan and heat over medium heat. Slice each banana in half across, then slice lengthwise into 4 pieces and add them to the syrup. Cook over medium-low heat until the bananas are soft but still intact, 7 to 8 minutes. Remove from the heat and transfer to individual serving bowls. Ladle the almond milk sauce over the bananas and serve warm. (If making ahead, cool the bananas and the sauce completely before storing in separate containers and refrigerate. When ready to serve, heat in a microwave at high heat for 20 to 30 seconds, or in a saucepan over medium-low heat.)

MAKES 4 SERVINGS

1 cup Almond Milk (page 21)

2 tablespoons sugar

¼ teaspoon salt

3 to 4 drops almond extract

½ cup maple syrup

1 tablespoon amaretto

3 ripe bananas, peeled

COLD WEATHER RECIPES

During my first winter in Kentucky as a young foreign student, I experienced the weather phenomenon called the "wind chill factor." For a girl born and raised in the tropics, the snow, ice, hail, and sleet were hard to take, but once the wind kicked in and the temperature dropped even further, I could never seem to warm up.

Most Thai traditional healers have never left the tropics, so they have no experience of how frigid and bone-chilling winter weather can be. If they were to come in contact with truly cold weather, they would say that this kind of climate is not good for a Water element person, me, or Wind element people, you, because we both have vulnerable circulatory, respiratory, and nervous systems.

Bitter cold brought on by nature's Earth element dampens the spirits, bruises emotions, slows circulation, and affects body heat. A way to overcome a cold climate is to stay in balance with Mother Nature and the needs of your body's Earth element by including astringent, salty, sweet, and buttery tastes and flavors in your diet. Combine vegetables such as potatoes, sweet potatoes, rice, and pumpkin with your own home element's protective, healing herbs and spices—ginger, star anise, nutmeg, cinnamon, and peppercorns—which will assist in fighting off the chilly scenes of winter.

BREAKFAST

Warm oatmeal with raisins or dried cranberries mixed in, cream of wheat with a spoonful of maple syrup, and rice porridge, with their rich, creamy flavors, are good healing foods for Wind element people exposed to the wintry sting of nature's Earth element.

Sweet, quick carrot or zucchini bread made with the addition of a handful of chopped candied ginger and dried cranberries and the grated zest of an orange and spread with cream cheese will help keep you dry and warm on cold, wet mornings. Balance the elements and pre-lunch munchies with a mid-morning snack of a slice or two of the sweet bread. A warm fruit compote of apples and figs (page 34) will cuddle you like a fuzzy blanket on chilly mornings. Tangy, sour-tasting fruits add another layer of protective warmth when nature's Water element shares the Earth element's cold domain in early morning hours, so for beverages, look to the citrus juices (orange, tangerine, or grapefruit), pineapple juice, and cranberry-apple juice.

LUNCH

Be comforted by nature's Fire element, which rules the noon hours. Prepare dishes with bland- and bitter-flavor vegetables and mix and match them with the astringent, sweet, and salty tastes and creamy flavors of the Earth element to balance against nature's chill. Together they will fortify your sensitive Earth element against the cold. Steady your Wind element by adding spicy and cool/refreshing flavors. Your tolerance for the burning heat of chiles serves you well in cold weather. Together with the presiding Fire element of the noon hours, spices and highly flavored aromatics will counteract the cold, lessen bloating sensations, and steady body temperature.

Try adding 1 to 2 tablespoons of Roasted Chile Oil (page 65) to the Noodle Soup on page 82, preparing it with rice vermicelli and sliced chicken or pork tenderloin for a spicy warm-up on a cold afternoon. Another delicious soup would be *Gaeng Khae* (page 95), with 1 cup each thinly sliced bamboo shoots and green beans and 2 cups spinach added for the vegetable choice; increase the basil to 1 cup and the parsley to ½ cup for extra protection against the cold.

Curries are a wonderful choice as well. Make Red Curry (page 76) with pork tenderloin and diced apple instead of the vegetables, garnishing it with a quartered fresh red serrano chile along with the basil.

For a beverage, enjoy a comforting hot tea such as ginger, jasmine, apple and cinnamon, or green tea. Brew it with a dry-roasted cardamom pod for extra warmth and to aid in digestion.

For a midday snack, take a handful of gingersnaps or rice crackers, or a medley of dried fruits—pineapple, mango, and apricot—mixed with roasted almonds, pecans, or walnuts.

DINNER

Free your artistic nature and glamorize the dinner table with elegant dishes, colorful candles, and vases of fragrant blooms. If you have a fireplace, set it ablaze with a crackling fire. Spice your cooking with warming herbs and spices such as cinnamon, pepper, ginger, sage, and nutmeg. Hearty dishes made with root vegetables and winter squashes cooked with a pinch of warm seasonings will equalize the forces of the wintry Earth element. Try Hot and Sour Soup with Roasted Chile Oil (page 89) made with one 15-ounce can drained and rinsed straw mushrooms for the mushrooms and peeled and deveined medium shrimp, or Yellow Curry (page 80), adding 3 bay leaves and 6 cloves, bite-size pieces of chicken you've stir-fried in a bit of olive oil for 3 minutes, and 2 cups peeled and cubed (1½-inch) russet potatoes and ½ cup sliced tomato for the vegetables.

A taste of sourness will add a gourmet touch to dinner dishes while balancing nature's Water element, which governs the evening hours.

For a beverage, chamomile, lemon balm, or mint tea helps digestion, while its magical healing power relaxes and soothes away the day's tensions.

*ust a teaspoonful of *sambal badjak,* an Indonesian spicy relish sold at most Asian supermarkets and online, can turn an ordinary stir-fry or noodle dish into a fiery mouth- and stomach-warming event.

MALAYSIAN NOODLES

IN a small bowl, combine the *sambal badjak,* bean paste, and cayenne. Set aside.

HEAT a large skillet over high heat for 1 to 2 minutes, then add 1 tablespoon of the oil and heat for 10 to 12 seconds. Add the shallot and stir-fry until translucent. Add the chicken and stir-fry until it is partially cooked. Add the shrimp and stir-fry until they turn pink and are firm, then add the bean paste mixture and soy sauce and stir to mix. Add the noodles and stir-fry until the noodles soften. If the mixture appears dry, add a tablespoon or two of water. (If using pad thai noodles, add more water, a tablespoon or two at a time, until the noodles are soft and cooked.) Push the noodle mixture to one side of the skillet and add the remaining 1 teaspoon oil. Crack the egg over the oil, scramble, and, when the egg begins to set, fold the noodle mixture over it. Add the chives and bean sprouts and stir gently to incorporate. When the vegetables' colors brighten, transfer to a plate, garnish with the cilantro, and serve with lime slices.

MAKES 1 SERVING

1 teaspoon *sambal badjak,* **chipotle salsa, Roasted Chile Oil (page 65) with ½ teaspoon minced fresh Thai or serrano chile added**

1 teaspoon bean paste

⅛ teaspoon cayenne pepper

1 tablespoon plus 1 teaspoon canola, corn, rice bran, or sunflower oil

1 tablespoon minced shallot

¼ cup thinly sliced chicken

¼ cup small, shrimp, peeled and deveined

1 tablespoon dark soy sauce

1½ to 2 cups fresh wide rice noodles, loosely separated, or dried pad thai rice noodles, soaked in warm water to soften, rinsed, and dried thoroughly (page 85)

1 large egg

2 to 3 stalks Chinese chives, cut into 1-inch lengths, or ¼ cup scallions thinly sliced on the diagonal

⅔ cup bean sprouts, rinsed

1 tablespoon coarsely chopped fresh cilantro

1 to 2 lime slices

Sunny orange persimmon is intriguing to the artistic nature of Wind element people. Its mild, sweet, and crunchy texture is a delightful surprise. Together with just enough heat from the ginger, the perfuming lemongrass, and the bitter-sour kumquats, Wind element people will linger on at the table for more.

SHRIMP WITH JAPANESE PERSIMMONS AND CANDIED GINGER SALAD

PREHEAT the broiler.

COMBINE the shallot, lemongrass, lemon zest, and salt in a medium bowl and mix well. Add the shrimp and mix to coat evenly. Coat a baking sheet with vegetable oil spray and spread the shrimp on it in a single layer. Lightly spray the shrimp with the vegetable oil and broil until they are pink and firm, about 5 minutes. Let cool, then combine with the persimmons, endive, and candied ginger in a large bowl. Toss lightly. Add the dressing and toss again to combine. Transfer to a serving platter, garnish with the almond slivers, and serve.

MAKES 4 SERVINGS

1 shallot, minced

1 stalk lemongrass, tough outer layers removed, tender inner stalk minced

Grated zest of 1 lemon

1 teaspoon salt

1 pound medium shrimp, peeled and deveined

Vegetable oil spray

2 Japanese persimmons, peeled and thinly sliced

2 Belgian endive, thinly sliced

2 to 3 pieces candied ginger, thinly sliced

¼ cup or more Kumquat, Ginger, and Clove Preserve Dressing (page 59)

¼ cup slivered almonds, toasted in a small skillet over medium heat until lightly golden

Sage's healing power clarifies the mind after a day of chores and responsibility, leading you back to the present moment and helping you to relax and let go.

PEAR AND SMOKED FISH SALAD

PREHEAT the broiler.

COMBINE the sage, ginger, salt, nutmeg, pepper, vinegar, and oil in a large bowl. Add the pear slices and toss to coat. Transfer to a baking sheet, spray them with vegetable oil, and place under the broiler for 3 minutes. Turn the slices over and broil for another 3 minutes. Transfer back to the bowl and let cool. Add the smoked trout, radicchio, lemongrass, and mint; toss gently. Add the dressing and toss gently again to combine. Serve immediately.

MAKES 4 SERVINGS

1 tablespoon minced fresh sage

1 tablespoon peeled and minced fresh ginger

¼ teaspoon salt

¼ teaspoon freshly grated nutmeg

¼ teaspoon white pepper

1 tablespoon balsamic vinegar

1 tablespoon olive oil

3 Anjou pears, peeled, cored, and cut into long, thin slices

Vegetable oil spray

3 smoked trout fillets, skin removed and cut into pieces

2 cups thinly sliced radicchio

1 stalk lemongrass, tough outer layers removed, tender inner stalk minced

½ cup fresh mint leaves, torn

¼ cup or more Citrus Dressing (page 58)

This is the Thai version of chicken soup made in many cuisines and considered the perfect remedy for a cold. It is prepared with a combination of healing herbs and spices with the tastes, flavors, and aromas belonging to Wind element. It is also a potent seasoning, protecting the respiratory system as well as healing respiratory impairments.

RESTORATIVE SOUP Gaeng Tom Klong

IN a large saucepan, combine the water, shallots, *krachai,* galangal, lemongrass, and chiles and bring to a boil. Reduce the heat to medium-low, cover, and simmer for 20 minutes.

ADD the salt, fish sauce, lime leaves, plums, and sugar, cover, and cook over low heat for another 15 minutes. Stir in the tamarind puree and taste for a pleasing balance of sour, salty, and slightly sweet. Add the catfish, increase the heat to medium-high, cover, and cook for another 5 minutes. Ladle into serving bowls, garnish with the cilantro, and serve with hot white, brown, or red rice.

MAKES 4 SERVINGS

5 cups water

3 shallots, peeled and slightly crushed

3 to 4 *krachai* (Chinese keys or lesser galangal), or 5 thin slices fresh ginger with the peel on, slightly crushed

10 thin slices galangal or fresh ginger with the peel on

3 stalks lemongrass, tough outer layers removed, tender inner stalk sliced and slightly pounded

4 to 5 fresh serrano chiles, quartered lengthwise

1 tablespoon salt

¼ cup fish sauce

10 kaffir lime leaves, slightly crushed, or grated zest of 1 lime

1 cup sliced tart plums

¼ cup palm sugar, light brown sugar, or maple sugar

3 tablespoons Tamarind Puree (page 25)

1 pound catfish fillets, cut into bite-size chunks

¼ cup chopped fresh cilantro

S weet, buttery coconut is the prescription for Earth element's cold evenings. Ginger, a true friend in need for Wind element people, balances the richness of coconut, making it easy to digest.

COCONUT AND CANDIED GINGER MACAROONS

MAKES 30 COOKIES

2 large egg whites

Pinch of salt

⅔ cup granulated sugar

1 teaspoon almond extract

2 cups Grated Fresh Coconut (page 101)

2 tablespoons minced candied ginger

Vegetable oil spray

½ cup confectioners' sugar

PREHEAT the oven to 350°F.

IN a large bowl, beat the egg whites with an electric mixer on high speed until soft peaks appear. Add the salt and continue to beat. Slowly add the granulated sugar and almond extract and continue beating until stiff peaks form. Fold in the coconut and candied ginger, taking care not to deflate the whites.

LINE a baking sheet with aluminum foil and coat lightly with the vegetable oil. Pick up a tablespoonful of the mixture and mold it into a ball. Place on the greased baking sheet. Repeat with the remaining coconut mixture, spacing the balls 1 inch apart. Bake for 20 minutes. Remove from the oven and let cool slightly before dusting with the confectioners' sugar. Serve warm, or let cool completely before storing in an airtight container. They will keep for a week or more.

BLISS

I have known my friend's son Darren since he was born. Through the years, she has often shared with me how different he is compared to his older sister. To help her better understand her son, we used the Wheel to find his home element. I was not surprised, although my friend was, to discover that her son is a Wind element child with a cusp of Water element.

Never an easy-to-care-for baby, Darren clung to his mother and always needed extra hugs and caresses. He did not sleep through the night until he was almost one year old. To this day, the slightest sound will wake him and his mother has to soothe him back to sleep. As a baby, he always stopped fussing when she took him with her to the Buddhist temple. The singsong sounds of chanting monks immediately calmed and soothed him. Encouraged by this change, she began taking him regularly. Each visit resulted in the same contented reaction.

When he was old enough to crawl, he would move closer to the monks, sitting quietly, as if in a state of meditation. He also seemed to instinctively know when Friday arrived, suddenly gaining back his appetite. On Fridays, my friend follows Buddhist tradition and cooks vegetarian foods for her family. It is clearly the child's preferred diet.

The monks say that her son possesses an old soul. The serene atmosphere of the temple calms his Wind element spirit, channeling its force and redirecting its energy, and thus lessening his fear. In the temple's environment, his heart and mind are at peace. Wise, but still young, he does not comprehend his older spiritual self. Until he can be taught to understand his sensitive nature and appreciate who he is, the world will frighten and confuse him. His sensitivity, combined with his sharp intellect, stirs fear and anxiety. To help him trust his inner Wind element spirit, the monks advised my friend to guide her son to channel his energy in both spiritual and artistic endeavors. Through serenity and beauty, they said, his understanding will mature and blossom. Peace will then embrace his mind and spirit.

Some of you, as Wind element people, are like my young friend. Endowed with a wise old soul, learn to feel your inner Wind element spirit. Learn to know its force and tap its energy. Recognize your fear for the shadow that it is. Strive for a vision of understanding and connect with your "wise" spirit. The vision of understanding graces the Wind element person with sensitivity, tenderness, and compassion. Find your "quiet" sanctuary within and without. Grace your life with beauty and calmness. Pamper your body and nurture your mind and spirit, so that you will achieve "peace of mind." This is your mantra.

YOUR PHYSICAL SELF

Whether it is changes in the weather or your mood, the Wind element person's sensitive physical self shows it all. Work out a regular preventive treatment plan to keep your skin, nails, and hair healthy and beautiful.

A Wind element person's delicate skin is vulnerable to changes in weather, which results in chapped, dry, and wrinkled skin. To nurture and keep your natural glow from prematurely fading, treat yourself to a facial mask after being exposed to sun or a chilly wind, which will restore the natural moisture to your skin, leaving it smooth and soft.

MANDARIN ORANGE ESSENTIAL OIL FACIAL MASK

COMBINE all the ingredients, except for the cucumber slices, in a small bowl. Wash your face and dry it thoroughly. Apply the mixture liberally to your face, rubbing it in a circular motion, starting at your forehead and moving down your face and neck. Take care not to get the mask in your eyes. Lie down and place the cucumber slices over your closed eyes. Relax, breathe deeply and evenly, and let your mind drift into a peaceful rest. Leave the mask on for 15 minutes. Wash your face, dry it thoroughly, and apply Lemongrass Skin Toner (page 196), then a moisturizer.

MAKES 1 APPLICATION

1 egg white, slightly beaten

1 tablespoon honey

2 tablespoons fine rice flour

10 drops mandarin orange essential oil

2 slices cucumber

This winter mask revitalizes the skin, tightens pores, and leaves your face soft and silky.

AVOCADO-SPEARMINT FACIAL MASK FOR WINTER

COMBINE all the ingredients, except for the cucumber slices, in a small bowl. Wash your face and dry it thoroughly. Apply the mixture to your face and rub it in a circular motion, starting the forehead and moving down to your face and neck. Take care not to get any in your eyes. Lie down and place the cucumber slices over your eyes. Relax, breathe deeply and evenly, and let your mind drift into a peaceful rest. Leave the mask on for 15 minutes. Wash your face, dry it thoroughly, and apply Lemongrass Skin Toner (page 196), then a moisturizer.

MAKES 1 APPLICATION

2 tablespoons plain yogurt

1 tablespoon chopped fresh aloe vera

3 tablespoons pureed avocado

5 drops spearmint essential oil

2 slices cucumber

To unwind before sleep, treat yourself with this body scrub. It will exfoliate dead skin, leaving your skin smooth and soft, and quiet your mind, releasing you to a night of sweet dreams.

CHAMOMILE AND ROSE BODY SCRUB

MIX all the ingredients together in a medium bowl. Standing in the shower, apply a tablespoonful of the scrub at a time and rub in a circular motion, massaging your entire body, face, and hair. Concentrate the scrub around your neck, shoulders, and chest. Sit in a chair and breathe in the fragrance. Unburden your mind and rest for 10 minutes. Shower away the scrub. After drying, work in moisturizer over your entire body. With your body cleansed and mind calmed, you are ready for a good night's sleep.

MAKES 1 APPLICATION

½ cup almond puree (page 21)

1 tablespoon honey

4 to 5 sprigs fresh chamomile with leaves and blossoms, minced

½ cucumber, peeled and pureed

10 drops chamomile essential oil

10 drops rose otto, rosewood, or rose absolute essential oil

*T*his marvelous potion will plump up and moisturize your hands.

HONEY-APPLE TREATMENT FOR DRY OR WRINKLED HANDS

MIX all the ingredients together in a small bowl, then massage it into your hands, fingers, arms, and elbows. Leave the mixture on for at least 10 minutes. Relax and breathe in the refreshing fragrance. Wash and dry your hands, arms, and elbows before lavishly applying moisturizer.

MAKES 1 APPLICATION

1 egg white, slightly beaten

1 tablespoon fine rice flour

1 tablespoon honey

2 tablespoons pureed apple

10 drops rose otto, rosewood, or rose absolute essential oil

*E*nliven dry, brittle, and lackluster hair with this easy-to-make hair treatment and turn a bad hair day into a sensual, silky hair day. Apply when the weather changes, or as needed.

ALMOND, AVOCADO, AND LEMON HAIR TREATMENT

COMBINE all the ingredients in a medium bowl. Wet your hair and apply the mixture. Work it into your scalp and hair. Wrap a warm, wet towel around your hair and relax for 15 minutes. Rinse and shampoo.

MAKES 1 APPLICATION

⅓ cup almond puree (page 21)

2 tablespoons pureed avocado

⅓ cup Lemongrass Skin Toner (page 196)

½ lemon, pureed (rind and all)

For tired and achy feet, try this foot soak. You'll be ready to dance the night away.

LEMON-PEPPERMINT FOOT SOAK

Fill a large basin with warm water. Squeeze the lemon juice from the lemon halves into the basin and add the rinds and the lemon slices. Tear and lightly crush the rose petals, and sprinkle them into the water. Add the lemongrass, peppermint leaves, and rose and peppermint essential oils and stir with your hand to combine. Place your feet in the water. Massage the soles and heels with the lemon rinds. Sit back and relax until the water cools. Dry your feet thoroughly and massage them with moisturizer, or with almond oil mixed with tea tree essential oil.

2 lemons, 1 halved, 1 sliced

Petals of 3 roses

2 stalks lemongrass, tough outer layers removed, tender inner stalk sliced lengthwise and slightly pounded

Leaves from 1 bunch fresh peppermint, crushed

12 drops rose otto, rose absolute, or rosewood essential oil

15 drops peppermint essential oil

10 drops tree tea essential oil

¼ cup almond oil

mind and spirit

The simple act of breathing is your passage to understanding. Let each breath, drawn from the depth of your abdomen, lead you on a journey to your inner self. Your breath is the Wind within, the force of life. Follow its flow to the well of peace and tranquility, where fear is just a fleeting feeling. Use your breath to push fear from your mind. If the gathering storm threatens to darken your spirit, let the sweet and protective scents of nature lend you a helping hand. Breathe in their nurturing aromas; filter out noise, burdens, and pain, dwelling in the tranquility of your mindfulness.

Buy soaps, bath oils, toner for your skin, and body lotions with any of the essential oils below. While using them, remember to breathe deeply and let their perfume work its magic:

BASIL: Soothing as well as stimulating, it has antiseptic properties.

BERGAMOT: Aromatic and slightly sweet, it is the predominant flavor in Earl Grey tea. The infusion is good for colds, coughs, nausea, or sore throats. Apply externally to heal acne, cold sores, and insect bites. As an essential oil, bergamot dissipates anxiety, depression, and other stress-related conditions.

CARAWAY: With its calming qualities, it's good for relaxing tight muscles and easing stomachaches and menstrual cramps—try adding the seeds to a quick bread or cookie recipe.

LEMON: Aromatic and astringent, lemon is a stimulant and an antiseptic; used externally, it is uplifting and refreshing. The essential oil can be added to lotion to treat sunburn and to cleansers to clean oily skin or greasy hair. After its application, stay out of direct sunlight, because it heightens your sensitivity to the sun's rays. Lemon essential oil brightens the spirits.

LEMONGRASS: Aromatic, pungent, and stimulating, it refreshes and helps eliminate unpleasant odors. Used externally, it tones the skin, as well as cleanses oily hair and treats dandruff. Lemongrass calms frayed nerves and centers one back to the present.

LIME: Aromatic and astringent, as well as stimulating and cleansing, it refreshes and has an uplifting quality. After its application, stay out of direct sunlight, because it heightens your sensitivity to the sun's rays.

MANDARIN: Its refreshing, aromatic scent soothes and keeps the mind alert. Used externally, it helps repair your skin and complexion.

MELISSA ABSOLUTE (LEMON BALM): An aromatic antidepressant with uplifting and calming effects, it is used to lessen fear, nervousness, anger, and grief. It also eases the discomfort of menstruation when taken as a tea.

MUSTARD: It facilitates blood flow and is used to soothe stiffness and muscle and joint pains. Mustard seeds and oil are an emotional restorative.

PEPPERMINT: Aromatic and pungent, it is good for chills, colic, fever, nausea, diarrhea, dizziness, headache, sore throat, insomnia, and mild gastric problems, as well as motion sickness. Used externally, it's both stimulating and refreshing.

ROSE OTTO, ROSEWOOD, ROSE ABSOLUTE: Sweet and aromatic, it is considered an antidepressant. It is used on dry skin, sensitive complexions, and for wrinkles, and it helps relieve coughs and hay fever, depression, stress, nervous tension, and insomnia.

SPEARMINT: Aromatic and pungent, it energizes both the body and mind. Used externally, it revitalizes and refreshes, as well as helps cleanse and tighten facial pores.

SWEET ORANGE: Aromatic and astringent, it refreshes, uplifts, and is good for increasing low energy levels. In a massage oil, it eases digestion after a heavy meal. Used in a facial mask, it helps lessen wrinkled skin, especially after being in the sun.

TEA TREE: A stimulant, it warms and boosts one's spirit, as well as relieves abscesses, acne, blisters, burns, and cold sores. It is also helpful in easing coughing, sinusitis, and fever.

TURMERIC: Pungent, it is a stimulant, carminative, and antibacterial agent, and it cleanses the skin and helps improve its condition. Be cautious with the color, which might stain. Turmeric is believed to improve blood circulation and eases headaches.

MASSAGE

Touch is a gift of love. It quiets fear and comforts the mind and spirit. As a Wind element person, regular deep tissue massage is essential. Prepare your own healing essential oils and let their scents embrace you with serenity and peace.

Start with a base of ½ cup almond, sesame, or mustard oil. Mix with 5 to 10 drops of the essential oil best suited to your needs. Take the oil of your choice when going for a massage. Enjoy your massage, close your eyes, and let your body and mind revel in the gift of touch. Afterward, leave the oil on for at least an hour before showering. Remember to drink plenty of water afterward to detoxify your body.

For both oils, massage them all over your body, concentrating around the areas where the muscles are tight and tense, like the temples, behind the ears, the base of the neck down toward both shoulders, and along the upper and lower back.

FOR RELIEVING STRESS: If you feel over-burdened by the stress induced by too much work, combine ½ cup almond, sesame, or mustard oil and 10 drops each bergamot, mandarin orange, and lemon essential oils (for day use), or rose otto, rosewood, or rose absolute, peppermint, and chamomile essential oils (for night use) in a bottle. Seal tightly and shake well.

FOR CALMING THE SPIRIT: This massage oil will soothe anxiety, agitation, and even melancholy. Combine ½ cup almond, sesame, or mustard oil and 10 drops each bergamot, Melissa, and pepper-mint essential oils in a bottle. Seal tightly and shake well.

SACHETS

Create a fragrant sachet for drawers and closets, using a pouch made with lace or silk appliqués or crocheted with velvet yarn and adorned with beautiful beads. Fill it with several cotton balls infused with your favorite essential oil from the list below. Then tie with colorful ribbons in multiple pastel colors. The perfume will renew and refresh you each time you open drawers or closets.

FOR INTIMATE APPAREL: Sprinkle 10 drops each bergamot (calming), mandarin (soothing), and sweet orange (uplifting) essential oils.

FOR CLOTHING CLOSETS: Sprinkle 10 drops each lemon (cheering), spearmint, (revitalizing), and tea tree (stimulating) essential oils.

FOR NIGHTCLOTHES: Sprinkle 10 drops each chamomile (calming), bergamot (calming), and Melissa (refreshing and soothing) essential oils.

TRADITIONAL REMEDIES FOR MINOR AILMENTS

When you are tired and feel out of sorts, as a preventive measure against getting sick, relax, eat light and healthful meals, and use the following traditional treatments as needed. In case of illnesses, in addition to your doctor's prescriptions, these remedies will speed your recovery.

FOR COLDS: Fill a saucepan with water and bring to a boil. Add 12 slices ginger, slightly pounded; 2 stalks lemongrass, tough outer layers removed, tender inner stalk sliced and slightly pounded; and 9 shallots, peeled and slightly pounded. When you can smell the fragrance, remove the pan from the heat and add 7 drops each of bergamot and spearmint essential oils. Set the saucepan on a table; sit in front of it with a large towel draped over your head and the saucepan. Breathe in the steam deeply for 1 to 2 minutes. Uncover and breathe the fresh air for a minute, before re-draping the towel over your head and the saucepan. Repeat for 10 to 15 minutes. Rest and try to sleep.

FOR SUNBURN: Fill the bathtub with cool water. Add 15 drops each tea tree and mandarin orange essential oils to the bath along with 3 sliced lemons; 5 stalks lemongrass, tough outer layers removed, tender inner stalk sliced and slightly pounded; 3 to 4 aloe vera leaves, sliced lengthwise to extract the inner jelly-like liquid; and 3 cucumbers, sliced. Soak for 15 to 20 minutes, using the cucumber slices and aloe vera leaves to lightly massage your skin. Pat yourself dry before applying aloe vera lotion along with drops of lemon essential oil to your skin.

Note: I keep a pot of aloe vera growing by my kitchen door in case I burn or cut myself. I also have several growing in the little garden next to my restaurants for my staff. Just twist off a leaf and apply the oozing, clear liquid to a small cut or burn.

FOR COLD HANDS AND FEET: Combine 1 tablespoon mustard oil with 1 tablespoon minced fresh ginger and 4 drops each basil and caraway essential oils. Mix well. Warm for 20 seconds in a microwave, then massage onto your hands and feet. Put a pair of socks on your feet, and cotton gloves on your hands, and leave the oil on for at least 1 hour.

FOR ACHY JOINTS AND MUSCLES: Combine 1 tablespoon mustard oil, 6 drops each lemongrass, caraway, and clove essential oils, and 1 tablespoon minced ginger in a small bowl. Heat the mixture in a microwave for 20 seconds. Massage the warm mixture onto the affected area. Leave on for at least 1 hour.

FOR INSOMNIA: Combine 5 drops each chamomile, bergamot, peppermint, and lemon verbena essential oils. Massage the mixture onto the neck, shoulders, chest, hands, and feet. Breathe in the magical scents, relax, close your eyes, empty your mind, and follow the rhythm of your breath. It will lull you to sleep.

CHAPTER SIX

The soft light lifted the veil of night, rousing *Paa* (Auntie) Jim, the cook, from her sleep. Trying not to wake the rest of the family, she rose early from her sleeping mat and quietly crept to gather kindling from the yard. Shuffling toward the kitchen's patio, she piled the wood in a terra-cotta brazier, nestling it among dried leaves and branches, and struck a match. The hungry flames from the newly lit fire fed on the kindling.

One by one, she added pieces of charcoal and gently blew on the flames, causing the fire to billow, snap, and pop with glee, turning the black coals into glowing red ones. Heat warmed her smooth face. By and by, ribbons of gray and white smoke swirled, drifting away from the kitchen and filling the crisp morning air with the smell of burning wood. As the sky brightened, the crackling flame fueled a pot of bubbling rice porridge for breakfast.

Throughout the day, as hard coals disintegrated into soft gray ashes, Paa Jim kept the fire glowing with fresh additions. By midday, and then again in the evening, the live hot coals were transferred to several braziers to fuel more cooking fires. It wasn't until twilight faded into darkness that she finally let the fire smolder and die, until it too, like the stars overhead, turned white and cold.

Paa Jim and millions of other Thai cooks start each day by building *fai*, or fire, to prepare meals. *Fai* is also the word for the Fire element, which is described by Thai traditional healers, as "the fuel that burns what we eat into nutrients for our body." Just as the fire's heat warmed Paa Jim's face, so the Fire element circulates through our bodies, heating us and regulating our bodies' temperatures.

FIRE

My mother was a Fire element person. She was born and raised in northern China, where there were four seasons, including a cold, snowy winter. Moving to tropical Thailand was difficult for her. Until she and my father relocated to the temperate climate of northern California, her life in the tropics was a constant battle with heat. For starters, steaming humidity and blistering heat can turn a Fire element person's sensitive skin into a red, clammy, perspiring mess.

Mother's hair turned completely gray by the time she was in her mid-thirties, a typical occurrence among Fire element people. Her regular visits to the hairdresser kept the gray hidden and her otherwise wiry hair tamed. Her morning toiletry and makeup routine were regimented and fastidious.

Her dresser was stacked with bottles and jars of oils, cleansing creams, and face powders, used in a valiant battle to clear her oily skin and clogged pores, another typical condition of the Fire element person. While sewing late one night on her beloved sewing machine, she accidentally pierced through the nail of her middle finger. As the wound healed, the nail grew back as good as new, and remained strong and healthy throughout her life. This type of resilience is another of the Fire element's physical attributes.

Mother was always preoccupied with the never-ending demands of raising a family and our antiques business. Her fierce determination and self-confidence, other admirable traits of Fire element people, gave her the will to educate her three children beyond our social and economic status. To increase sales in the family business, she brilliantly and regularly came up with marketing ideas to attract customers. With

her heavy workload and responsibilities, she would be the last to bed, stealing quiet moments to read her favorite history books while the rest of the family slumbered. As a typical Fire element person, five to six hours of sleep was all she needed. Her sleep was often filled with vivid and imaginative dreams, which she recalled with great detail. Thais believe this ability is a gift bestowed upon Fire element people. Arising from the depths of the unconscious, a spiritual messenger is said to guide Fire element people through the unpredictable course and demanding duties of daily living.

If the Fire element is your home element, you may recognize some of my mother's characteristics as similar to your own. Fire element people glow with immense energy, which radiates physically, emotionally, and spiritually. Although many of you are of average physique, your fiery presence shines large with an aura of vigor and exuberance. Charismatic, self-assured, intense, and vibrant, your strong sense of purpose in life and natural gifts of leadership generate admiration and awe.

Just as fire can burn out of control, leaving a trail of destruction, so can the volatile emotions of Fire element people. Your natural ability to lead can, at times, rob you of patience, tolerance, and empathy for others. Like the raging

flames, your anger and quick judgment of another's behavior can be devastating and feed smoldering, hurtful feelings harbored within. Fire element people need to channel their incendiary and dazzling flames into positive action, generous, charitable causes, and intelligent projects.

Just as a warm fireplace comforts our bodies and gladdens our spirits on cold wintry days, so does the presence of Fire element people, who are in touch with their physical and emotional selves. The rest of us need your warmth, dynamic personality, and witty and intelligent minds. And if, for some reason, you feel your Fire element about to flare out of control, or if your mood takes a sudden impatient or angry turn, express that fiery force in a vigorous physical workout. There's nothing like exercise such as yoga, swimming, fast walking, or running to burn off excessive steam.

Fire element people can be seduced by their own brainpower, so practice letting go. Give the intellectual side of your brain a rest by using the brain's creative side. Work with your hands and engage in artistic projects with visible and pleasurable results such as cooking, gardening, drawing, knitting, carpentry, or pottery.

FOOD FOR HEALTH

Just as Paa Jim expertly built the fire each day to cook for her family, you can follow her example and perfect the inner fire within you. Care for it with patience and consistency. Choose the right kind of kindling. For Fire element people, this means a dietary road map that maintains and regulates the body's inner heat. Lean, clean fuel sources will result in well-functioning digestive systems and evenly regulated body temperatures, the two most sensitive dynamics of the Fire element person.

Since Fire element people tend to have bottomless appetites, in order to control your weight and tendency toward heartburn and constipation, Thai folk doctors would advise against snacking between meals. Adopt the habit of leaving the table just a little hungry, rather than completely satiated. Instead of a heavy dinner, your main meal should be lunch, when nature's Fire element rules the midday hours. Keep in mind, however, that during lunch hours you will be under the double influence of your fiery home element and the time of day when fire reigns. This will exaggerate an already demanding appetite and also overload your easily taxed digestive system.

Among the foods that should be avoided or eaten sparingly are red meat, alcohol, and coffee. They are "warming foods" that spike the heat in Fire element people. Nightshade vegetables such as potatoes, tomatoes, eggplant, peppers, and chiles are believed to aggravate the inflammation of joints and muscles, another potential problem for your home element.

Sour, salty, sweet, spicy, and fermented foods also generate heat. These should be eaten in moderation and during rainy, damp, or cold weather, when you need extra fuel to keep you inner body's thermometer in sync with the weather.

A healthful diet consists of foods that stabilize Fire element people's digestive system and keep body heat constant. They include foods with natural bland, bitter, and cool/refreshing flavors. Bitter flavors are believed to cleanse and purify the blood, and to relieve fever. In other words, eat bitter-flavor vegetables to regulate your body's inner heat and temperature.

Eat bland flavors to protect the respiratory system and ease digestion. For Fire element people, bland-flavor vegetables help maintain a healthy digestive disposition and prevent constipation and heartburn.

Cool/refreshing flavors and aromas are believed to nurture the heart, calm emotions, eliminate stress, and restore tranquility. They also quench thirst, quiet the overactive Fire element, and keep fiery emotions steady and constant. Medicinal herbs spiked with peppery flavors are cool and refreshing. Refer to the chart on pages 264 to 265 for a listing of bitter-, bland-, and cool/refreshing-flavor vegetables, fruits, and herbs.

Grains such as barley, oats, rice, granola, couscous, and quinoa should be eaten, as they are more suitable and digestible for Fire element people. Buckwheat, wheat, corn, and rye, on the other hand, are considered warming, and they are to be avoided or eaten in moderation. Go easy with yeast breads because yeast is considered warming, adding to the already heat-prone Fire element person. If you must have some, toast it. Among the bean, nut, and seed families, mung, red, and yellow beans, soybeans, and sunflower seeds keep the Fire element's temperature level. Using rice bran, sunflower, safflower, and soybean oils when you cook will do likewise.

With the countless fires she has built throughout the years, Paa Jim has become expert at using her breath to kindle the coals and keep the fire constant. Fluids, for the Fire element person, are like Paa Jim's breath, maintaining the delicate balance of body heat and circulation. Too much can extinguish the fire, creating swelling, fluid retention, and an unbalanced body temperature. Not enough fluid and the body's inner heat spikes. The circulatory system gets sluggish and joints or muscles might start to feel inflamed. Your already insatiable appetite can also be intensified by bursts of combustible heat brought on by your home element's desire.

Fire element people are blessed with the discipline to maintain their emotional and spiritual health. Endowed with your sense of purpose, organizational skills, and a quick mind, there is no project or obstacle you can't handle. Together with your will and the wisdom of Thai healers, you can forge an eating plan that will synchronize and harmonize all of your dynamic appetites. Using your impressive initiative, you can create a lifestyle that radiates with good health as brilliant and nurturing as the sun's rays.

HOT WEATHER RECIPES

While hot, sunny days may delight others, the rising heat brought on by nature's Fire element coupled with your own home element can turn your body into a blazing furnace, making you long for cool shade and shelter from the sunlight. Remember your two major areas of vulnerability: your digestive system and body temperature. Both can flare out of balance from this double dose of Fire element. Shading yourself with an umbrella or wearing a hat and carrying a fan when venturing outdoors will help keep you cool. So will dressing in light pastel colors.

Think cool, stay cool, and eat cool. Try not to succumb to your increased hunger pangs. Keep your body hydrated, which will also curb your cravings. Reduce or eliminate red meat, alcohol, and rich, buttery-flavored foods on these hot summer days. Eat salty, sour, sweet, and buttery-tasting foods sparingly, as they can spike inner body heat. Instead, select from your home element's taste for bland, bitter, and cool/refreshing fruits and vegetables. These include summer melons, crisp greens, and refreshing herbs. Together, they make great summer eats and will keep you cool and unruffled even in the most oppressive heat.

BREAKFAST

Start your morning with a cool/refreshing breakfast. A glass of apple, apple-cranberry, or Watermelon Juice (page 45) is a good beginning. For something hot, have a cup of breakfast blend, Earl Grey, jasmine, or green tea. Cold cereals, including Rice Krispies or granola made with oats, combined with sunflower seeds, fresh berries or sliced peaches, and nonfat or soy milk, or rye toast or crackers with dabs of butter or low-fat cream cheese mixed with minced fresh mint and candied ginger, will ignite energy while moderating your highly charged temperament. Enjoy smoothies made from sweet, succulent summer melons, peaches, plums, nectarines, and/or apricots combined with cool cucumber or celery, with a touch of mint or basil, to fan the Fire element with a steady, refreshing

current. Balance the presence of nature's Water element, which presides over the breakfast hours, by adding sour tastes such as citrus juice.

For a powerhouse breakfast, combine a smoothie drink like Mumbo Jumbo Melon and Banana (page 39) with an egg white omelet dressed with parsley and Parmesan cheese.

LUNCH

As the sun reaches its zenith, you experience a triple crown of the Fire element (your home element, hot weather, and the lunch hour), bringing with it the possibility that an uncontrollable fire may spread through your system. Just as nature's wild fires feed on combustible fuels and air, you may burn with intense hunger pangs. Listen to the Thai healers' advice: For Fire element people to stay balanced in this extreme situation, you must contain the spreading inner fire by feeding it clean fuels on a regular schedule. Eating lunch as your main meal at the same time each day, especially during the hot weather, is a sound practice.

Nevertheless, your hungry Fire element can push your appetite to the point where it is difficult to stop eating, adding unwanted pounds to your other problems. Eating mean but lean will contain your urges and weight. Fight your hunger attacks with cool/refreshing dishes. Watercress, lettuce, cucumbers, sweet melons, jicama, chayote, peas, green beans, and carrots are summer fruits and vegetables that will serve you well.

Nothing calms a voracious appetite like hot soup. The warm, comforting broth is filling, keeping you from overeating higher calorie dishes. Hot soup on a hot, humid day is a Thai tradition, especially when prepared with a selection of bitter- or bland-flavor vegetables. It's one of the best ways to keep the body cool. Try Noodle Soup (page 82), making it with rice vermicelli and minced turkey or thinly sliced chicken, adding 5 or 6 torn lettuces leaves when you add the mustard greens and bean sprouts.

Crisp salads are like breezy streams of cool trade winds fanning you on hot summer days. Both the Fragrant Rice Salad (page 50) and Sweet 18 Salad (page 51) will shelter you from the heat inside and out. Winning combinations of salads can be made with crisp lettuce or bitter/pungent watercress mixed with sweet and crunchy jicama, water chestnuts, summer melons, or cooked lotus roots. Salads prepared with bland-, bitter-, and cool/refreshing-flavor vegetables will keep you from getting overheated and will regulate your body temperature. Mix them with a savory dressing of sweet, salty, and sour to balance your other body elements. Try these combinations:

- Equal amounts of carrot, jicama, and chayote peeled and thinly sliced into matchsticks, thinly sliced sweet onion, and slivered fresh mint tossed with Miso-Ginger Salad Dressing (page 60) and garnished with roasted pumpkin seeds

- Shredded grilled chicken, peeled and thinly sliced lotus root that you've boiled just until tender, and bitter salad greens tossed with Miso-Ginger Salad Dressing (page 60)

Liven up dishes with herbs such as mint, basil, thyme, tarragon, parsley, and cilantro. With a little practice and creativity you too can rejoice in summer's heat.

For beverages, choose from Lemongrass Tea (page 46), Chrysanthemum Tea (page 46), Watermelon Juice (page 45), mint tea mixed with a splash of orange juice, hibiscus tea, or water laced with slices of cucumber and mint sprigs. Hot herbal or green tea will aid digestion and calm overheated nerves.

If you must eat between meals, small tea sandwiches made with crackers and chopped cucumbers, radishes, or watercress mixed with low-fat cream cheese or goat cheese, or a plate of fresh watermelon slices, will ease hunger attacks.

DINNER

When the evening hours arrive, the triple influence of the Fire element is thankfully reduced to a double influence. Relax and enjoy the evening's cooling trend. Rally family and friends for a light supper graced by finger foods, cold soups, or summer salads. Fill a pitcher with chrysanthemum tea or one of the hot weather smoothies, like Mumbo Jumbo Melon and Banana Smoothie (page 39), using a stick or two of slightly pounded lemongrass to stir the beverage. Perk up bland- and bitter-flavor fruits and vegetables with sour-tasting fruits and vegetables. They will also complement nature's Water element's presence during the dinner hours.

Serve cold soups such as sparkling cucumber soup with sorrel or summer melon soup tingling with a surprising sweet dash of orange juice. A squeeze of lime can awaken the zest in ordinary lettuce. No need to be tempted by the forbidden nightshade vegetables such as tomatoes and eggplant, known to aggravate the inflammation of joints and muscles, when salads can be graced with the fresh, tangy tastes of summer fruits such as pineapple, peach, kiwi, or mango.

To end the evening, a cup of hot jasmine, green, or herbal tea is a pleasant finale to supper and soothes the overworked digestive systems of Fire element people.

TASTE	VEGETABLES	FRUITS	HERBS/SPICES	GRAINS	
BITTER	Belgian endive, broccoli raab, Brussels sprouts, collard greens, escarole, dandelion, mustard greens, kale, radicchio		Kaffir lime leaves, lemon zest, lime zest, orange zest, rosemary, star anise		
BITTER/ASTRINGENT	Tea				
BITTER/BUTTERY					
BITTER/COOL/ REFRESHING	Bitter melon, bitter salad mix, frisée		Aloe vera, Asiatic pennywort		
BITTER/SPICY	Arugula				
BLAND	Bottle gourd, chayote, fuzzy melon				
BLAND/ASTRINGENT	Artichoke, cauliflower, chrysanthemum leaf, Swiss chard, green bean, yard-long bean, wing bean	Unripe guava			
BLAND/BITTER	Broccoli, Chinese broccoli, eggplant				
BLAND/BUTTERY	Mushroom, potato, taro	Unripe papaya			
BLAND/COOL/ REFRESHING	Bamboo shoots, bean sprout, bok choy, Boston bibb lettuce, butter lettuce, Chinese okra, cucumber, green leaf lettuce, iceberg lettuce, okra, Napa cabbage, red leaf lettuce, romaine lettuce, summer squash, tatsoi, watermelon rind, water spinach, winter melon				
BLAND/SWEET	Hearts of palm, kholrabi, rutabaga				
COOL/REFRESHING			Borage, pandanus		
COOL/REFRESHING/ AROMATIC			Lemon balm, lemongrass, lemon verbena		
COOL/REFRESHING/ ASTRINGENT	Lotus root, pea shoot				
COOL/REFRESHING/ SPICY	Daikon, mache, radish, watercress				
COOL/REFRESHING/ SPICY/AROMATIC	Chinese chive, chive		Cilantro, culantro, dill, Italian basil, peppermint, spearmint, Thai basil, parsley, tarragon, thyme		
COOL/REFRESHING/ SWEET	Fennel bulb	Jicama, canary melon, cantaloupe, Crenshaw, honeydew, loquat, sugarcane, water chestnut, watermelon			
BUTTERY				Barley, oat, couscous	
BUTTERY/ASTRINGENT				Quinoa	
BUTTERY/COOL/ REFRESHING				Rice	
AROMA					
BITTER/AROMATIC					
PUNGENT/WARMING					
SWEET/AROMATIC					
WARMING/AROMATIC					
WARMING					

SEEDS/NUTS	BEANS/LEGUMES	COOKING OILS	ESSENTIAL OILS	SEASONINGS
	Cocoa, fava			
Almond				
Sunflower, pumpkin	Mung, red, soy	Safflower, sunflower, soy		
			Cajuput	
			Camphor, clove, cinnamon, eucalyptus, ginger, nutmeg, sandalwood, thyme	
			Jasmine, rose otto, rosewood, rose absolute	
			Rosemary	
			Tea tree	

$\mathcal{P}$repare the filling and dressing the night before, and store them in separate containers. When ready to eat, arrange the filling on the lettuce leaves, mix filling and dressing together and enjoy. Your lunch will be the envy of your friends and colleagues.

SINGAPORE-STYLE LETTUCE POUCHES

BLEND together the hoisin, sesame oil, cayenne, and marmalade in a small bowl.

IN a large bowl, combine the chicken, crabmeat, tofu, bean sprouts, and radishes and toss lightly. Drizzle the sauce over the mixture and toss to coat. Mound the mixture in the center of each of the lettuce leaves. Top with the scallions and cilantro. Loosely wrap the lettuce leaf around the filling and enjoy.

MAKES ABOUT 12 POUCHES;
ABOUT 4 SERVINGS

3 tablespoons hoisin sauce

¼ teaspoon sesame oil

½ teaspoon cayenne pepper (optional)

3 tablespoons orange marmalade

1 cup shredded cooked chicken

1 cup crabmeat, picked over for shells

1 cup diced baked tofu

1 cup bean sprouts, blanched in boiling water for 10 to 20 seconds and drained

1 cup thinly sliced radishes

½ cup minced scallions

½ cup coarsely chopped fresh cilantro

12 iceberg lettuce leaves

Lemongrass adds a refreshing and alluring fragrance to the shrimp, while balancing the presence of all home elements.

GRILLED SHRIMP ON LEMONGRASS STALKS

COMBINE the shrimp, rice flour, ginger, salt, pepper, cilantro, mint, sesame oil, and egg white in a food processor and process into a paste. Transfer to a bowl. Line a plate with wax paper and lightly spray with vegetable oil. Wet your hands, then scoop a tablespoon of the shrimp paste and mold it around the slender top of the lemongrass stalk to form a small ball. Place it on the oiled wax paper. Repeat with the remaining paste and lemongrass. (If making ahead, cover and refrigerate. It will keep for half a day or more.)

HEAT a stovetop grill pan over high heat. When the pan is very hot, carefully pick up each lemongrass stalk and lightly spray the shrimp paste ball with vegetable oil. Put on the hot pan. Turn the stalks with tongs to ensure even grilling. When the outside is slightly charred and the shrimp feels firm when pressed, about 6 minutes, remove to a serving platter and serve with the Honey Pepper Sauce.

MAKES 10 SKEWERS

½ pound medium shrimp, peeled, deveined, and thoroughly dried

2 tablespoons rice flour

1 teaspoon peeled and minced fresh ginger

½ teaspoon salt

½ teaspoon white pepper

¼ teaspoon cayenne pepper

1 tablespoon minced fresh cilantro leaves and stems

1 tablespoon minced fresh mint

1 teaspoon sesame oil

1 egg white, lightly beaten

12 stalks lemongrass, tough outer layers removed

Vegetable oil spray

Honey Pepper Sauce (page 239)

A single bite of *mieng* salmon displays Thai ingenuity in creating a dish with perfectly balanced taste and flavor. Bitter endive and spicy ginger and onion answer your Fire element's requirements. Sour lime and tart apple acknowledge the presence of nature's Water element during the evening hours. Buttery peanut nurtures the Earth element within you.

Mieng SALMON

LINE a platter with the endive leaves. Fill each with a cube each of the lime, ginger, and apple. Add a quarter of a pearl onion and a peanut. Top with a cube of salmon. When ready to eat, pick up the endive and eat in one or two bites.

MAKES 24 STUFFED LEAVES; 4 TO 6 SERVINGS

24 Belgian endive leaves

24 small cubes lime, with the peel on

24 small cubes young ginger, or regular ginger, salted for 5 to 6 minutes, rinsed, and dried thoroughly

24 small cubes tart apple, with the peel on

6 pickled pearl onions, quartered lengthwise

24 dry-roasted unsalted peanuts

24 small cubes smoked salmon (not lox)

$\mathcal{A}$ cool and refreshing salad of white- and green-colored vegetables and fruits tempers the summer heat, delights the eyes, and washes away exhaustion after a long, hot day.

CHICKEN SALAD WITH KIWI-GINGER DRESSING

HEAT the grill to medium.

COAT the chicken with the oil, then sprinkle it with the salt and pepper. Grill until the chicken is cooked through and slightly charred, turning it once, 10 to 12 minutes. Let cool, then cut into thin slices and place in a large bowl.

TOAST the sesame seeds in a small skillet over medium heat, shaking the skillet back and forth, until they are golden, about 5 minutes. Transfer to a plate to cool.

ADD the lettuce, jicama, basil, and cilantro to the chicken. Toss gently, then add the dressing and sesame seeds. Toss to mix, transfer to a serving platter, and serve.

MAKES 4 SERVINGS

1 teaspoon safflower oil

1 large or 2 small boneless chicken breast(s)

¼ teaspoon salt

⅛ teaspoon white pepper

¼ cup sesame seeds

1 small head iceberg lettuce, shredded to make 2 cups

1 cup peeled jicama cut into matchsticks

2 tablespoons slivered fresh basil leaves

2 tablespoons coarsely chopped fresh cilantro

¼ cup or more Kiwi-Ginger Dressing (page 61)

*I*f there is a creative way to make a delectable salad that balances nature's Water element (the time of day) with your own home element's needs, this is it. Crispy, sweet jicama and tangy, fruity pineapple tossed with watercress's bitter flavor make a nice accompaniment for the delicate, succulent scallops.

WATERCRESS, JICAMA, PINEAPPLE, AND GRILLED SCALLOP SALAD WITH KIWI-GINGER DRESSING

HEAT the grill to medium.

COMBINE the scallops, salt, garlic, and oil in a medium bowl. Place a fine-mesh rack on the grill rack. Wait for 5 minutes for the rack to get very hot. Place the scallops on the rack and grill until slightly charred, whitish, and firm to the touch, 5 to 6 minutes. Remove from the heat. When cool, cut each into halves or quarters. (If making ahead, store in a container with lid and refrigerate. The scallops will keep for several hours.)

TOSS together the watercress, jicama, pineapple, and lemongrass in another medium bowl. Add half the dressing and toss lightly. Transfer to a serving plate and top with the scallops. Drizzle the remaining dressing over and serve immediately.

MAKES 4 SERVINGS

1 pound large scallops

¼ teaspoon salt

½ teaspoon minced garlic

1 tablespoon safflower or soybean oil

1 cup tightly packed watercress

1 cup peeled jicama cut into matchsticks

½ cup slivered fresh pineapple

1 stalk lemongrass, tough outer layers removed, tender inner stalk thinly sliced and separated into rings

¼ cup or more Kiwi-Ginger Dressing (page 61)

*T*here is enough substance provided by the avocado, crabmeat, and yogurt in this light, summery soup to appease the appetite of any Fire element person.

COLD CUCUMBER, MELON, AND SORREL SOUP

COMBINE the crabmeat, avocado, chives, 2 teaspoons of the mint, the lemon zest, the pinch of salt, and the yogurt in a small bowl. Mix well and set aside.

PUT the cucumber, melon, sorrel, almond milk, honey, pepper, the remaining 1½ teaspoons salt, and the remaining mint in a food processor and process until smooth. Transfer to chilled serving bowls and garnish with the crabmeat mixture. Serve immediately.

MAKES 4 SERVINGS

½ cup crabmeat, picked over for shells

⅓ cup diced avocado

2 teaspoons minced fresh chives

⅓ cup minced fresh mint

Grated zest of 1 lemon

1½ teaspoons plus a pinch of salt

2 tablespoons low-fat plain yogurt

4 cups peeled, seeded, and chopped cucumber

2 cups ripe honeydew melon chunks

1 cup frozen honeydew melon chunks

1 cup chopped sorrel or iceberg lettuce tossed with 1 tablespoon fresh lemon juice

1 cup Almond Milk (page 21)

1 tablespoon honey

⅛ teaspoon white pepper

m y daughter, Angela, had her first taste of cold peach soup when she was nine years old, sitting on a sunny deck overlooking the Monterey peninsula. This exceptionally delicious soup lit up her face as bright as the glittering lights dancing on the blue sea.

COLD PEACH AND GINGER SOUP WITH ALMONDS

COMBINE the yogurt, 1 tablespoon of the honey, and the mint in a small bowl. Set aside.

PUT the remaining ingredients, except for the almond slivers, in a food processor and process until smooth. Transfer to chilled serving bowls and garnish with a dollop of the yogurt mixture. Sprinkle the almond slivers over the yogurt and serve immediately.

MAKES 4 SERVINGS

½ cup low-fat plain yogurt

2 tablespoons honey

1 tablespoon slivered fresh mint leaves

2 tablespoons peeled and minced fresh ginger

4 cups peeled ripe peach chunks, chilled

1 teaspoon fresh lemon juice

1 cup cold pineapple juice

1 cup low-fat frozen vanilla yogurt

⅓ cup slivered almonds, toasted in a small skillet over medium heat until lightly golden

Fire element people, with their flair for the unusual, might think baking strawberries would yield something quite ordinary. But they won't be able to keep from smiling after their first taste of these sweet fruits, perfumed by orange zest and paired perfectly with tart balsamic vinegar.

BAKED STRAWBERRIES

PREHEAT the oven to 380°F.

SPREAD the almond oil over a 9 x 14-inch baking pan. Combine the vinegar, amaretto, and orange zest in a large bowl. Add the strawberries, toss to coat them, and let sit for 20 to 30 minutes, tossing them occasionally. Sprinkle the brown sugar over the strawberries, toss, and spread them with the sauce on the oiled pan. Bake until the strawberries turn slightly soft, 15 to 20 minutes. Remove from the oven and let cool.

SCOOP the ice cream into individual bowls. Spoon several tablespoonfuls of the warm strawberries with the sauce over the ice cream and serve immediately.

MAKES 4 SERVINGS

1 tablespoon almond or hazelnut oil

1 tablespoon balsamic vinegar

2 tablespoons amaretto

1 tablespoon grated orange zest

3 cups strawberries, hulled and cut in half

½ cup firmly packed light brown sugar

1 pint low-fat vanilla ice cream

my friend Steve is a great cook. This is his recipe. I altered it to better suit Fire element's requirements of bitter taste and cool/refreshing flavor by adding lemon zest and mint. The berries can be substituted with a combination of cubed pears and sliced bananas. Greek yogurt has a rich and thick texture. If you cannot find it, substitute with drained regular yogurt.

FRESH BERRIES WITH SWEETENED YOGURT

COMBINE the berries in a large bowl and toss gently to mix. Divide into four serving bowls.

PUT the yogurt, condensed milk, gelatin, lemon juice, lemon zest, and mint in a blender and blend at high speed to combine. Spoon the yogurt mixture over the berries and refrigerate for at least 1 hour or no more than 4 hours before serving.

MAKES 4 SERVINGS

One 6-ounce carton blueberries

One 6-ounce carton blackberries

One 6-ounce carton raspberries

1 cup plain low-fat Greek yogurt

¼ cup plus 1 tablespoon sweetened condensed milk

1 envelope Knox unflavored gelatin

¼ cup fresh lemon juice

1 teaspoon grated lemon zest

2 to 3 fresh mint leaves, slivered

RAINY WEATHER RECIPES

Rainy days brought on by the Wind element are easier times for Fire element people than for those with other home elements. Heavy, intense rain, however, can douse the internal flames, causing the body to lose its natural resistance and warm balance. You might catch a cold, or, if you are prone to allergies, rain might aggravate them. When going out into the damp outdoors, keep your body's Fire element warmly lit by covering your head, neck, and chest.

Food and drink for rainy days should definitely include your home element's food group of bland and bitter flavors, with a touch of the Water element's sour tastes and Wind element's pungent flavors. Bland-flavor foods such as bean sprouts, okra, mushrooms, bamboo shoots, and Chinese cabbage fortify your vulnerable digestive system. When damp days turn chilly, strengthen the respiratory system with the sour tastes of rose hips, cranberries, tamarind, fresh berries, citrus, and pineapple. Go lightly on sour tastes when wet days are humid and warm; they will raise the body's temperature. Instead, eat more of your home element's bitter-flavor vegetables, like radicchio, escarole, or bitter greens. They will take the edge off the heat while aiding the circulatory system and treating any congestion in the respiratory system.

Use warm- and pungent-flavor herbs and spices for seasoning. Ginger, cloves, cinnamon, nutmeg, allspice, and peppercorns all help to keep things calm when the Wind element whips up rainy weather.

Dishes cooked with these seasonal fruits and vegetables, brimming with Fire element's tastes and flavors, can brighten even the worst wet days. When the weather gets dreary, foods with your home element's tastes, flavors, and aromas will supplement your strong energy reserves, keep your mind and spirits firing at maximum capacity, and reinforce your typically robust health.

BREAKFAST

Stay snug and dry on rain-drenched mornings by insulating your usually warm and glowing home element with a protective shield. With your high energy level, a hearty breakfast is a must; rich and buttery-flavor eggs, rice porridge, or warm cereal like quinoa or oatmeal will keep your inner fires lit and protect your Earth element's joints, muscles, and tendons from getting stiff and achy. It will also put a lid on your cravings until noontime rolls around. Try adding dried cranberries or cherries to your quinoa and honey, or raisins and bananas to your oatmeal. Warm slices of toasted banana or apricot bread made with whole-wheat flour or oat bran will also hit the spot.

Limit your intake of stimulants like coffee. Even in the rain, you have the tendency to become overheated. Instead, use a juice-making machine to extract the essence from sweet and tangy seasonal fruits and vegetables in such combinations as pineapple/orange/jicama/mint, kiwi/orange/cucumber/French tarragon, or carrot/apple/celery. A cup of hot herbal tea or warm rice milk or Soy Milk (page 24) is a good accompaniment to cereals or lightly toasted slices of homemade fruit bread.

Smoothies are also an excellent choice, and bananas, which strengthen your Earth element body structure, are a good base for them. Give Berry and Papaya Smoothie (page 40) with a shake of cinnamon a whirl, then make up your own combinations.

LUNCH

During lunchtime, the sun dominates the sky, a forceful presence even on miserably wet and stormy days. Your task is to keep that fiery energy flowing without being short-circuited by soggy, moist air. Protect your sensitive circulatory and digestive systems; eat dishes prepared with seasonal greens bursting with healing bitter and soothing bland flavors. Even when nature's Wind element hurls sheets of rain, you can stay warm by eating dishes with pungent and cool/refreshing flavors.

Soups and curries are a wonderful choice. You can't beat a noodle soup on a cold day. Add rice vermicelli and thinly sliced chicken to the recipe on page 82 and substitute thinly sliced bamboo shoots and Napa cabbage for the bean sprouts and mustard greens. *Gaeng Liang* (page 94) would also be satisfying—make it with equal amounts of diced zucchini and oyster mushrooms and 1 Chinese okra, peeled and sliced into chunks, or 5 to 6 regular okra pods, diced. Or try *Gaeng Koa* (page 72), with 1½ cups sliced plums and 1½ pounds large green-lipped New Zealand mussels or 1 pound small black mussels as the main ingredients.

For a beverage, hot Lemongrass Tea (page 46) made with honey and lemon, mandarin orange tea, or ginger tea soothes the chest, throat, and the digestive tract.

For a midday snack, grapes or sliced apple or jicama, will sate hunger urges. A handful of sunflower seeds or sesame cookies with a cup of hot Lemongrass Tea or mint tea will reenergize, also taming any emotional upheaval caused by the double influence of nature's Wind element (the weather and the afternoon hours).

DINNER

Nature's Wind element, with its ever-present possibility of rain, is joined by the Water element during

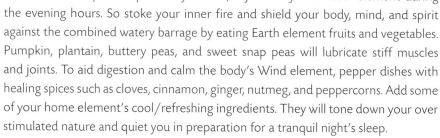

the evening hours. So stoke your inner fire and shield your body, mind, and spirit against the combined watery barrage by eating Earth element fruits and vegetables. Pumpkin, plantain, buttery peas, and sweet snap peas will lubricate stiff muscles and joints. To aid digestion and calm the body's Wind element, pepper dishes with healing spices such as cloves, cinnamon, ginger, nutmeg, and peppercorns. Add some of your home element's cool/refreshing ingredients. They will tone down your over stimulated nature and quiet you in preparation for a tranquil night's sleep.

Creamed soups made with mushrooms, carrots, watercress, or beets, with almond milk substituting for heavy cream, are healthful and sustaining. Japanese miso soup is another good choice; instant miso soup packages can be found in both American and Asian supermarkets. Adding a tablespoon of dried seaweed or cubed soft tofu to boiling miso soup will enrich its texture while fortifying your Earth element's body structure. And chicken soup's healing properties will protect you against catching a cold.

For a beverage, cranberry-apple juice, pineapple juice, grape juice, or hot ginger tea with a teaspoon of sweet honey will brace your respiratory system against the damp evening air.

*T*his salad is easy to make using leftover rice. If it has been refrigerated, bring to room temperature. Summer vegetables, fruits, and herbs add freshness and tang, combining nature's Fire element (climate) and Water element (time of day) with that of your home element.

COLD RICE SALAD

COMBINE all the dressing ingredients in an airtight container and shake together vigorously. Refrigerate until ready to use. Stir to mix well before adding to the salad.

COMBINE all the salad ingredients in a large bowl. Add the dressing and mix well. Let sit for 5 to 7 minutes before serving.

MAKES 4 SERVINGS

DRESSING

1 teaspoon Dijon mustard

½ teaspoon paprika

1 teaspoon salt

1 teaspoon honey

1 teaspoon grated lime zest

3 tablespoons apple juice

2½ tablespoons fresh lime juice

1 tablespoon olive oil

SALAD

2 cups cooked white, brown, or red rice (page 29)

½ cup diced celery

¼ cup diced carrot

½ cup diced hearts of palm

½ cup chopped scallions

½ cup chopped fresh cilantro

½ cup peeled, seeded, and diced cucumber

½ cup peeled and diced mango

1 cup diced cooked chicken or turkey or baked tofu

⅓ cup fresh tarragon leaves

¼ cup slivered fresh Thai basil or peppermint leaves

½ cup Dry-Roasted Coconut Flakes (page 101)

This is a guilt-free soup that tastes as rich as cream soup made with heavy cream. Bland-flavor mushrooms nurture the Fire element with help from spicy garlic, shallot, parsley, and mint. The soup keeps well refrigerated and tastes even better the next day.

CREAMY MUSHROOM AND CARROT SOUP

HEAT the oil in a large saucepan over medium-high heat for 1 to 2 minutes. Add the garlic and shallots and cook, stirring, until the garlic is golden and the shallots turn translucent, about 1 minute. Add the fennel, mushrooms, and carrot and stir to mix. Season with the salt and curry powder. Stir to mix, then add the parsley and mint. Mix to combine, then stir in 2 cups of the almond milk. Cover, reduce the heat to medium-low, and cook until the vegetables are soft, about 30 minutes. If the liquid evaporates too much, add a bit more of the almond milk. Remove from the heat and let cool slightly.

TRANSFER the soup to a blender, add the remaining almond milk, and puree. Transfer back to the saucepan. Cover and heat over low heat. When the soup comes to a boil, turn off the heat.

COMBINE the yogurt, honey, and lemon juice and zest in a sauce bowl.

WHEN ready to eat, stir to mix well, ladle the soup into individual serving bowls, and garnish the top with a dollop of the yogurt mixture.

MAKES 4 SERVINGS

1 tablespoon safflower oil

2 cloves garlic, minced (1 tablespoon)

2 shallots, minced (about ⅓ cup)

½ cup chopped fennel bulb

4 cups mixed sliced white and brown mushrooms

1 large carrot, finely chopped (about 1 cup)

1½ teaspoons salt

¼ teaspoon Madras curry powder

¼ cup chopped fresh Italian parsley

¼ cup chopped fresh mint

3½ cups Almond Milk (page 21)

¾ cup low-fat Greek yogurt or drained regular yogurt

1 teaspoon honey

1 teaspoon fresh lemon juice

1 teaspoon grated lemon zest

$\mathcal{A}$ light dinner is the way to go for Fire element people. These vegetable cakes can be served as an appetizer or as a main course with Creamy Mushroom and Carrot Soup (at left).

SAVORY VEGETABLE CAKES

COMBINE the daikon, carrot, mushrooms, and green beans together in a large bowl. Mix well, then add the salt, curry power, rice flour, and milk. Mix to combine before adding the egg whites, cilantro, and lime zest. Mix well. Set the mixture aside.

LINE a strainer with several layers of paper towels and set it by the stove. Heat the oil in a large skillet over high heat for 3 to 4 minutes. Put a heaping tablespoonful of the mixture in the hot oil, frying them up in several batches. Try not to overcrowd the skillet. Deep-fry until golden, 7 to 8 minutes. Using a slotted spoon, transfer them to the paper towels to drain. Serve hot, with the relish.

MAKES 18 TO 20 CAKES; 4 TO 6 SERVINGS

1 cup peeled and shredded daikon

1 cup peeled and shredded carrot

1 cup thinly sliced mushrooms

1 cup thinly sliced green beans

1 teaspoon salt

1 tablespoon Madras curry powder

½ cup fine rice flour

2 tablespoons milk, Soy Milk (page 24), or Almond Milk (page 21)

3 large egg whites, slightly beaten

1 tablespoon minced fresh cilantro

Grated zest of 1 lime

4 to 6 cups safflower, sunflower, or soybean oil

Cucumber Relish (page 54) made with 1 sliced shallot and 1 tablespoon chopped fresh cilantro

Gather family members and friends to help make these wraps. They are so good that they might just disappear into the maker's mouth instead of appearing on the plate. They're impressive appetizers, but you can also serve them as a main course, with a light salad. ✺ Choose rice papers that are loosely packaged, have the whitest color and no dark specks, and have few broken pieces or holes in the center of the sheets. After opening the package, save the remaining sheets in a zip-top plastic bag and store them in the pantry. ✺ To soften rice paper for making fresh rolls or fried spring rolls, bathe the sheet in a bowl filled with very warm water, then lay it flat on your work surface. When the sheet turns slightly soft, you can fill the center with filling. You can soften several sheets of rice paper at a time.

CRAB WRAPS

IN a medium bowl, combine the crabmeat, salt, lemon zest, paprika, cilantro, and mayonnaise. Cut each rice paper in half. Fill another medium bowl with very warm water. Bathe a piece of rice paper in the water and lay it on your work surface. Repeat with several more rice papers. As they start to soften, fill the center of each with a teaspoon or more of the crab mixture. Fold the rice paper over the filling to form a snug square. Tie a chive around it to resemble a gift package. Put on a plate lined with wax paper. Cover with a dish towel. Repeat with the remaining rice papers and crab mixture. (If making ahead, cover the wraps with plastic wrap and refrigerate for up to 4 hours. When ready to serve, pat them lightly with water to soften.)

MAKES ABOUT 30 WRAPS

1½ cups crabmeat, picked over for shells

¼ teaspoon salt

Grated zest of 1 lemon

½ teaspoon paprika

1 tablespoon minced fresh cilantro

⅓ cup mayonnaise

Fifteen 6-inch round rice papers

30 fresh chive strands, blanched in boiling water for 10 to 20 seconds and drained

Spicy arugula balances nature's Wind element. Bland-flavor mushrooms equalize the needs of the Fire element, whereas creamy and bland avocado fulfills Earth, Water, and Fire elements' needs.

GRILLED MUSHROOM, AVOCADO, AND ARUGULA SALAD

HEAT the grill to medium-high.

SPRAY the mushrooms with vegetable oil spray and put them on a fine-mesh rack set on the grill rack. Turn frequently to prevent burning. When they are slightly charred and softened, 10 to 12 minutes, transfer to a plate to cool.

QUARTER each of the smaller mushrooms. Thinly slice the portobello into long strips. Put them in a large bowl. Add the avocado and arugula and toss gently. Add the dressing and toss again. Transfer to a platter and serve.

MAKES 4 SERVINGS

2 cups white or brown mushrooms

1 large portobello mushroom, stem removed

Vegetable oil spray

1 cup peeled and diced avocado

1 cup tightly packed torn arugula

⅓ cup Mint-Cilantro Dressing (page 62), or more to taste

Cabbage and peas, with their mild flavor, are a restorative to the digestive systems of Fire element people.

CHICKEN SOUP WITH SHRIMP, CABBAGE, AND SUGAR SNAP OR SNOW PEAS

BRING the broth to a boil in large saucepan over medium-high heat. Add the salt and soy sauce. (If using canned broth, taste and season accordingly.) Reduce the heat to medium and add the carrot, celery, and onion. Cook for 5 minutes, then add the cabbage and peas. When it comes back to a boil, reduce the heat to medium-low, cover, and simmer for 5 minutes. Uncover and add the shrimp. Cook until they turn pink and firm, 3 to 4 minutes. Turn off the heat. Stir in the white pepper and scallion. Transfer to a tureen, garnish with the fried garlic, and ladle into individual serving bowls.

MAKES 4 SERVINGS

6 cups homemade (page 26) or canned low-sodium, low-fat chicken broth

1 teaspoon salt

1 tablespoon soy sauce

1 medium carrot, diced

1 stalk celery, diced

1 small onion, diced

1 cup thinly sliced cabbage

1 cup tightly packed sugar snap or snow peas

About ¼ pound small shrimp, peeled and deveined

¼ teaspoon white pepper

1 scallion, minced

1 tablespoon fried garlic (page 100)

Fresh asparagus reminds me of a spring rain. Its mild, slightly bitter, and sweet taste is delicious paired with this delicate sauce made with crabmeat.

STEAMED ASPARAGUS WITH CRAB SAUCE

PEEL the asparagus with a vegetable peeler. Fill a pot halfway full with water and bring to a boil. Place the asparagus stalks in a pie plate and into the steamer basket. Steam until they are tender, 10 to 12 minutes. Turn off the heat and leave the asparagus in the steamer to keep warm.

HEAT the sesame oil in a medium saucepan over high heat for 10 to 12 seconds. Add the ginger, soy sauce, salt, crabmeat, and broth. (If using canned broth, taste and adjust the amount of salt accordingly.) Stir to mix, and reduce the heat to medium. In a small bowl, blend together the cornstarch and water. When the broth comes to a boil, stir in the cornstarch mixture and stir until the broth thickens. Add the egg white and stir to mix. When the egg is cooked, turn off the heat.

TRANSFER the cooked asparagus to a serving plate. Pour the sauce over and garnish with the pepper. Serve hot.

MAKES 4 SERVINGS

12 stalks white asparagus

1 teaspoon sesame oil

1 teaspoon peeled and minced fresh ginger

1 tablespoon soy sauce

½ teaspoon salt

1 cup crabmeat, picked over for shells

1 cup homemade (page 26) or canned low-sodium, low-fat chicken broth

1 tablespoon cornstarch

2 tablespoons water

1 egg white, lightly beaten

Pinch or two of white pepper

In Thailand, grilled bananas are sold and eaten as snacks from the crack of dawn through the day and night to the wee hours of the next morning. This is because banana is easily digestible—a wholesome fruit for everyone.

GRILLED BANANAS

IN a small saucepan, combine the salt, brown sugar, and almond milk; cook over medium-low heat, stirring, until the sugar is dissolved. Remove from the heat.

PREPARE a smoldering fire in a charcoal grill or preheat a stovetop grill pan over medium-low heat.

PEEL the bananas and save a couple of the peels. Put the bananas on the grill and grill until they turn slightly brown on all sides, about 5 minutes. One by one, place each grilled banana back in one of the reserved peels, put a plate on top, and press down to flatten the banana. Put the banana back on the grill and brush with the brown sugar syrup, turning and brushing the banana until it's completely covered. Grill until warm all the way through. Put the bananas in a shallow plate and pour the remaining syrup over them. Serve warm.

MAKES 4 SERVINGS

¼ teaspoon salt

3 tablespoons light brown sugar

⅓ cup Almond Milk (page 21)

12 firm, slightly underripe baby bananas or 6 firm, slightly underripe regular bananas

*C*ooked Anjou pears infused with lovely lemongrass and galangal revive the Fire element person's smoldering flames.

GLAZED PEARS IN LEMONGRASS AND GALANGAL SYRUP

PUT the lemongrass, galangal, lemon zest, and water in a large saucepan and bring to a boil. Reduce the heat to low and simmer for 30 minutes. Remove the lemongrass, galangal, and lemon zest. Increase the heat to medium, add the sugar, and stir to mix. When the sugar is dissolved, add the pears, cover, reduce the heat to medium-low, and cook for 5 minutes. Uncover and continue to cook until the liquid turns syrupy, 20 to 25 minutes, turning the pears occasionally.

SERVE warm or cold with vanilla ice cream or whipped cream.

MAKES 4 TO 6 SERVINGS

4 stalks lemongrass, tough outer layers removed, tender inner stalk thinly sliced and slightly pounded

10 to 15 thin slices galangal or fresh ginger, slightly pounded

3 to 4 strips lemon zest

2 cups water

²/₃ cup sugar

3 ripe Anjou pears, peeled, cut in half, and cored

Low-fat vanilla ice cream or whipped cream

*I*t might seem odd to serve ice cream on a wet, cold day, but in fact it is just the right dessert in which to indulge. This is because ice is thought to add warmth to our bodies. Spicy basil is especially good for Fire element people, relieving dizziness and indigestion and easing colds.

BASIL ICE CREAM

COMBINE the milk, basil, ¼ cup of the sugar, and the salt in a medium saucepan and bring to a boil. Reduce the heat to medium and cook until the basil is limp and soft, about 9 minutes, stirring constantly to keep the milk from curdling. Remove from the heat and let cool for 45 minutes.

TRANSFER the mixture to a blender and blend until the basil is pureed.

IN a large bowl, beat the yolks and the remaining sugar with an electric mixer until thick and pale. Add the milk mixture in a steady steam and continue to beat until smooth and well mixed. Return the mixture to the saucepan and cook, stirring constantly, over low heat until the mixture coats the back of a spoon, 2 to 3 minutes; do not let it boil. Remove from the heat and pour through a fine-mesh strainer into a metal bowl. Refrigerate or set in a larger bowl of ice water and ice cubes. Chill completely. When it is cold, add the cream and mix well.

TRANSFER the mixture to an ice cream maker and freeze, following the manufacturer's instructions. Transfer to an airtight container and put in the freezer for at least 2 hours before serving.

MAKES ABOUT 3 CUPS

2 cups whole milk

⅓ cup tightly packed chopped fresh basil

⅔ cup sugar

Pinch of salt

4 large egg yolks

½ cup heavy cream or half-and-half

COLD WEATHER RECIPES

Cold weather is prime time for Fire element people. Your home element, like Paa Jim's burning charcoals, is firing your inner brazier with constant flames. Because of your warm constitution, you can usually dress lightly, with only a sweater or two, and stroll gleefully into the cold.

Although this is your season, be wise and keep your energy stoked and steady by feeding it the right kind of fuel. Besides your own home element's food groups, you might be surprised to find yourself craving warm-, sweet-, and buttery-flavor foods. This is because your body's Earth element is begging for extra lubrication to maintain joints, muscles, and tendons. Recipes using a variety of beans and nuts, including red beans, black beans, lentils, lima beans, kidney beans, and peanuts, will appease this need and make your mouth water with desire.

Tangy fruits such as pomegranates, oranges, lemons, tamarind, and limes never look as tempting as they do when it's cold outside. Their sour taste, like a bellows, will fan the body's Fire element, while keeping your respiratory system warmed and humming along.

In addition to paying attention to your body, it's a time to discipline your mind. Keep your desires and needs in balance. Baby your sensitive digestive system and keep the juices flowing with warming spices

such as ginger, cinnamon, cloves, nutmeg, pepper, cardamom, lemongrass, shallot, cumin, and mace. All have medicinal properties, which will balance out your extra intake of rich and buttery flavors.

Cold, wintry days are a gift for Fire element people. Exploding with sudden swells of energy, your creative spirits sparkle as brilliantly as crystal icicles. There seems to be no limit to the projects you can tackle. Ride the waves of your fiery power and do good work. Take a daily exercise break to burn excessive calories, protect against possible burnout, and stay in shape. Prevent exhaustion and fatigue by adding some of Wind element's pungent and aromatic herbs, such as mint and basil, to your cooking.

BREAKFAST

Invigorated by the chilly morning air, fortify yourself with a filling breakfast. Blend the sweet and tangy sour tastes of the dominant Water element presiding over the morning hours (such as orange or tangerine with cranberry, pomegranate, or apple juice) with Earth element's rich and buttery flavors, such as rice milk or Soy Milk (page 24), for a perfect breakfast drink or smoothie. This is also the season to treat yourself to a cup or two of coffee. Kindle your boundless energy with foods of your home element mixed with foods that placate nature's Earth element's cold, wintry weather. Tuck into a plate of eggs and turkey bacon or sausage links. Craving a stack of pancakes or waffles? Go ahead and indulge, but make them with light and fluffy rice flour (see page 31). Toss a warming spice such as ground cinnamon or nutmeg into the batter for good measure. Or enjoy a big bowl of oatmeal, topping it with sliced bananas or peaches and a bit of maple syrup for sweetener.

LUNCH

In a tornado of motion and crackling with energy, your home element moves into high gear with the return of nature's Fire element during the noon hours. The double influence, however, can lead to double perils. Although you are famished and ready to sit down for a big lunch, choose wisely. Feed your body the right selections by combining your home element's food groups with the Earth element's (the weather) multiple tastes and flavors of sweet, salty, astringent, and buttery. A wonderful way to do this is in a salad. One of my favorite combinations is shredded cooked chicken, arugula, and slivered fresh mint, cilantro, and Italian parsley leaves tossed with Roasted Chile Oil Dressing (page 57) and garnished with Dry-Roasted Coconut Flakes (page 101).

Now would be the time to indulge in rich, hearty curries. Use ginger, galangal, garlic, shallot, and onion to balance the rich flavors and keep your body temperature steady. They will also protect your respiratory system against the wet, cold air. Enjoy Panang Curry on page 74, preparing it with 2 cups cleaned squid cut into bite-size pieces, 2 cups green beans blanched in boiling water for 30 seconds and thinly sliced on the diagonal, and 2 fresh Thai or other hot chiles, slivered. Or try Yellow Curry (page 80), made with chicken and 1 cup each pumpkin chunks (1-inch) and thinly sliced bamboo shoots, along with 2 bay leaves and 3 cloves.

For a beverage, hot ginger, rose-hip, cinnamon-orange, or mint tea will settle down an overly active digestive system.

The Wind element stirs up the mid-afternoon hours with gusts of swirling power. For a midday snack to cool overcharged batteries, clear your mind, and elevate your mood, enjoy a cup of hot, warming mint tea. Cinnamon sugar or anise cookies can also lift the clouds and quiet the currents of an overtaxed afternoon.

DINNER

Your home element, glowing like the silvery moon in the cold, wintry night, draws both family and friends closer to you. Celebrate your gathering with a feast. Turn a winter harvest of mushrooms, lotus shoots, root vegetables, and apples into dumplings and spicy soups or stews. Add sprinkles of nutmeg, star anise, cinnamon, cloves, and mace to warm the body and calm the spirit.

Mix and match your favorite vegetables and fruits with nature's Earth and Water elements ruling the cold dinner hours. Sour-tasting citrus adds a burst of flavor to warm, buttery, and sweet winter squashes. All fuel your Fire element, keeping it burning bright and adding sparks to your exuberant personality.

For a beverage, hot apple cider served with a cinnamon stick, tea spiced with cardamom, or an herbal tea scented with jasmine or rose will nurture the digestive tract and quiet the mind for a good night's sleep.

$\mathcal{L}$ong before chefs in America decided to deconstruct traditional recipes to create new, inventive dishes, a small Bangkok restaurant hidden in an alley near the government building complex did it with an old-fashioned one-bite snack recipe called *Mieng Khum* (page 48). It has all nine basic tastes, flavors, and aromas, balancing all the body's elements.

CRISPY FRIED CATFISH WITH MIENG KHUM SAUCE

PREHEAT the oven to 400°F.

IN a large bowl, combine the minced shallot, lime zest, 1½ tablespoons of the lime juice, the salt, and safflower oil. Add the fish, mix to coat the pieces well, and marinate in the refrigerator for at least 20 minutes, but no more than 1 hour.

PUT a rack on a baking sheet and lay a fine-mesh metal rack on top. Spray lightly with vegetable oil spray.

PROCESS the macadamia nuts in a food processor until finely chopped. Transfer to a bowl and mix with the flour. Coat the pieces of fish evenly with the mixture and put on the rack. Spray the fish with vegetable oil spray and bake until the outside is golden and the inside is cooked through, 10 to 12 minutes. Remove from the oven and keep warm.

MEANWHILE, combine the *mieng khum* sauce and orange juice in a small saucepan over medium heat and stir until it comes to a boil. Remove from the heat and stir in the remaining 2 tablespoons lime juice.

Toss the endive, ginger, mango, and sliced shallots together in a medium bowl, then transfer to a serving platter. Add the fish. Drizzle with the sauce and garnish with the chile and coconut. Toss lightly and serve.

MAKES 4 SERVINGS

3 shallots, 1 minced, 2 thinly sliced

Grated zest of 1 lime

3½ tablespoons fresh lime juice

½ teaspoon salt

1 tablespoon safflower or soybean oil

1 pound catfish fillets, cut into small bite-size pieces

Vegetable oil spray

1 cup macadamia nuts

¼ cup all-purpose flour

¼ cup *Mieng Khum* sauce (page 48)

⅓ cup orange juice

1 cup thinly sliced endive

1 tablespoon peeled and thinly slivered fresh ginger

½ cup peeled and shredded green mango or tart green apple

1 to 2 fresh Thai or 1 fresh serrano chile(s), minced

1 tablespoon Dry-Roasted Coconut Flakes (page 101)

*T*hese little one-bite pouches can be made ahead and kept in the freezer to be pulled out for a last-minute get-together. They'll disappear as quickly as they come out of the steamer.

SHAO MAI WITH SHRIMP, MUSHROOMS, AND BAMBOO SHOOTS

PUT the shrimp in the food processor and process until smooth. Transfer to a medium bowl and add the remaining *shao mai* ingredients, except for the wontons and wax paper. Mix well to combine. Put a tablespoon of filling in the center of each wonton. Gather the wrapper around the filling. Give it a slight squeeze around the center to adhere the pleats onto the filling, while at the same time you pressing the top lightly with a spoon. Press the bottom down gently to flatten it. Dab a bit of water on the bottom and set it on a piece of wax paper. (You can freeze the *shao mai*. Set them on a baking sheet and freeze, then transfer them to a zip-top plastic bag. They'll keep in the freezer for a month.)

COMBINE the sauce ingredients in a small bowl. (It will keep, refrigerated, in an airtight container for a couple of days.) Fill the steamer pot of a Chinese steamer three-quarters full with water and bring to a boil. Place the *shao mai* on the steamer rack. Do not let them touch one another. Place the filled steamer rack on top of the boiling steamer pot. Cover tightly and steam for 5 minutes (1 minute more for frozen *shao mai*). Serve hot with the dipping sauce.

MAKES ABOUT 35 PIECES

SHAO MAI

1 pound medium shrimp, peeled, deveined, and patted dry

8 to 9 dried shiitake mushrooms, soaked in warm water, patted dry, and finely chopped (about ½ cup)

1 cup thinly sliced bamboo shoots, rinsed, patted dry, and finely chopped

½ teaspoon salt

½ teaspoon white pepper

1 tablespoon peeled and minced fresh ginger

1 scallion, minced

⅓ cup minced fresh cilantro

1 tablespoon soy sauce

1 teaspoon sesame oil

1 teaspoon cornstarch

1 large egg white, slightly beaten

1 package wonton wrappers (about 40 sheets)

Thirty-five 1½-inch squares wax paper

DIPPING SAUCE

¼ cup soy sauce

2 tablespoons distilled white vinegar

½ teaspoon sesame oil

1 teaspoon peeled and minced fresh ginger

If you're wondering what to make for Fire element people who have a very selective palate and prefer foods that are neat and easy to eat, try these samosas. The warm, spicy ginger, curry spices, cayenne, and mint, all of which are the perfect taste and flavor for Fire element people, will make them glow with happiness.

THAI SAMOSAS WITH CRAB AND APPLE

IN a large bowl, mix together all the ingredients, except for the filo, vegetable oil spray, and Honey Pepper Sauce.

PLACE a damp towel on your work surface and set the filo sheets on it. Cover with another damp towel. Carefully remove a sheet of filo and place it directly on your work surface. Spray it lightly with vegetable oil and place a second sheet of filo on top. Spray lightly with vegetable oil and place a third sheet on top of that. Cut the filo across into 2½-inch-wide strips. Place about 1 tablespoon of the filling at the end of each strip and fold the bottom right edge over the filling to form a triangle. Fold the triangle over toward the top, then fold from left to right. Fold again, this time from right to left, then left to right, like folding a flag. Place the samosa on a cookie sheet and spray lightly with vegetable oil. Repeat with the remaining filling and filo sheets. (You can freeze the samosas on the cookie she et, then transfer them to a zip-top plastic bag. They'll keep in the freezer for a month.)

PREHEAT the oven to 375°F.

BAKE the filo triangles until they are golden and crisp, about 15 minutes (add another minute if you're cooking them frozen). Serve hot with the Honey Pepper Sauce.

MAKES 35 PIECES

1½ cups crabmeat, picked over for shells and any excess liquid squeezed out

1 cup minced tart green apple, with the peel on

1 teaspoon peeled and minced fresh ginger

1 teaspoon Madras curry powder

½ teaspoon cayenne pepper

½ teaspoon salt

1 teaspoon cornstarch

½ cup minced fresh mint

30 sheets frozen filo dough, thawed

Vegetable oil spray

Honey Pepper Sauce (page 239)

Bland, bitter, buttery, sweet, and sour, all in one bountiful arrangement, this salad will keep Fire element's inner heat burning with precision.

ARTICHOKE HEART, HEARTS OF PALM, ENDIVE, CABBAGE, AND APPLE SALAD

PUT the almonds on a baking sheet and toast in a preheated 375°F oven until golden, about 5 minutes. Remove to cool.

Combine the artichoke hearts, hearts of palm, endive, and cabbage and toss lightly. Add the dressing and toss again. Transfer to a platter, garnish with the almonds, and serve.

MAKES 4 SERVINGS

¼ cup slivered almonds

1 cup canned artichoke hearts, rinsed, patted dry, and quartered

1 cup canned hearts of palm cut into rounds

1 Belgian endive, thinly sliced lengthwise

1 cup thinly sliced cabbage

¼ cup or more Apple-Tamarind Dressing (page 56)

my father loved cabbage of every variety cooked in any manner. While I was growing up, our family had cabbage soup for dinner every evening. My father lived to be 102 years old.

STIR-FRIED CHICKEN, CABBAGE, AND BEAN THREADS

HEAT a large skillet or wok over high heat for 1 minute. Add the oil and wait for another minute. Add the garlic and ginger and stir-fry until the garlic is golden. Add the chicken and stir-fry until it is partially cooked. Add the onion and cabbage, stir to mix, then add the soy sauce and wine. Continue to stir-fry until the chicken is fully cooked, the cabbage softened but slightly firm, and onion translucent, 3 to 4 minutes. Add the bean threads and stir until they are soft and translucent. Add the cilantro and toss to mix. Transfer to a platter and serve with hot white, brown, or red rice.

MAKES 4 SERVINGS

1 tablespoon rice bran, safflower, sunflower, or soybean oil

2 cloves garlic, minced

3 to 4 thin slices fresh ginger, peeled and minced

²⁄₃ cup thinly sliced boneless, skinless chicken breast

1 small onion, thinly sliced

2 cups thinly sliced cabbage

1 tablespoon soy sauce

2 tablespoons white wine

1 cup bean threads (page 86), softened in cool water, dried, and cut into manageable lengths

¼ cup coarsely chopped fresh cilantro

Yellowish green frilly-leaved frisée, with its slightly bitter taste, boosts the body's immune system. Grape peel, with the slightly astringent tannin surrounding the grape's sweet juicy flesh, has been claimed to do likewise. For Fire element people, this marvelous combination tends to your needs.

SHRIMP, GRAPE, AND FRISÉE SALAD WITH APPLE-TAMARIND DRESSING

COMBINE the shrimp, grapes, and frisée in a large bowl. Toss lightly and add the dressing. Toss again. Add the sunflower seeds and fried shallots and garlic. Toss and serve.

MAKES 4 SERVINGS

1 cup cooked medium shrimp

1 cup seedless grapes, cut in half

1½ cups torn frisée leaves and stems

¼ cup or more **Apple-Tamarind Dressing** (page 56)

1 tablespoon shelled roasted sunflower seeds

1 tablespoon fried shallots (page 100)

1 tablespoon fried garlic (page 100)

Recently, Thais fell in love with the avocado when Mexican food finally came to Bangkok. Although it is a pricey commodity in gourmet markets, Thais love to sprinkle sugar on avocado, spooning the nutty-buttery flesh out and eating it as a dessert. So it seems rather appropriate to add avocado to an otherwise traditional Asian chicken and rice soup.

CHICKEN RICE SOUP WITH AVOCADO

BRING the broth to a boil in a large saucepan over high heat. Add the ginger, garlic, fennel, carrot, onion, chayote, 1 teaspoon of the salt, the paprika, and 1 teaspoon of the oregano. (If using canned broth, taste and adjust the seasonings accordingly.) Cover, reduce the heat to low, and simmer for 10 minutes.

IN a medium bowl, combine the ground chicken with the remaining ¼ teaspoon salt and 1 teaspoon oregano, the pepper, and 1 tablespoon of the cilantro. Mix well before adding 2 tablespoons of the rice. Mix well.

UNCOVER the saucepan and increase the heat to medium. Use a small ice cream scooper to form the chicken mixture into balls, and gently drop them into the hot broth. Cover, reduce the heat to low, and simmer for another 10 minutes. Uncover and add the remaining rice. Cook for 5 minutes, then add the avocado. Cook for another 1 to 2 minutes. Ladle the soup into individual serving bowls and garnish with the remaining cilantro. Serve hot with the lime slices and minced chiles, if using, on the side.

MAKES 4 SERVINGS

5 cups homemade (page 26) or canned low-sodium, low-fat chicken broth

3 thin slices fresh ginger

1 clove garlic, slightly mashed

½ cup diced fennel bulb

1 cup diced carrot

½ cup diced onion

1 chayote, peeled, seeded, and diced

1¼ teaspoons salt

¼ teaspoon paprika

2 teaspoons dried oregano

½ pound ground chicken

¼ teaspoon white pepper

⅓ cup chopped fresh cilantro

½ cup cooked long-grain rice

1 ripe avocado, peeled, pitted, and diced

1 lime, thinly sliced

1 to 2 fresh Thai or 1 fresh serrano chile(s) (optional), minced

The cool months of November and December are rice-harvesting time. Fresh rice grains are made into prized desserts, such as rice pudding cooked with rich coconut cream and palm sugar. For a lighter version, I substitute the coconut cream with almond milk and use grenadine syrup to perfume it, which also turns it a pretty pink color. ⁓⁓⊱ Long-grain Thai glutinous rice can be bought in Asian supermarkets or online.

COCONUT RICE PUDDING

PUT the rice in a large bowl and add boiling water to cover. Stir to combine. Let sit until the grains have expanded, about 10 minutes. Drain and rinse several times with cold water. Shake to remove the excess water. Transfer to a medium saucepan and add the remaining ingredients, except for the coconut. Bring to a boil, stirring frequently. Reduce the heat to medium and cook, stirring frequently, until the rice grains are soft and the liquid thickens, about 20 minutes. Stir in the coconut. Serve warm.

MAKES 4 SERVINGS

½ cup long-grain Thai glutinous rice

3 cups Almond Milk (page 21)

2 tablespoons grenadine syrup

½ cup sugar

Pinch of salt

Meat from 1 young coconut, slivered (page 119)

The Chinese set off firecrackers during celebrations to scare off evil spirits, leaving a clear path to usher in good spirits. Banish the residue of a tiring day with these sweet little nuggets and celebrate your evening with sparks of contentment and joy.

FIRECRACKERS

IN a medium bowl, combine the sesame seeds, walnuts, dates, apricots, and salt. Lightly spray your hands with vegetable oil. Pick up a teaspoon or more of the mixture and roll it into a 2-inch-long, ¼-inch-wide sausage. Place on a plate. Repeat until the mixture is used up.

PLACE a wonton wrapper on the work surface in front of you with a corner pointing toward you. Position one of the "sausages" on that corner. Roll the wrapper over the filling toward the top, making a long cylinder. Dab a bit of water on the wrapper to seal it. Twist each side of the cylinder slightly to shape it like a candy wrapper. Repeat with the remaining wrappers and filling.

HEAT the oil in a wok or large skillet over high heat. Place a strainer lined with several layers of paper towels nearby. Test the oil for readiness by putting a wooden chopstick in it. When oil bubbles form around the chopstick, the oil is ready. Slide several firecrackers into the hot oil and deep-fry until golden. Using tongs or a slotted spoon, transfer them to the paper towels to drain. Repeat with the remaining firecrackers. Reduce the heat if the firecrackers seem to be browning too quickly.

TRANSFER the firecrackers to a plate and dust with the confectioners' sugar. Serve warm or cold. (These will keep in an airtight container or zip-top plastic bag for several days.)

MAKES 18 TO 20 PIECES

¼ cup black or white sesame seeds, toasted in a small skillet over medium heat until fragrant

½ cup finely chopped walnuts

¾ cup finely chopped dates

3 to 4 dried apricots, minced

Pinch of salt

Vegetable oil spray

1 package wonton wrappers (about 40 sheets)

4 cups safflower, sunflower, or soybean oil

2 tablespoons confectioners' sugar

BLISS

One evening, when I was about eight years old, and as my family settled down cozily after supper, the peace of our small shop and home was shattered by loudly honking cars and hysterical shouting. Mother sprinted to the door with father and me following close behind. As she cracked the door ajar, the noise blasted in with a gust of wind. Our front door faced the main street, which was jammed with cars, tricycles, and carts piled high with household goods. Streams of people carrying their belongings and dragging children by the hands raced amidst the traffic, unconcerned for their safety. The evening sky was painted with a strange reddish orange glow, and the air was choked with soot and the smell of burning wood.

Several blocks up from our street near the outdoor market, a fire had started and was devouring blocks like bundles of dry kindling. When the fire trucks finally arrived, the firemen found the water hydrants defective and unusable. They drove away, hoping to fill the empty tanks with water from the lake at the nearby park. In the meantime, the fire raged out of control. Gusts of hot, smoke-filled wind swirled across Father's face as he stood transfixed and pale with fear.

In the midst of the chaos, Mother suddenly turned very quiet. As she looked toward the horizon and watched the red flames and smoke creeping ever closer, she turned to Father, who was contemplating what to do. Instantly and without a trace of doubt in her voice, she shooed my brother, sister, and me back into our home and ordered us to change into our school clothes and pack our books.

We were to leave with Father the instant she gave the signal. We were to walk, not run like others, toward our aunt and uncle's home several blocks away. Faced with the possibility that our family would lose everything to the fire, all she cared about was our safety and for her children to be prepared to return to school the next morning. I have never forgotten her reaction. Despite the terror of the situation, she was serene and poised and took quick command. Her ability to rein in her fierce and furious energy and turn it into clear and calm action was astounding. She possessed absolute and unquestionable self-confidence.

Fire element people have amazing dual capabilities. If given the opportunity, you can burn out of control, incinerating everything and everyone, including yourself. On the other hand, like my mother, you are endowed with the rare ability to lead and act, especially in times of crisis. You have the immense gift of being able to take control of that inner fire of yours, transcend obstacles, and transform your awesome power into a constructive force.

Your mantra is *Jai Yen Yen,* which means "a cool and calm heart." To channel your fiery energy into a positive path requires the vision of knowledge. Knowledge opens your mind to clarity and wisdom, enabling you to control a firestorm of emotions. A tranquil heart allows you to soothe the dangerous, smoldering, soot-covered path of your powerful Fire force. Once you learn to nurture your energy with healing foods, thoughts, and personal care, you will be able to enhance and control your inner fire, which blazes with such bold brilliance.

YOUR PHYSICAL SELF

Keep your sensitive skin supple and young with daily cleansing and rejuvenation. Irrigate the pores with Lemongrass Skin Toner (page 196). Afterward, apply facial lotion with cooling balms that include aloe vera, carrot, cucumber, and watermelon.

*T*his facial treatment is believed to eradicate wrinkles, nurture the skin, and keep you looking youthful. Apply once a month.

TAMARIND, HONEY, AND YOGURT FACE MASK

COMBINE the tamarind, honey, and yogurt in a small bowl. Wash and dry your face, neck, and upper shoulders. Gently rub the mixture, starting from the forehead, over your face, then down toward the neck and upper shoulders. Be careful not to get it in your eyes. Lie down in a cool room, close your eyes, and put the cucumber slices over your eyes. Breathe deeply and evenly to empty the thoughts from your mind. Rest and relax for 10 to 15 minutes. Rinse off your face with warm water. Pat dry and apply toner and moisturizer.

MAKES 1 APPLICATION

2 tablespoons Tamarind Puree (page 25)

1 tablespoon honey

2 tablespoons plain yogurt

2 slices cucumber

*T*o exfoliate grime from your skin and to unclog oily pores, treat yourself to this enriching and refreshing face mask once a week or as needed.

COOLING FACE MASK

COMBINE all the ingredients, except for the cucumber slices, in a small bowl. Mix and blend well.

WASH and dry your face, neck, and upper shoulders. Gently apply the mixture in circular motions, starting from the forehead, then over the face and working down toward the neck and upper shoulders. Be careful not to get the mask in your eyes. Lie down in a cool room. Breathe deeply and evenly. Close your eyes and put the cucumber slices over your eyes. Empty your mind of thoughts and concerns. Rest and relax for 10 to 15 minutes. Wash the mask off with warm water. Pat dry and apply toner and moisturizer.

MAKES 1 APPLICATION

1 tablespoon mashed fresh aloe vera

1 tablespoon pureed carrot

1 teaspoon fresh lime juice

1 tablespoon fine rice flour

1 tablespoon honey

2 cucumber slices

*T*o keep your skin from becoming parched and inflamed when the weather is hot and dry, use this facial treatment, especially after spending long hours outdoors. This face mask is so gentle that you can use it every day.

CUCUMBER AND FRUIT FACE MASK

COMBINE all the ingredients, except for the cucumber slices, in a small bowl. Mash and mix until well blended.

WASH and dry your face, neck, and shoulders. Gently apply the mixture in circular motions, beginning with the forehead, then over the face and down toward the neck and upper shoulders. Be careful not to get the mask in your eyes. Lie down in a cool room, close your eyes, and put the cucumber slices over your eyes. Breathe deeply and evenly. Empty your mind of all thoughts and concerns. Rest, enjoy the cool and refreshing mask, and relax for 10 to 15 minutes. Wash the mask off with warm water. Pat dry and apply toner and moisturizer.

MAKES 1 APPLICATION

1 tablespoon mashed ripe banana

1 tablespoon pureed apple

1 tablespoon mashed watermelon

1 teaspoon fine rice flour

1 tablespoon mashed cucumber

2 cucumber slices

After a long day's work, shower and then pamper yourself with this hand treatment. Your hands will feel soft and silken, as if you haven't lifted a finger all day.

ALMOND PUREE AND BANANA HAND TREATMENT

MIX all the ingredients together in a small bowl. Rub and massage the mixture into your hands, nails, cuticles, and wrists. Put on a pair of disposable plastic gloves. Leave the mixture on for at least 30 minutes or longer. Rinse and pat dry. Apply moisturizing lotion.

MAKES 1 APPLICATION

2 tablespoons almond puree (page 21)

1 tablespoon mashed banana

1 tablespoon honey

3 to 4 drops peppermint essential oil

Because your home element has the capacity to radiate intense heat, it can elevate the body's temperature to greater degrees than most of us. Therefore, your warm, sensitive skin is prone to reacting to sudden and unexpected climatic changes, resulting in red, dry, chapped, freckled, oily, and easily scarred skin. You are also susceptible to skin rashes, especially in hot weather. To keep your body toned and protected from nature's whims, treat yourself to aromatic baths like this one.

ROSE, JASMINE, AND CUCUMBER BATH SOAK

FILL the bathtub with warm water. Slightly crush the rose petals and scatter them over the water. Add the remaining ingredients. Immerse yourself in the aromatic bath. Lightly scrub your body and face with the blossoms and cucumber slices. Close your eyes, breathe in the perfume deeply and evenly, and let the fragrance guide your mind toward a peaceful bliss. Soak until the water cools. Pat yourself dry and let the relaxed feeling wash over you.

MAKES 1 APPLICATION

Petals of 6 to 10 roses

2 to 3 cups jasmine blossoms or 10 drops jasmine essential oil

1 to 2 cucumbers, peeled, thinly sliced, and slightly crushed

15 drops rose otto, rosewood, or rose absolute essential oil

For oily and stringy hair, use this treatment, once a week if necessary, or once a month as a preventative.

HONEY, APPLE, AND ROSE OTTO HAIR TREATMENT

COMBINE all the ingredients in a small bowl. Wet your hair, then scrub and massage the mixture into your scalp and hair. Wrap your hair with a warm, wet towel and keep the treatment in for 20 minutes. Rinse and shampoo.

MAKES 1 APPLICATION

1 egg white

1 tablespoon fine rice flour

1 tablespoon honey

½ apple, peeled, cored, and pureed

15 drops rose otto or rose absolute essential oil

Dryness and split ends can send hair flying out of control. To nurture your hair, treat yourself to this rich hair care. For problem hair, use once a week. As a preventative measure, a once-a-month treatment will keep your hair silken soft and manageable.

EGG YOLK, COCONUT, AND ROSEMARY HAIR TREATMENT

MIX all the ingredients together in a small bowl. Wet your hair, then massage the mixture into your scalp and hair. Wrap your hair with a warm, wet towel and leave the treatment in for 20 minutes. Rinse and shampoo.

MAKES 1 APPLICATION

1 egg yolk

1 tablespoon honey

3 tablespoons plain yogurt

2 tablespoons Coconut Cream (page 22)

10 drops rosemary essential oil

Tired, perspiring feet will be ready for dancing after a treatment with this soothing foot soak.

REFRESHING TEA TREE FOOT SOAK

FILL a basin with warm water and add all the ingredients. Wash and dry your feet before soaking, scrubbing, and massaging them with the cucumber, rose petals, and aloe vera. Sit back and relax until the water cools. Pat dry, then apply moisturizing lotion.

MAKES 1 APPLICATION

1 cucumber, peeled, thinly sliced, and slightly crushed

Petals of 3 roses, crushed

One 6-inch piece aloe vera, thinly sliced across and slightly mashed

15 drops tea tree essential oil

mind and spirit

In November, Thais celebrate the Festival of Light. Villagers gather to make an enormous paper balloon. They then build a bonfire, and individuals take turns fanning smoke into the balloon. While doing so, they meditate, emptying their minds of misdeeds, fear, anger, and other negative feelings. As the balloon fills with smoke, it gently rises toward the open sky, carrying with it the destructive thoughts and emotions and leaving the people with a sense of release, hope, and tranquility.

When you feel the fearful and angry storm beginning to build, take hold of these emotions and do as the Thais do—breathe out the negatives, filling an imaginary balloon, and send them up and away into the sky. Wash away destructive energy and cleanse your body with tender, loving touches. Healing hands can rejuvenate your enthusiasm and caress your spirit with love and joy.

Select soaps, lotions, or candles scented with the following essential oils best suited for your life circumstances. In general, for a very active Fire element person, use sandalwood- or rosemary-scented soap when showering in the morning. To restore and relax an overcharged mind, cool down and refresh with rose-, mint-, or jasmine-scented soap and lotion. Burn jasmine- or rose-scented candles in your bedroom prior to sleep; the dreamy aromas will wrap you in comfort and air out worries.

CAJUPUT: Bitter, warm, and aromatic, it is a stimulant and antiseptic. It relieves respiratory congestion, loosens phlegm, and eases muscle stiffness and pain. It should not be used on children.

CAMPHOR: Pungent, sour, and warming, it is an analgesic, antiseptic, and decongestant and clears the mind, eases headaches, and relieves coughs, chest colds, asthma attacks, and insomnia.

CLOVE: Pungent and warming, it is a stimulant and analgesic that relieves muscle pain and respiratory ailments, including asthma and bronchitis. It is good for nervous tension and fatigue.

CINNAMON: Pungent and warming, this stimulant is used to treat colds, fever, digestive ailments, and muscle pain, and is believed to relieve constipation, exhaustion, and flatulence.

EUCALYPTUS: Pungent and warm, it is a stimulant and antiseptic and relieves respiratory ailments, muscular stiffness, and pain. Because it's an antiseptic, it's also applied to burns, wounds, and sores to heal and disinfect. Caution: Some might develop a skin allergy. When used on irritated, red, or chapped skin, it might burn slightly. It is a good remedy for exhaustion and fatigue.

GINGER: Pungent and warm, it is a stimulant and an analgesic, good for the respiratory, circulatory, and digestive systems. Ginger relieves stress, calms the mind, and eases insomnia.

JASMINE: Sweet, aromatic, and uplifting, it is ideal for treating stress, fatigue, and exhaustion.

NUTMEG: Pungent, warming, and stimulating, it is uplifting, restorative, and good for muscle inflammation, and it relieves nausea and indigestion. Nutmeg essential oil is very potent and should be used sparingly. It is especially good for men, and it should never be used by pregnant woman, children, or the elderly. Nutmeg relieves nervous tension and exhaustion.

ROSE OTTO, ROSEWOOD, ROSE ABSOLUTE: Sweet and aromatic, it is considered an antidepressant as well as a cleanser and antidote for dry skin, sensitive complexions, and wrinkles. It also helps relieve coughs and hay fever, depression, stress, nervous tension, and insomnia.

ROSEMARY: Warming and aromatic, it is a stimulant believed to be good for the circulatory, digestive, and nervous systems. Used as a restorative for the mind, it helps concentration, relieves dizzy spells, and restores appetite. Used externally as a hair oil, it helps stimulate hair growth.

SANDALWOOD: Sweet, slightly woody, and warming, this stimulant is used for chapped, oily, or sensitive skin, as well as to make scars fade. It is also believed to relieve anxiety, nervous tension, stress, and insomnia and can heighten the ability to concentrate and focus. The Chinese use it as a treatment for a stomachache, vomiting, sore throat, and bronchitis.

TEA TREE: This warming stimulant relieves abscesses, acne, blisters, burns, and cold sores. It's also helpful in treating coughing, sinusitis, and fever. It is an energy booster.

THYME: Pungent, warming, cleansing, and purifying, it is used externally as a massage oil to relieve stomach discomfort, indigestion, and congestion. Uplifting, it eases depression.

MASSAGE OIL

For Fire element people, whose minds are always at work and whose sensitive and tender hearts sometimes feel as if they are being neglected and taken for granted, touch is the magical trail that leads back to a cool, calm place. Heavy-pressure massages with selected essential oils can help alleviate headaches, muscle stiffness, and pain from stress, leaving your home element once again glowing with clarity.

For all three oils, massage them all over your body, concentrating around the areas where the muscles are tight and tense, like the temples, behind the ears, the base of the neck down toward both shoulders, and along the upper and lower back.

TO REJUVENATE, UPLIFT, AND REENERGIZE (ESPECIALLY FOR MEN) AFTER A STRENUOUS WORKOUT: Combine ½ cup jojoba oil with 10 drops each cinnamon and clove essential oils in a bottle. Seal tightly and shake well.

TO REFRESH, CLEANSE, AND PURIFY THE MIND AND SPIRIT: Combine ½ cup jojoba oil with 10 drops each rose otto, rosewood, or rose absolute, jasmine, and thyme essential oils in a bottle. Seal tightly and shake well.

TO RESTORE ENERGY, BOOST THE CIRCULATORY SYSTEM, AND RELIEVE HEADACHES: Combine ½ cup jojoba oil with 5 drops each rosemary, clove, and eucalyptus essential oils in a bottle. Seal tightly and shake well.

SACHETS

Make pastel-colored silk, cotton, or brocade sachets filled with cotton balls scented with your choice of essential oils. Tie each one with a strand of contrasting ribbon or yarn. Hang them in clothing closets or stash them in dresser drawers. Whiffs of the aromatic scents will refresh the mind and uplift the spirit.

FOR WORK AREAS: Place sprigs of rosemary or bundles of cinnamon sticks tied with ribbons in your work area to heighten concentration. Put a sachet scented with 6 to 7 drops sandalwood essential oil to relieve stress and tension near your worktable.

FOR CLOTHING CLOSETS: Hang sachets scented with 10 drops each of clove (contentment, creativity, happiness, uplifting) and thyme (uplifting, restorative) essential oils.

FOR INTIMATE APPAREL: Use sachets of 10 drops each of sweet and uplifting jasmine and refreshing rose essential oils.

FOR NIGHTCLOTHES AND LINENS: Combine 7 drops rose essential oil and 2 oz. drinking water. Spray them with a rose-scented mist for a heavenly night's sleep.

TRADITIONAL REMEDIES FOR MINOR AILMENTS

The following suggestions are gentle remedies to help relieve symptoms and speed recovery, but they should be used in conjunction with treatment prescribed by a doctor.

FOR MUSCLE ACHES, PAIN, AND INFLAMMATION: Combine 2 tablespoons pulverized fresh ginger and 3 drops each lemon, rosemary, and camphor essential oils in a small bowl and heat in the microwave oven 20 to 30 seconds. Massage the mixture in a circular motion on the affected areas. Cover with a warm blanket, rest, and leave the oil on for 1 hour.

FOR CONGESTION: Fill a basin with hot water. Add 10 drops each eucalyptus and lemon essential oils; 3 stalks lemongrass, tough outer layer removed and tender inner stalk sliced and pounded to bruise; and 6 shallots, peeled and pounded to bruise. Cover your head with a towel over the basin and deeply inhale the scented steam. After a minute or two, uncover and breathe in fresh air. Cover your head with the towel over the basin once again and breathe in deeply for a minute or two. Repeat the process until the steam dissipates. If necessary, repeat 3 to 4 times a day until the congestion disappears.

FOR MENSTRUAL CRAMPS: Mix 1 tablespoon jojoba oil with 5 drops each rosemary and cinnamon essential oils. Rub gently in a circular motion around the abdomen and lower back area. Cover the areas with a warm blanket, rest, and leave the oil on for at least 30 minutes.

ONLINE SHOPPING and INFORMATION for ASIAN MARKETS

www.time4thai.com
Bangkok Center Grocery
104 Mosco Street
New York, NY 10013-4321
212-349-1879

www.GroceryThai.com
10929 Vanowen Street, Suite 143
North Hollywood, CA 91605
818-469-9407

www.thaiessence.com
Thai Essence
440 Bohemian Highway
Freestone, CA 95472
707-874-3113

www.mythaimart.com
MyThaiMart LLC
467 Saratoga Avenue #123
San Jose, CA 95129

www.templeofthai.com
Temple of Thai
877-811-8773

www.newasiancuisine.com
Asian supermarket with branches in
California, Georgia, Nevada, and
Washington

www.99Ranch.com

ARIZONA

House of Rice Store
3221 North Hayden Road
Scottsdale, AZ 85251
480-947-6698

CALIFORNIA

Tuk Tuk Thai and Asian Market
1581 University Avenue
Berkeley, CA 04703
510-666-1125

Bangkok Market
4757 Melrose Avenue
Los Angeles, CA 90029
213-662-9705

Khanh Phong Supermarket
429 Ninth Street
Oakland, CA 94067
510-839-9094

Vien Dong Supermarket
5382 University Avenue
San Diego, CA 92105
619-583-3838

FLORIDA

Asia Market
9525 SW 160th Street
Miami, FL 33157
305-232-2728

GEORGIA

New Asian Market
5461 Riverdale Road
Atlanta, GA 30349

ILLINOIS

Chicago Oriental Wholesale Market
1835 South Canal Street
Chicago, IL 60616
312-733-9633

NEW JERSEY

Asian Food Markets
1409 Route 70 East
Cherry Hill, NJ 08034
856-657-1388

NEW MEXICO

99 Banh Oriental Supermarket
5315 Gibson Boulevard Southeast
Albuquerque, NM 87108
505-268-2422

NEW YORK

Bangkok Center Grocery
102 Mosco Street
New York, NY 10013
212-349-1979

OREGON

Hong Phat Market
9819 NE Prescott Street
Portland, OR 97220
503-254-8280

Uwajimaya
10500 SE Beaverton-Hillsdale Highway
Portland, OR
503-643-4512

TEXAS

My Thanh Oriental Market
10901 North Lamar Boulevard
Austin, TX 78753
512-454-4804

Hung Phong Oriental Market
243 Ramount
San Antonio, TX 78218
210-655-8448

Viet HOA International Foods
8300 West Sam Houston Parkway
South Houston, TX 77072
832-448-8838

UTAH

Kim Long Oriental Market
3450 South Redwood Road
Salt Lake City, UT 84119
801-972-8440

WASHINGTON

Vientian Asian Grocery
6059 Martin Luther King Jr. Way
Seattle, WA 98118
206-723-3160

Uwajimaya
600 5th Avenue South
Seattle, WA 98104
206-624-6248

INDEX

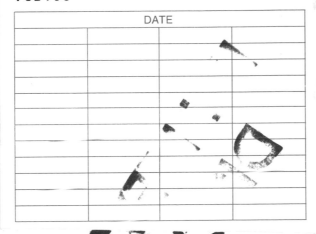

Shankman and O'Neill children's books

www.shankmanoneill.com

Also by Ed Shankman and Dave O'Neill

The Boston Baloonies
I Met a Moose in Maine One Day
The Cods of Cape Cod

Also by Ed Shankman, with Dave Frank

I Went to the Party in Kalamazoo

Ed Shankman was born in the Bronx, New York, and lives today in Verona, New Jersey. As a creative director in the advertising industry, he has directed creative efforts for some of the world's best-known companies. Beyond the office, he has always spent his time chasing creative inspiration as a writer, guitar player, and painter.

Dave O'Neill has worked as a graphic designer and illustrator since receiving his bachelor of fine arts degree from William Paterson University in 2001. A native of Mount Olive, New Jersey, he now hangs his hat and sharpens his pencils in Montclair.

Visit Shankman and O'Neill on the Web at www.shankmanoneill.com.

If you come to Vermont
Near a lake called Champlain,
And you cut through the woods
On an old country lane,

There's a chance you will see
My friend Champ and me
Playing happy and free
By the old maple tree.

From morning 'til night,
We find new ways to play.
And I know for a fact
That he'll be here today!

Now I'm happy to say
Champ comes back every day.
He meets me out here,
And it's here that we stay.

Then Champ got a hug
From the bird and the bug,
And we all watched the clouds
From our soft grassy rug.

Then we came to a place
That was well known to me—
That meadow of mine
And the old maple tree!

I cannot explain
How the magic beast found it,
But we played beside it
And raced all around it.

As we finished our food
And continued to roam,
I was suddenly gripped
By the urge to be home.

We dined on the run,
As we breezed through the trees,
Licking pure maple syrup
Off sharp cheddar cheese.

You can search the world over
And all seven seas,
But you won't find a treat
That is better than these!

We whittled some wood
With the cows on the ridge.

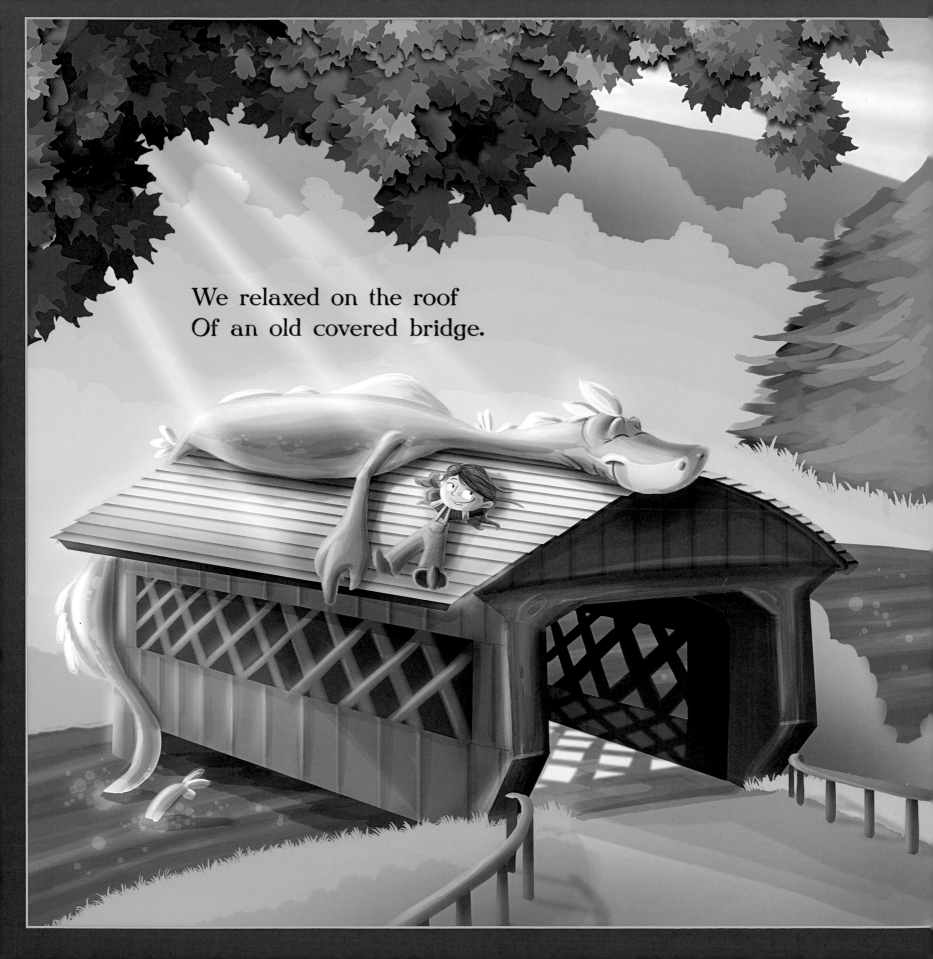

We relaxed on the roof
Of an old covered bridge.

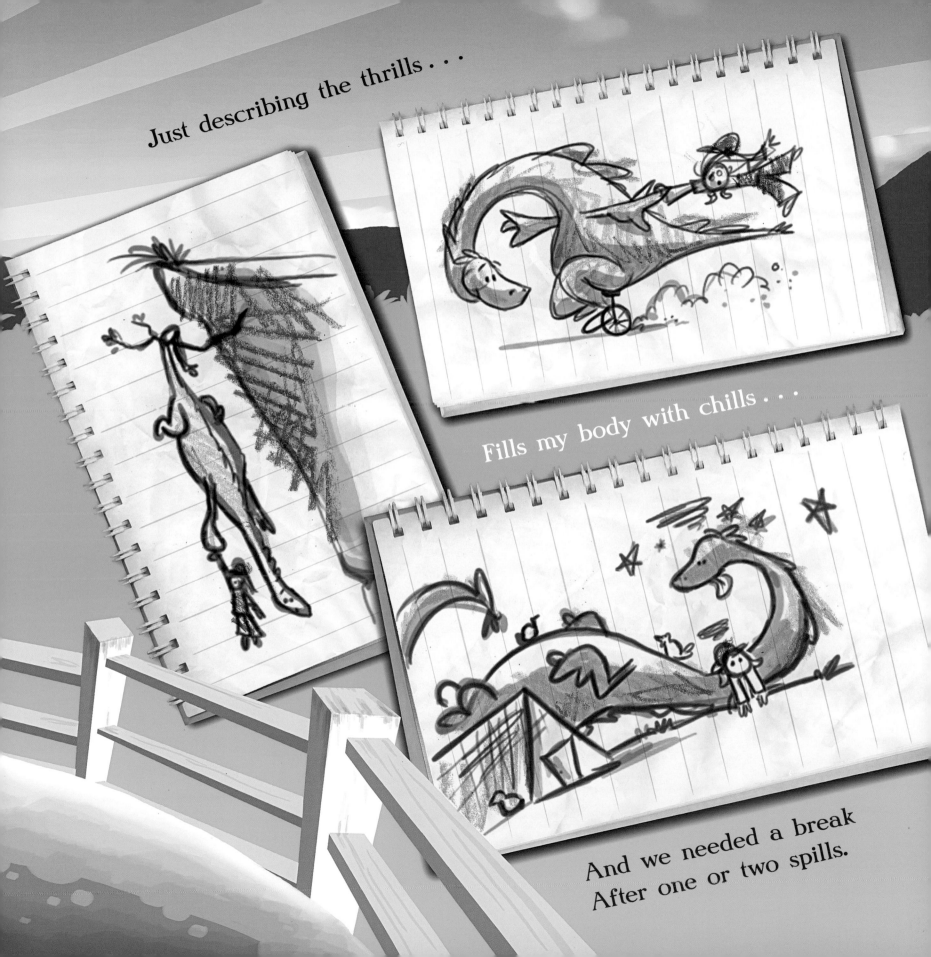

Just describing the thrills . . .

Fills my body with chills . . .

And we needed a break
After one or two spills.

We dashed through the fields,
Past the farms and the mills.

Then we romped through the valleys
And rolled down the hills.

The dazzling scene
Was amazingly green.
It was green far and wide.
It was green in between.

When I say it was green
Do not doubt what I mean,
Because this was the greenest green
You've ever seen!

Now riding a monster
Is hardly worth doing
Unless you take note of
The view that you're viewing.

Vermont lay before me
In all of its glory
Like one of the pictures
In this very story!

It gave me a fright,

But it turned out
all right,

If you don't mind
a dreadfully
frightening height!

But what was he doing?
Did he want to meet me?
Or scare me or chase me?
Or squash me and eat me?

I knew who he was
From his myth and his fame.
Although few had seen him,
We all knew his name.

This could be none other
Than one and the same.
It was Champ—the legend
Of old Lake Champlain!

... With a very long neck,
And two very large eyes,
And a body that was
Of unusual size.

He was tall as a house.
He was wide as a barge.
He was totally, awesomely,
Frightfully large.

Yes, something or somebody,
To my surprise,
Was there in the water,
And starting to rise . . .

And then just like that,
The wind ripped off my hat,
And that hat hit the water
In two seconds flat!

I was gonna jump in,
So I put down my pack,
But then something or somebody
Threw the hat back!

It was long, it was wide,
It was deep, it was clear.
I was glad I had come.
I was glad to be here!

And so, at long last,
I arrived at the lake,
The great Lake Champlain!
There could be no mistake.

I chose to go west
Because that's what felt best,
But I don't know my west from my east
So I guessed.

Then I walked just as far
As I could without rest,
While I ate all the apples
A kid could digest.

So on that very day,
Without further delay,
I collected my things
And I went on my way.

I left without knowing
How long I might be
Away from my meadow,
My friends, and my tree.

. . . and the grass down below is as soft as a rug.

I spent many mornings there,
Cozy and snug,
Watching the clouds
With a bird and a bug.

But one sunny morning
Right out of the blue,
I had a strange longing
To see something new.

Its branches are curled
In a powerful hug . . .

In the hills of Vermont
Near a lake called Champlain,
If you cut through the woods
On an old country lane,

You'll come to a meadow
With one maple tree
That's almost as high
As a person can see.

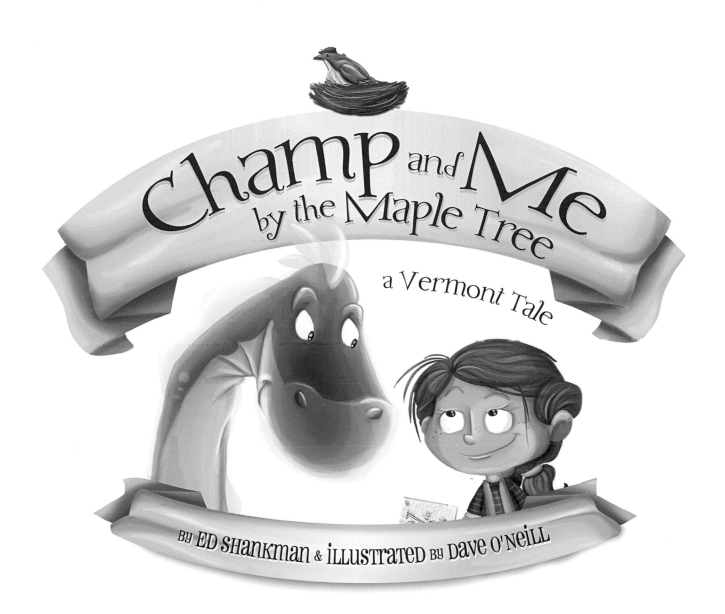

Champ and Me by the Maple Tree

a Vermont Tale

BY ED SHANKMAN & ILLUSTRATED BY DAVE O'NEILL

children's books

www.shankmanoneill.com

Commonwealth Editions
Beverly, Massachusetts

Copyright © 2010 by Ed Shankman and Dave O'Neill

ISBN 978-0-9819430-5-3

Designed by John Barnett/4 Eyes Design

Printed in Korea

Published by Commonwealth Editions, an imprint of Memoirs Unlimited, Inc.,
266 Cabot Street, Beverly, Massachusetts 01915
Visit us on the Web at www.commonwealtheditions.com.
Visit Shankman and O'Neill on the Web at www.shankmanoneill.com.

10 9 8 7 6 5 4 3 2 1

this book belongs to